Praise for AGAINST THE GRAIN...

"*Against the Grain* will be invaluable to all who ponder how to bring Christian social teachings to bear on the most urgent political, economic, and cultural issues in contemporary life. In these marvelously readable essays, Weigel challenges reigning opinion on a wide range of issues, offers fresh insights drawn from the Catholic intellectual heritage, and opens a conversation 'with all partisans of the free and virtuous society, of whatever creed or no creed.'"

— **Mary Ann Glendon, Professor of Law, Harvard University**

"*Against the Grain* is a wonderful collection of George Weigel's essays over the past thirteen years. This book shows once again that Weigel is the most articulate and astute Catholic lay theologian and public intellectual at work in the English-speaking world today. For members of other but related traditions, Weigel brings Catholic political and social teaching into the type of discussion that is supposed to characterize a free, multi-faith society. *Against the Grain* is a true synthesis of theory and practice. Weigel saves his practical points from becoming pedestrian by backing them up with theory, and he saves his theoretical insights from becoming arcane by showing their practical application in dealing with real life issues here and now."

— **David Novak, J. Richard and Dorothy Shiff Professor of Jewish Studies, University of Toronto**

"An essential voice in the perennial debate over what matters most, George Weigel is a serious man with provocative things to say about the way we live now and, perhaps more important, about the way we should live now but do not. *Against the Grain* is a bracing collection of pieces worth reading — and remembering."

— **Jon Meacham, Editor of *Newsweek***

AGAINST
THE
GRAIN

ALSO BY GEORGE WEIGEL

Tranquillitas Ordinis: *The Present Failure and Future Promise of American Catholic Thought on War and Peace*

Catholicism and the Renewal of American Democracy

American Interests, American Purpose: Moral Reasoning and U.S. Foreign Policy

Freedom and Its Discontents: Catholicism Confronts Modernity

Just War and the Gulf War (with James Turner Johnson)

The Final Revolution: The Resistance Church and the Collapse of Communism

Soul of the World: Notes on the Future of Public Catholicism

Witness to Hope: The Biography of Pope John Paul II

The Truth of Catholicism: Ten Controversies Explored

The Courage To Be Catholic: Crisis, Reform, and the Future of the Church

Letters to a Young Catholic

The Cube and the Cathedral: Europe, America, and Politics without God

God's Choice: Pope Benedict XVI and the Future of the Catholic Church

Faith, Reason, and the War Against Jihadism: A Call to Action

AGAINST
THE
GRAIN

Christianity and Democracy,
War and Peace

GEORGE
WEIGEL

A Crossroad Book
The Crossroad Publishing Company
New York

The Crossroad Publishing Company
16 Penn Plaza – 481 Eighth Avenue, Suite 1550
New York, NY 10001

Printed in the United States of America on acid-free paper.

The text of this book is set in 12.5/15.5 Adobe Garamond.
The display face is Mrs. Eaves.

Library of Congress Cataloging-in-Publication Data

Weigel, George, 1951-
  Against the grain : Christianity and democracy, war and peace / George Weigel.
  p. cm.
  Includes bibliographical references and index.
  ISBN-13: 978-0-8245-2448-7 (cloth)
  ISBN-10: 0-8245-2448-9 (cloth)
  1. Democracy – Religious aspects – Catholic Church. 2. Christian sociology – Catholic Church. 3. Just war doctrine. 4. Catholic Church – Doctrines. I. Title.

BX1793.W44 2008
261.7 – dc22
                                                    2007051568

1 2 3 4 5 6 7 8 9 10   15 14 13 12 11 10 09 08

For

Amy Sherman

Christopher Ditzenberger

Derek Mogck

Ann Derstine Batlle

Ever Horan Johnson

Carrie Gress Stibora

Stephen White

Contents

Introduction

Against Several Grains

St. Anselm famously described theology as *fides quaerens intellectum* [faith seeking understanding], a definition on which there has been little improvement over the past millennium. The theological essays collected here are "Anselmian" in the sense that they're attempts to show how Catholic understandings of the human person and human society, human origins and human destiny — all of which derive from the basic Christian confession of faith — can shed light on controverted and urgent questions of public life. The goal of these explorations, then, is understanding: understanding ordered to action in the spheres of culture, economics, and politics.

The essays in their original forms were written over a period of some fifteen years. I have taken the liberty of revising each essay for this volume, indicating in a brief preface to each chapter something of its genesis and evolution. There has been no attempt to smooth things out, however, so the alert reader will sometimes find the argument of one essay being revisited in one or another of its stable-mates. Still, repetition need not be boring repetition, and I trust that's the case here.

Truth be told, I came to this business of "political theology" somewhat accidentally. In my graduate school days at the University of St. Michael's College in Toronto, my primary interest was systematic theology, and specifically Christology. However, on being hired as a (very) junior subaltern on the faculty of St. Thomas

Seminary School of Theology in Kenmore, Washington, I was asked to teach the core course in social ethics, an assignment that led me into an ongoing intellectual encounter with Catholic social thought, and with the social doctrine of the popes from Leo XIII through John Paul II (with whom the encounter was both personal and intellectual). From 1977 through 1989, I worked with the World Without War Council and the James Madison Foundation on issues of war and peace, ethics and international relations. In the latter years of that period, beginning with my 1984–85 sabbatical year at the Woodrow Wilson International Center for Scholars in Washington, I was fortunate enough to become engaged in the work of the cluster of scholars gathered and led by Richard John Neuhaus in New York, first at the Center on Religion and Society, later at the Institute on Religion and Public Life. During my years as president of the Ethics and Public Policy Center (1989–96), I had the opportunity to deepen various of these conversations, many of which have continued well into the first decade of the 21st century. My work on the biography of Pope John Paul II from 1996 to 2000 gave me a privileged look inside the Vatican and initiated yet another series of still-ongoing conversations, especially about world politics. Thus the essays collected here reflect, in one way or another, the education I have received in all of these venues. I trust that no one will be offended if I say that it has been an education superior to that which is on tap in many, perhaps most, university doctoral programs.

I suppose that, at the outset, a word about nomenclature is required. (Note to reviewers on deadline: pay attention *here*.) I am often described as a "Catholic neoconservative" or "theocon." Garry Wills, reeling from the election of Pope Benedict XVI in 2005, suggested in an overwrought essay in the *New York Review of Books* that several similarly branded colleagues and I were "situated at the contact points between the similar ruling systems of the

Vatican and the White House" — a claim that, however momentarily flattering, was in fact preposterous. Replying to Dr. Wills in my syndicated column, I proposed that my friends and I had been trying to advance six Big Ideas with respect to the past, present, and future of the American democratic experiment and the Catholic Church. They're worth repeating here as a kind of in-house summary of what we neo-cons or theocons or whatever think we're up to:

1. The Founders and Framers did not intend the United States to be built around a "naked public square" in which religiously informed moral argument is ruled out-of-bounds in public life. The Supreme Court should recognize that the First Amendment was intended to create the legal framework and support the cultural conditions necessary for the free exercise of religion — "no establishment" being one means to the end of free exercise.

2. The abortion license defined by *Roe v. Wade* is a grave injustice because it established a spurious constitutional "right" to take innocent human life willfully, and thus violated a first principle of justice. Similar threats to the first principles of justice, which can be known by reason, are entailed in euthanasia and in embryo-destructive stem cell research. These issues can and ought to be debated and adjudicated on genuinely public moral-philosophical grounds, without appeals to ecclesiastical authority or "sectarian" doctrine.

3. The free economy is superior to state-based economies because it creates wealth more efficiently, distributes it more equitably, and reflects the economic creativity built into us as rational and moral beings. If you believe the poor are people with potential, and if your goal is to empower the poor to unleash the creativity that is theirs, you work to incorporate the poor into those networks of productivity and exchange that we call the "free economy"; you don't keep poor people trapped on the welfare plantation.

4. The classic just war tradition, a tradition of statecraft aimed at securing the peace of order that is composed of freedom, justice, and security, remains the normative Catholic method of moral reasoning about world politics. Its criteria and its internal logic also provide a public moral grammar by which free societies can debate their responsibilities in a dangerously conflicted world.

5. The pontificate of John Paul II was not a pontificate against modernity, but a pontificate advancing a distinctively modern appraisal of modernity, one that included both affirmation and critique. This, in fact, was the strategy of the Second Vatican Council: the Church's openness to the modern world ought to be complemented by a challenge to modernity to open its windows to the world of transcendent truth and love.

6. The Catholic Church has a "form" given it by Christ. All genuinely Catholic reform — whether institutional or intellectual — is by reference to that "form."

Most of these issues come on stage at various points in the essays that follow, but perhaps this brief summary will help locate my thinking and my primary concerns, as I understand them, at the outset. Those interested in a more detailed explication of the Catholic neoconservative position may wish to consult my essay "The Neoconservative Difference: A Proposal for the Renewal of Church and Society," in *Being Right: Conservative Catholics in America* — a 1995 book that, among other things, illustrated the real differences between "neoconservatives" and others conventionally lumped together on the "Catholic right."[1]

But enough of ideological navigation. How are these essays "against the grain"?

They cut against several grains, actually.

They challenge the tendency to reduce political science to a subset of statistics. And while many of the reference points below are taken from the social doctrine of the Catholic Church, that social doctrine has itself been deeply influenced by the great conversation about the ends, methods, and nature of politics that began in Athens almost three millennia ago. So if these explorations in political theology help revive the ancient craft of political theory, that is no bad thing.

Many of these essays challenge the notion of "functional" or "procedural" democracy — the claim that democracy is essentially a matter of procedures, such that a well-constructed democracy is a machine that can run by itself. This functionalist or proceduralist view tends to reflect (or at least intersect with) two other notions: that freedom is essentially a matter of willfulness or choice, and that the larger (and always controverted) questions of personal and public goods can be bracketed in democratic public life or consigned to a sphere of "privacy." This was not the view of the American Founders, who staked their claim to independence on the relevance to public life of certain self-evident truths about the human person; and it is certainly not the view of Catholic social doctrine. So, in what follows, I have made several probes toward a richer, thicker, and, I believe, nobler understanding of the democratic experiment — probes that I hope will be of interest throughout the democratic world.

The essays on world politics, war, and peace also cut against several grains. They challenge the genuine pacifist of principle (whom I can respect amidst our disagreement). More urgently, these essays challenge the functional pacifism embedded in much of what has passed for just war thinking in Catholic, ecumenical, and secular-philosophical circles in recent decades. In cutting against those sundry grains, these essays also cut against the grain of that form of foreign policy realism, often called Realpolitik, in which it is insisted that world politics is necessarily an arena of amorality. Which, of course, is impossible, for world politics, like all politics, is a human enterprise, and nothing genuinely human takes place beyond the horizon of moral scrutiny.

For those familiar with the terrain of debate in Catholicism in the United States, perhaps the most obvious over-against here is the liberal consensus that has dominated much of Catholic political theology since the 1970s. That that consensus has run out of intellectual gas seems obvious to me from browsing the pages of both popular and scholarly journals in the mid-years of the first decade of the 21st century. But perhaps the magnitude of what has been lost here — and lost to both Church and society — has not been fully appreciated.

In the best Catholic book ever written on American democracy, *We Hold These Truths,* the late John Courtney Murray, S.J., argued that the United States, as a "proposition" country, constantly had to return to its moral and cultural roots in order to renew itself for the challenges of a given moment. Those moral and cultural roots, Murray argued, had found their deepest and most nourishing subsoil in the Christian civilization of Europe, rather than in the political philosophies of the Enlightenment. The Enlightenment had taught the Church some important things about the organization of just societies; perhaps better, the Enlightenment and its political achievements had compelled the Church to retrieve and renew elements in its theory of social and political life that had lain fallow for centuries. But that American democracy — and, by extension, the democratic project in history — owed a large debt of gratitude to what Christianity had done to form what we call "the West," Murray did not doubt. The reference points here are American, but the issues posed for understanding democracy and living it nobly are universal:

> The Bill of Rights was an effective instrument for the delimitation of government authority and social power, not because it was written on paper in 1789 or 1791, but because the rights it proclaims had already been engraved by history on the conscience of a people. The American Bill of Rights is not a piece

of 18th century rationalist theory; it is far more the product of Christian history. Behind it one can see, not the philosophy of the Enlightenment but the older philosophy that had been the matrix of the common law. The "man" whose rights are guaranteed in the face of law and government is, whether he knows it or not, the Christian man, who had learned to know his own personal dignity in the school of Christian faith.[2]

The problem, as Murray saw it in the 1950s, was that the moral-cultural "consensus" that had sustained American democracy for more than two centuries was getting more than a little frayed. Positivism and pragmatism had sapped the consensus in the academy, with results seeping into public discourse, and thence into the citizenry. As Murray put it, "The American university long since bade a quiet goodbye to the whole notion of an American consensus, as implying that there are truths that we hold in common, and a natural law that makes known to all of us the structure of a moral universe in such wise that all of us are bound by it in a common obedience."[3] But as the older forms of the consensus became frayed — in part because of what Murray presciently foresaw as the intellectual disintegration of mainline liberal Protestantism in America — a new champion of the truths we must hold in common would emerge, Murray hoped: the Catholic community in America, which still was in possession of those truths and still retained the capacity to argue them in public in a genuinely public way.

That hope did not survive the intellectual and cultural whitewater that we call "the Sixties." And so by the end of another low decade, the 1970s, a new generation of Catholic social ethicists, often contemptuous of Murray and like-minded classicists, had taken over the American Catholic academy, the scholarly journals, and the high-brow Catholic popular press, represented by *America* and *Commonweal.* Some of these social ethicists argued that the Catholic tradition needed to be complemented (they actually meant "corrected") by what they deemed the "Marxist tradition" of rights. Others dismantled the just war tradition and then reassembled the pieces in such a way that the new framework delivered the appropriate liberal answers to the dilemmas of the last stages of the Cold War. Still others found in John Rawls and Richard Rorty more congenial intellectual conversation partners than Augustine and Aquinas, Leo XIII and Pius XI, Jacques Maritain and Yves Simon. Murray had been right: the liberal Protestant form of the American democratic "consensus" had collapsed, under the pressures of its own intellectual implausibility and the new utilitarianism. What Murray did not foresee, in the Fifties, was that the Catholic intellectual community would join the Gadarene rush over the cliffs of relevance.

This abandonment of a great intellectual heritage was deeply problematic for the Church in the United States, and indeed for the public mental health of American democracy. It occurred at the same time that "1968" and its afterburn were creating a vast rupture in European intellectual and cultural life, rendering the old continent increasingly incapable of linking its contemporary democratic commitments to its deepest cultural roots (because, according to the children of 1968, those roots were contemptible). The net effect of these defaults on both sides of the Atlantic was to leave Catholic social ethics vulnerable to the siren song of Marxist analysis — at precisely the moment when (as we now know) the Marxist project in history was on the verge of implosion. The most pronounced effects of all this were felt in Latin America, during the heyday of the theologies of liberation, but there were real effects in North America and western Europe, too, effects the radioactive traces of which can still be found today.

The impetus that compelled a return to the classic sources of Catholic wisdom in thinking about the problems of democracy came, in the United States, Europe, and elsewhere, from an unlikely source: a Polish pope, John Paul II, who had spent much of his pre-papal life living under (and contesting) two of the great 20th-century totalitarianisms, Nazism and communism. Yet in the aftermath of the collapse of communism, which he had helped accelerate, John Paul began to articulate a Catholic theory of democracy that drew respectful attention around the world — with the possible exception of the aforementioned Catholic social-ethical guilds. John Paul II's thought and example were decisive prods to my own thinking, and in fact it was the example of John Paul II that led me back to Murray, whom I helped retrieve from the oblivion to which he had been consigned by his successors (and inferiors). Thus the challenge to the regnant liberal consensus among U.S. Catholic scholars that follows — a challenge that applies to Europe and Latin America, too — has a distinctive Polish and Slavic, as well as American Catholic, texture and flavor. Let me emphasize, however, that my principal purpose in these essays has not been to chastise my liberal brethren, but to work out my own thinking in ways that I hope are helpful to others, wherever they locate themselves on whatever spectrum of opinion.

Over the decade and a half in which these essays were written, my conversation partners, as well as my audience, have happily expanded beyond North America. In revising these essays, I have tried to keep in mind situations other than the American circumstance, although it is inevitable that a certain parochialism will intrude from time to time. Still, the more I meet the world Church, the more I am impressed with the fact that, beneath the obvious surface differences, there are very similar arguments about living freedom under way throughout the billion-plus *communio* of the Catholic Church. So I hope that these explorations will be of interest to fellow-Catholics throughout the world.

And, indeed, to fellow partisans of the free and virtuous society, of whatever creed or no creed. What Pope Leo XIII once called the "social question" is genuinely global today. That the conversation about the global social question must be ecumenical and interreligious (and in the broadest sense of both terms) should go without saying. What should also go without saying is that that broader conversation will be fruitful only if the best of specific traditions of thought engage each other with respect and clarity. That is what I have tried to provide here: explorations in political theology that can, I trust, be catholic in the interest they evoke, even as they emerge out of a distinctively Catholic perspective.

Chapter One

The Free and Virtuous Society

This essay offers an overview of the principal themes of modern Catholic social doctrine and a survey of the original contributions of Pope John Paul II to that doctrine, while suggesting several areas in which the social doctrine of the Catholic Church requires extension and development in its second century.

The essay was originally prepared for an international conference on the future of Catholic social doctrine, held in Rome in April 2002 at the Pontifical Athenaeum Regina Apostolorum; the conference was co-sponsored by the Athenaeum and the Ethics and Public Policy Center. In its "Roman" form, the essay was published in the Spring 2003 issue of Logos, *the journal of the Catholic Studies Program of the University of St. Thomas in St. Paul, Minnesota.*

The essay was subsequently revised and expanded for delivery in May 2004 as the Fourth Annual Tyburn Lecture at London's Tyburn Convent. Tyburn Convent maintains a perpetual adoration chapel and memorial to the Catholic martyrs of Reformation-era England in the heart of London, a few yards from the "Tyburn Tree" and the site of many martyrdoms. In this

"London" form, the essay was published in a collection of the first four Tyburn Lectures, entitled First Things: The Moral, Social and Religious Challenges of the Day.

I have continued to develop and revise the essay over the years, as its material forms the basis of the introductory lecture at the annual Tertio Millennio Seminar on the Free Society, held every summer in Kraków. It's in that "Cracovian" form that I present it here.

C HRISTIANS HAVE BEEN THINKING THROUGH their relationship to the worlds-within-worlds of politics, economics, and culture for nearly two millennia. The nature of that unavoidable entanglement, and the distinctive character of the Christian's presence in "the world," came into focus early. As the *Letter to Diognetus*, most likely written in the second century, reminds us, Christians are always "resident aliens" in the world, for while Christians honor just rulers, obey just laws, and contribute to the common good of whatever society in which they find themselves, a Christian's ultimate loyalty is given to a Kingdom that is elsewhere. Christians believe that history can be read in its fullness only in the light of faith in the Risen Christ, the Lord of history. And in that perspective, history is both the arena of God's action and the antechamber to our true home, the "city of the living God" (Heb. 12:22). Those who know that about history live in history in a distinctive way.[1]

One might think that this two-edged conviction about the present and the future absolves Christians from responsibility for politics, economics, and culture, and some Christians have in fact regarded a quietistic withdrawal from the world and its affairs as a demand of discipleship. Catholic faith takes a different stance, however. The Catholic Church believes that it is precisely because Christians live their lives "in the world" by reference to transcendent Truth and Love that Christians can offer their neighbors a word of genuine hope amidst the flux of history. Because Christians live both *in* time and *ahead of* time — because Christians are the people who know how the human story turns out, *viz.*, in the final vindication of God's salvific purposes — Christians are in a unique position vis-à-vis history, politics, economics, and culture. As Hans Urs von Balthasar has put it, amidst the world's accelerating development Christians are the people who "can confront [that development] with a divine plan of salvation that is co-extensive with it, that indeed always runs ahead of it because it is eschatological."[2]

Over the centuries, there have been numerous Christian proposals for understanding the Church's relationship to the world of politics, economics, and culture; H. Richard Niebuhr's classic, *Christ and Culture*, still offers a useful typology of the five principal approaches.[3] One of the most intellectually important Christian efforts to shed the light of the Gospel on public life has been the tradition of Catholic social doctrine. Reaching back to the classical and medieval masters for its inspiration while putting their insights into conversation with the realities of the contemporary world, modern Catholic social doctrine has always had a distinctive public quality to it, beginning with Leo XIII's pioneering 1891 encyclical, *Rerum Novarum* [Of New Things, referring to the new social, economic, and political circumstances of modernity]. Unlike other Christian explications of the Church's position in the world, which speak essentially to the believing community, Catholic social doctrine has been thoroughly ecumenical in the full sense of the *oikumene:* Catholic social doctrine has understood itself as being "not for Catholics only." Although the phrase does not appear until the time of Pope John XXIII, the social doctrine of the Church has always been addressed to "all men and women of good will." It is a genuinely public proposal, using analyses and arguments about public goods and the means to achieve them that can be engaged by any intelligent person.

From the mid-19th century and the years prior to Pope Leo's writing *Rerum Novarum* down to the present, Catholic social doctrine has evolved in a collaborative dialogue between the successors of Peter and theologians. Here, I would like to suggest where that dialogue and the papal teaching that has evolved from it have led us in the early 21st century, so that we can better understand the areas where Catholic social doctrine requires development in the years immediately ahead. The focal point of these reflections will be the social, political, and economic thought of the late Pope John Paul II, whose teaching on the free and virtuous society influenced the global discussion of these questions for more than a quarter-century.

The Contribution of John Paul II

The social magisterium of John Paul II assumed, even as it developed, the foundational principles that had shaped the Church's social doctrine since Leo XIII. John Paul also cemented a fourth principle into the foundations of Catholic social doctrine.

The first classic principle of Catholic social doctrine is the *principle of personalism*, which can also be called the *human rights principle*. According to this principle, all right thinking about society — in its cultural, economic, and political aspects — begins with the inalienable dignity and value of the human person. Right thinking about society does not begin with the state, the party, or the tribe; neither does it begin with ethnicity, race, or gender. Rather, it begins with the human person, considered as an individual possessing intelligence and free will, and therefore inherent dignity and value. Society and its legal expression, the state, must always be understood to be in service to the integral development of the human person. The state, in particular, has an obligation to defend the basic human rights of persons, which are "built into" us by reason of our very humanity. "Rights," in the Catholic understanding of the term, are not benefices distributed by the state at its whim or pleasure; they are goods to be protected and/or advanced by any just state.

The second classic principle of Catholic social doctrine is the *principle of the common good*, or what might be called the *communitarian principle*; it complements and completes the personalist principle. Because men and women grow into the fullness of their humanity through relationships, each of us should exercise our rights in such a way that that exercise contributes to the general welfare of society, and not simply to our individual aggrandizement. Living in service to the common good is essential for the good of society, as well as for the integral development of persons. Thus, in the classic Catholic view, society is a "natural" phenomenon, not a remedial reality (as it is, for example, in the political philosophy of Thomas Hobbes).

The third classic principle is the *principle of subsidiarity*, which can be called the *free-associational principle* or *principle of civil society*. Although its vision of a richly textured and multi-layered human society reaches back to medieval Christian experience, this principle first appeared in papal teaching in Pope Pius XI's 1931 encyclical, *Quadragesimo Anno,* which marked the fortieth anniversary of *Rerum Novarum.* The principle of subsidiarity, which is an extension and development of the traditional Catholic claim that the state exists to serve society, teaches us that decision-making in society should be left at the lowest possible level (i.e., the level closest to those most affected by the decision), commensurate with the common good. Classic American federalism — in which local and state governments handle many aspects of public policy, while the national government exercises certain strictly defined functions — is one empirical example of the principle of subsidiarity at work. Articulated under the lengthening shadow of the totalitarian project in the first third of the 20th century, the principle of subsidiarity remains today as a counter-statist principle in Catholic social thinking. It directs us to look first to private sector solutions, or to a private sector/public sector mix of solutions, rather than to the state, in dealing with education, health care, and social welfare.[4]

These were the foundational principles inherited by John Paul II, principles Karol Wojtyła had taught in his pre-episcopal days as a seminary lecturer on social ethics. As pope, John Paul added a fourth principle to the foundations of the Church's social doctrine: the *principle of solidarity,* or what might be called the *principle of civic friendship.* A society fit for human beings, a society capable of fostering integral human development, cannot be merely contractual and legal, John Paul taught; it needs a more richly textured set of relationships. It requires what French philosopher Jacques Maritain used to describe as "civic friendship": an experience of fellow-feeling, of brotherhood, of mutual participation in a great common enterprise. A genuinely human society flourishes when individuals dedicate the exercise of their freedom to the defense of others' rights and the pursuit of the common good, and when the community supports individuals as they grow into a truly mature humanity — that is what living "in solidarity" means.[5] This commitment to the principle of solidarity is one important way in which the social doctrine of the Catholic Church is clearly distinguished from that prominent current of modern political thought that reduces all social relationships to the contractual. (Americans instinctively understood the false picture of democratic society proposed by a strictly contractual understanding of society on September 11, 2001, when great acts of heroism and compassion were done by people who clearly knew that their relationship to their fellow-Americans, and to America, was not reducible to the terms of a contract.)

On the foundation of these four principles, John Paul II developed the social doctrine of the Church in five of his encyclicals. Three of these were "social encyclicals" *stricte dictu;* two other encyclicals addressed grave issues at the heart of the contemporary "social question." Rather than summarizing each of these documents, the focus in what follows will be on the original contributions of John Paul II to Catholic social doctrine.[6]

In his first social encyclical, *Laborem Exercens* [On Human Work], issued in 1981, John Paul offered the Church and the world a rich phenomenology of work. Challenging the view that work is a "punishment" for original sin, the Pope taught that work is both an expression of human creativity and a participation in the sustaining creative power of God.[7] Work is less to be understood as constraint, and more to be understood as an expression of our freedom. Through our work, John Paul urged, we do not simply *make* more; we *become* more.[8] Thus work has a spiritual dimension, and when we identify our work and its hardships with the work, the passion, and the death of Christ, our work participates in the development of the Kingdom of God.[9]

In his 1988 social encyclical, *Sollicitudo Rei Socialis* [The Church's Social Concern], John Paul defined, for the first time in Catholic social doctrine, a "right of economic initiative," which he described as an expression of the creativity of the human person.[10] At a macro level, the Pope insisted that the network of free and voluntary associations that make up civil society is essential to economic and political development; the Pope also taught that development economics and economic development strategies cannot be abstracted from questions of culture and politics. Nor can the problems of underdevelopment be understood, in Catholic perspective, as a question of victimization only; integral human development, John Paul wrote, requires Third World countries to undertake rigorous legal and political reforms. Participatory government, the Pope suggested, is crucial to integral development of society.[11]

In what seems, in retrospect, a prophetic anticipation of the communist crack-up, John Paul II warned in *Sollicitudo Rei Socialis* against the dangers to integral human development (at both the individual and societal levels) of a "blind submission to pure consumerism," a theme to which he would return frequently in the 1990s.[12] In another anticipation of the post–Cold War debate, *Sollicitudo Rei Socialis* also urged the developed world not to fall into "selfish isolation"; "interdependence" (a phenomenon that would evolve into "globalization") has a moral, not merely material, character, the Pope taught. No country or region can ever be read out of history or simply abandoned.[13]

John Paul II's most developed social encyclical, *Centesimus Annus* [The Hundredth Year], was published in 1991; it had three purposes — to mark the centenary of *Rerum Novarum,* to survey the world scene at the end of the 20th century, and to launch the Church's social doctrine into a new century and millennium. In this document, John Paul developed seven original themes that pointed the social doctrine of the Catholic Church firmly in the direction of the future:

1. What the Church proposes to the world is the *free and virtuous society.* The two are inseparable. However powerful the contemporary human quest for freedom may be, that longing for freedom will be frustrated, and new forms of tyranny will emerge, unless the free society is also a virtuous society.[14]

2. The free and virtuous society is composed of three interlocking and interdependent parts — a democratic political community, a free economy, and a robust public moral culture. The key to the entire edifice is the cultural sector. Because free politics and free economics let loose tremendous human energies, a vibrant public moral culture is necessary in order to discipline and direct those energies so that they serve the ends of genuine human flourishing.[15]

3. Democracy and the free economy are not machines that can run by themselves. It takes a certain kind of people, possessed of certain virtues, to run self-governing polities and market economies so that they do not self-destruct. The task of the moral-cultural sector is to form these habits of heart and mind in people, and the primary public task of the Church is to form that moral-cultural sector. Thus the Church is not in the business of proposing technical solutions to questions of governance or economic activity; it is not within the Church's competence to decide whether bicameral legislatures are superior to unicameral legislatures, or whether parliamentary systems are preferable to presidential systems, or where the top marginal tax rate should be set. The Church is in the business of forming the culture that can form the kind of people who

can craft political, economic, and social policy against a horizon of transcendent moral truths, truths that can be known by human reason.[16]

4. Freedom must be tethered to moral truth and ordered to human goodness if freedom is not to become self-cannibalizing.[17] If there is only "my" truth and "your" truth, but nothing that we both recognize as "the" truth, then we have no basis on which to settle our differences other than pragmatic accommodation; then, when pragmatic accommodation fails (as it must when the issue is grave enough), either I will impose my power on you or you will impose your power on me. Truth and goodness shape the moral horizon against which the deliberations of free peoples can take place in an orderly and productive way.

5. Voluntary associations — the family, business associations, labor unions, social and cultural groups — are essential to the free and virtuous society. They embody what John Paul called the "subjectivity of society," and they are crucial schools of freedom, in which we learn the habits and skills necessary to live well in free societies.[18]

6. Wealth in the contemporary world is not simply to be found in resources, but rather in ideas, entrepreneurial instincts, and skills. The wealth of nations is no longer primarily a matter of stuff in the ground; the wealth of nations resides in the human mind, in human creativity.[19]

7. Poverty in the 21st century is primarily a matter of exclusion from networks of productivity and exchange; it is not to be understood simply or simplistically as a matter of having an unequal and inadequate portion of what are imagined to be a fixed number of economic goods. Thus we should think of the poor, not as a problem to be solved (as modern social welfare states tend to do), but as people with potential to be unleashed. Welfare programs should aim at developing the habits and skills that allow the poor to participate in networks of productivity and exchange.[20]

In his 1993 encyclical on the renewal of moral theology, *Veritatis Splendor* [The Splendor of Truth], John Paul II also had important things to say about the free and virtuous society. To take but one example: how, the Pope asked, are we to defend the core democratic principle of the equality of all citizens in a world in which people are manifestly unequal (in wealth, in intelligence, in beauty, in energy, in skill, etc.)? John Paul's answer — that the equality of citizens before the law is most securely grounded in our common human responsibility to avoid intrinsically evil acts, acts that are always and everywhere wrong no matter what the intention or circumstance — is an intriguing proposal for democratic theory to consider.[21]

Finally, in his 1995 encyclical *Evangelium Vitae* [The Gospel of Life], John Paul made his most developed statement on the relationship of constitutional and statutory law to the moral law, and on the relationship of the moral law to the free and virtuous society. Democracies risk self-destruction, the Pope warned, if moral wrongs are defended and promoted as "rights." Reducing human beings to useful (or useless, or troublesome) objects for manipulation erodes the moral culture that makes democracy possible. Moreover, a law-governed democracy is impossible over the long haul when a certain class of citizens claims the right to dispose of other classes of citizens through the private use of lethal violence. Abortion and euthanasia are two examples of this deadly syndrome; the production of so-called "research embryos" destined from conception for experimentation and death is another, as is embryo-destructive stem cell research. A "culture of life" is thus essential for democracy and for human flourishing. Unless the state has no other means to defend itself against predatory individuals, the use of capital punishment erodes the culture of life and should thus be avoided.[22]

John Paul II's social teaching took the Catholic Church into new territory. There was no sense in these five encyclicals of a nostalgia for the arrangements of the *ancien régime;* nor was there the slight-est hint of a longing for the way-things-were before the emergence of the modern state and the modern economy. *Centesimus Annus,* in particular, brought a new empirical sensitivity to the papal social magisterium, which from Leo XIII through Paul VI had some-times been characterized by a certain abstractness about political and economic life. A Church widely perceived as a foe of democ-racy in the 19th-century had become, through the Second Vatican Council and the social magisterium of John Paul II, perhaps the world's foremost institutional defender of human rights, and a so-phisticated participant in the worldwide debate over the nature and functioning of democracy.[23]

Indeed, one can widen the lens ever further and suggest that, at the beginning of the 21st century, the social doctrine of the Catho-lic Church had a comprehensive quality and a salience in public life that would have amazed Leo XIII, that 19th-century "prisoner of the Vatican." As the 20th century gave way to the 21st, there were three proposals for organizing the human future that had global reach and were supported by the institutional infrastructure neces-sary to have a worldwide impact. One proposal was the pragmatic utilitarianism that defined much of moral discourse in western Eu-rope and North America, even as it was carried worldwide through Western popular culture and certain aspects of economic global-ization. The second was the proposal of political Islamism, with its vision of a universal caliphate. And the third was the proposal of Catholic social doctrine: a way of living freedom that ties freedom to truth and truth to goodness, and a way of thinking about the human prospect that can be engaged by every person of good will because it is based on first principles of justice that can be known by reason, principles that provide a kind of "grammar" for the public debate over public policy. It does not risk a charge of Catho-lic special pleading to suggest that the course of the 21st century and beyond will be determined in no small part by the answer to the question, how will each of these proposals shape the emerging global culture?

The Development of Catholic Social Doctrine

What, then, is the work that John Paul II left the rest of us to do as we consider the development of the Catholic Church's social thought today? Let me suggest here a pastoral/catechetical issue, a methodological issue, and a set of specific policy issues where the wisdom of Catholic social doctrine is urgently needed, but the social doctrine itself remains, at present, insufficiently developed.

The Pastoral/Catechetical Issue: The Reception of Social Doctrine

The first thing to be done about Catholic social doctrine in the 21st century is to ensure that it is far more thoroughly received throughout the world Church.

In the United States, it is often said that Catholic social doctrine is Catholicism's "best-kept secret." There is an unfortunate amount of truth in that. The social doctrine of the Church is rarely preached and poorly catechized. It is possible to complete a pre-ordination theology program without having taken a semester-long course on the Church's social doctrine. Courses in the social doctrine of the Church are rarely a staple of secondary or college-level Catholic education. The social doctrine of the Church is barely mentioned in most programs that prepare adults for baptism or for reception into full communion with the Church. In all of this, alas, the Church in the United States is not alone.

The *Compendium of the Social Doctrine of the Church* prepared by the Pontifical Council for Justice and Peace and published in 2004 is itself a testimony to the world Church's failure to draw deeply enough from the wells of its own wisdom in the related fields of culture, economics, and politics. If the Church had truly received the social doctrine of the 20th-century popes, would such a compendium have been necessary? (Indeed, John Paul II once told guests over lunch that a compendium was necessary because "the bishops don't know the social doctrine of the Church"). The entire Church, including the world episcopate, is simply not as conversant with the Church's social doctrine as it must be, if the Catholic Church's proposal is to have the impact it should on shaping the emerging global culture.

This question of reception is both general and specific. In addition to a generalized failure to make the social doctrine "live" in the local churches, intellectually and pastorally, there has been a specific failure to reckon with the distinctive contributions of Pope John Paul II to Catholic social teaching. In more than a few Catholic intellectual and activist circles in western Europe, North America, and Latin America, it often seems as if *Centesimus Annus* had never been written. In these quarters, the quixotic search for a "Catholic third way" somewhere "beyond" capitalism and socialism continues, and the teaching of *Centesimus Annus* on the free economy is virtually ignored. Several interventions at the 2001 Synod of Bishops also suggested a striking unfamiliarity with John Paul II's social doctrine and its emphasis on the poor as people with potential who are to be empowered to enter local, national, and international networks of productivity and exchange. In the 2001 Synod, "globalization" was often discussed absent the empirical sensitivity evident in *Centesimus Annus*. Indeed, insofar as one purpose of *Centesimus Annus* was to challenge dependency theory and other forms of Marxist-influenced economic analysis in Latin American Catholicism, it must be said that the encyclical has, to date, not been altogether successfully received in the new demographic center of the world Church.

Thus a more thorough reception of the 20th-century papal social magisterium, with specific reference to the social magisterium of John Paul II, is an imperative for 21st-century Catholicism.

The Methodological Issue: Refining Principles through Rigorously Empirical Analysis

The world Church owes western European Catholicism a great debt of gratitude for taking the lead from the mid-19th to the mid-20th centuries in developing Catholic social theory in its modern form. That influence continues today, as the demographics of the relevant organs of the Holy See devoted to social doctrine demonstrate. No serious student of Catholic social doctrine can doubt that those steeped in the intellectual traditions that produced Wilhelm Emmanuel von Ketteler and Oswald von Nell-Breuning, Jacques Maritain, Yves Simon, and other such giant figures will have much to contribute to the development of Catholic social thought in the 21st century.[24]

That continental European legacy must be complemented, however, by an intensified dialogue with Catholic social thinking as it has evolved in the United States. While there is no scientific survey of the matter, it is not unlikely that the social doctrine of John Paul II had its greatest public impact in America. Several of the encyclicals cited above were debated in the secular American press with an interest and rigor that was not always evident in other parts of the world Church; indeed, few great world newspapers took John Paul II with such intellectual seriousness as the *Wall Street Journal,* arguably the world's most important business newspaper. A journal that regularly explores the implications of John Paul II's social doctrine, *First Things,* is the most widely read religious-intellectual journal in America, and indeed one of the most widely read intellectual journals, period. In the United States, book-length analyses of Catholic social doctrine are debated in intellectual and public policy circles far beyond the formal boundaries of the Catholic Church and shape debates within both Congress and the White House. All this suggests a dynamic ferment of reflection that, in dialogue with its European antecedents, will be important in developing the social doctrine of the Church in the new century.

American Catholic social ethicists and theologians and their colleagues from throughout the Anglosphere will bring to the development of Catholic social doctrine in the 21st century an inductive, empirical approach to social analysis that will complement the more deductive, abstract analysis that has characterized continental European approaches to Catholic social thought. Differing Anglo-Saxon and continental European concepts of human rights and of the nature of law, and differing American and European experiences of the social welfare state and the management of the free economy, will be put into conversation in ways that should produce an intellectually richer result.[25]

In suggesting the importance of this North American–European axis of dialogue, I do not intend to demean the crucial contributions to Catholic social thought that must come from Latin America and from the new churches of Africa and Asia in the 21st century. I do mean to emphasize the impressively serious discussion of the social doctrine of John Paul II that took place among some American Catholic intellectuals, and the importance of that work for the world Church of the next decades, in common intellectual enterprises and in shaping the reflections of the relevant offices in Rome.

Five Specific Issues

1. Catholic International Relations Theory. The events of 9/11 and the response to them throughout the world Church have reminded us that Catholic international relations theory must be refined and developed if the Church is to bring the moral wisdom of its tradition to the pursuit of the peace of freedom, justice, order, and security in world affairs. John XXIII's 1963 letter, *Pacem in Terris* [Peace on Earth], is not usually considered a "social encyclical" or an integral part of the Church's social doctrine. But here, too, a development of thinking is in order. If the social doctrine of the Church is prepared to address issues of globalization in the economic sphere, it must also be prepared to help statesmen and citizens think through the transition from world dis-order to a measure of world order in the sphere of international politics. Given the nature of the 21st-century world, the "social question" now includes the question of world order.

The first requirement in this area of intellectual development is to retrieve the classic Catholic notion of peace as *tranquillitas ordinis:* the tranquillity of that "order" within and among nations that is composed of freedom, justice, and security.[26] In this context, it is also essential to renew the Catholic understanding of the just war tradition as a tradition of statecraft in which all the instruments of legitimate public authority, including the instruments of proportionate and discriminate armed force, are analyzed for their ability to contribute to the building of *tranquillitas ordinis* on a global scale. Among many other things, this renewal of understanding will mean recovering the classic intellectual structure of the Catholic just war tradition, which begins with a demonstration of legitimate public authority's obligation to defend the innocent and pursue justice. The just war tradition must, in other words, be renewed as a reflection on obligatory political ends, rather than be further reduced (as it has been in recent decades) to a thin casuistry of means. *Ad bellum* [war-decision] questions must once again take their proper theological priority in moral analysis over *in bello* [war-conduct] issues, if the latter are going to be understood properly.

This, in turn, will require a development of the just war tradition itself. Questions of "legitimate authority" are in need of urgent investigation. Where, in world politics today, is the locus of moral legitimacy for the conduct of just and limited war? Are there occasions when military action absent the sanction of the

U.N. Security Council can serve the ends of *tranquillitas ordinis?* Moreover, how are we to understand the classic components of "just cause"? Does the first use of military force to prevent the use of a weapon of mass destruction satisfy the classic concept of a "just cause" as "repelling aggression"? In order to think through the full implications of John Paul II's proposal that "humanitarian intervention" is a moral obligation in the face of impending or actual genocide or mass starvation, is it necessary to recover the older "just cause" notion of "punishment for evil" as a legitimate *casus belli?* How should the *ad bellum* criterion of "right intention" shape the peacemaking that ought to follow the proportionate and discriminate use of armed force in a legitimate cause? What does the *ad bellum* criterion of "last resort" mean in a world where unstable, aggressive regimes may possess weapons of mass destruction, the means to deliver them over long distances, and the capacity to transfer them to terrorist organizations? Are there circumstances in which "last resort" can mean "only" resort, given the nature of the regimes involved? Indeed, does the just war tradition challenge the Westphalian notion of the sovereign immunity of the nation-state, in itself and in light of the emergence of states that are innate threats to world order because of their ideology and their weapons capabilities?[27]

These are all questions in need of urgent attention. Catholic international relations theory has lain fallow for the better part of four decades. It is time to revive it and develop it as an important component of the social doctrine of the Church.

2. Interreligious Dialogue and the Global "Social Question." Activist Islam, or Islamism, is one of the other proposals for the human future with global "reach" in the early part of this new millennium. This suggests that the social doctrine of the Church must take its place in interreligious dialogue, if that dialogue is to be anything more than an ineffectual exercise in political correctness. This, in turn, suggests that the Catholic-Islamic dialogue in the immediate future must be framed, from the Catholic point of view, in frankly strategic terms.

Can the Catholic Church, in other words, be of some modest assistance to those Islamic scholars, lawyers, and religious leaders who are working — often at great risk — to develop a genuinely Islamic case for religious toleration in something approximating what we in the West would call "civil society"? If a world safe for diversity and pluralism requires more than a billion Muslims to become good Rawlsian secular liberals, then we really do face the grim prospect of a global clash of civilizations. Thus, from the vantage point of Catholic social doctrine, the crucial question for the Islamic future is whether Islam can find within its sacred texts and legal traditions the internal resources to ground an Islamic case for crucial aspects of the free and virtuous society, including religious toleration and a commitment to the method of persuasion in politics.

Some may wonder whether the Catholic Church has anything of particular interest to bring to this discussion. What it has to offer is its own recent history — for it took the Catholic Church until 1965 to develop and articulate a thoroughly Catholic concept of religious freedom and to draw out the implications of that concept of religious freedom for the organization of public life. Indeed, one can draw a (very) rough analogy between pro–civil society Islamic scholars and religious leaders today and those Catholic intellectuals and bishops who were probing toward some sort of *rapprochement* with religious freedom and democracy as the old order was crumbling in Europe throughout the 19th century. There may be lessons to be learned from this experience — which eventually led to a dramatic development of social doctrine in Vatican II's Declaration on Religious Freedom — that could and should be brought into the Catholic Church's global dialogue with the multi-faceted worlds of Islam.

3. The Emerging Global Economy and the Environment. *Centesimus Annus* raised a host of important questions for further exploration. Its phenomenology of economic life suggests the possibility that there are economic "laws" written into the human condition in a way analogous to the moral law. Teasing out what those laws might be should be one issue on the agenda of exploration in the years immediately ahead. Important experiments in welfare reform are now under way in various countries; monitoring those experiments in light of *Centesimus Annus*'s critique of the "Social Assistance State," its teaching on poverty-as-exclusion, and its endorsement of empowerment strategies for including the poor in networks of productivity and exchange will help develop the social doctrine in the early decades of the 21st century.

The condition of the world's poor is a moral scandal, not least because today, for the first time in human history, poverty is not necessary, not something fixed in the order of things. The Catholic Church thus has an obligation to lift up before the world the moral imperative of eradicating poverty. In doing so, however, Catholic social doctrine and its exponents should focus primary attention on questions of wealth creation rather than wealth distribution. Billions of human beings today are *not* poor, which is a tremendous moral as well as economic achievement. Rigorous empirical analysis of how wealth has been created, poverty reduced or conquered, and the formerly poor empowered to unleash the economic creativity that is theirs must inform the development of Catholic social doctrine in the 21st century. This does not mean exchanging Catholic social doctrine for Adam Smith and *The Wealth of Nations*. The Catholic Church must always remind the free economy that there are economic things that can be done but should not be done; it must always remind the free economy that it, too, is under moral scrutiny and that calculations of efficiency are not the only measure of integral human development. But to note, as the social doctrine must, that the tremendous energies unleashed by the free economy must be directed by a vibrant public moral culture and by law does not mean a Church opting for socialism; it means a Church teaching the moral principles essential for the ongoing reform of the free economy.[28]

The emerging social doctrine of the 21st century must also address much more directly the problem of corruption as an obstacle to development. In the 1990s, Latin America seemed poised on the edge of a genuine breakthrough, politically and economically; in the early 21st century, there are severe political and economic difficulties throughout Latin America and a resurgence of socialist and neo-Marxist ideology. Both local pastors and knowledgeable observers have said that one major cause of these difficulties is corruption: corruption in the legal and political systems, and a culture of corruption that distorts individual consciences. Here is perhaps the clearest example of the failure of the Catholic Church to receive and internalize its own social doctrine. That failure must be reversed if the bright promise of Latin America is to be realized in the century ahead.

Catholic social thinking must also shed some bad intellectual habits if it is to play its essential role in creating a global moral culture capable of disciplining and directing the globalization process. Catholic bishops and Catholic intellectuals must stop thinking of the so-called "gap" between the developed and the underdeveloped as the chief defining characteristic of the world economic situation, and ask again, with *Centesimus Annus,* how to unleash the potential of the poor so that they can participate in networks of productivity and exchange. The failed mercantilist and oligarchic systems in Latin America ought not be described (as they are in too many Catholic circles) as failures of "capitalism." Catholic thinkers and religious leaders (including those in the Vatican) must break the habit of thinking of the state as the first instrument of recourse in resolving problems of poverty, education, and health care. The Church should encourage individual and corporate philanthropies that support a thick network of voluntary organizations capable of empowering the poor, educating the illiterate, and healing the sick; according to its own logic, Catholic social doctrine must also promote the formation of legal and tax systems that encourage philanthropy and support independent-sector initiatives in the fields of health, education, and welfare. Catholic intellectuals and activists must resolve not to make intellectual common cause with the demographic, economic, and environmental prophets of doom who see nothing but decay and ruin in the present and the future. Employing the new empirical rigor exemplified by the social magisterium of John Paul II, Catholic social ethicists of the 21st century would recognize that life expectancy is increasing on a global basis, including the Third World; that water and air in the developed world are cleaner than in five hundred years; that fears of chemicals poisoning the earth are wildly exaggerated; that both energy and food are cheaper and more plentiful throughout the world than ever before; that "overpopulation" is a myth; that the global picture is, in truth, one of unprecedented human prosperity—and, recognizing these facts, Catholic social ethicists would ask, why? What creates wealth and distributes it broadly? What are the systemic political, economic, and cultural factors that have created this unprecedented prosperity, which is not (contrary to the shibboleths) limited to a shrinking, privileged elite? What can be done to make this prosperity even more broadly available?[29]

Finally, in this regard, Catholic social doctrine must follow through on the suggestion of *Centesimus Annus* that the spiritual challenge of a time of rising abundance will be to understand and live the truth that, while there is nothing inherently wrong with wanting to have more material goods, there is something morally wrong (and, ultimately, economically destructive) about imagining that *having more* is *being more*. The Church must, in other words, develop and inculcate a spirituality for abundance, in which the solipsism and selfishness too often characteristic of certain developed societies (and manifest, for example, in their demographic suicide) is challenged by the call to a rich generosity.

4. The Life Issues as Social Doctrine Issues. The new genetic knowledge and the biotechnologies to which it has given rise offer immense possibilities for healing and enriching human life; they also open the prospect of humanity sliding into a brave new world of manufactured and stunted human beings. Because the biotechnology challenge involves issues of public policy, the life issues must be seen in the 21st century as a crucial set of questions for Catholic social doctrine as well as for bioethics *stricte dictu.*

Here, perhaps the most urgent need at the moment is for a development and elaboration of the Catholic theory of democracy. In *Centesimus Annus,* John Paul II alerted the world to the dangers inherent in a purely instrumental view of democratic governance. In *Veritatis Splendor,* he suggested that a robust public moral culture, recognizing the moral truths inscribed in the human condition, is essential in defending such bedrock democratic principles as equality-before-the-law, as well as in managing passions and interests, fighting corruption, and maintaining democratic "inclusiveness." In *Evangelium Vitae,* the Pope demonstrated that abortion and euthanasia, by placing certain classes of human beings outside the protection of the law, threaten the very moral structure of the democratic project. Now is the time to develop these insights into a public moral vocabulary capable of challenging the utilitarianism that dominates debates on these questions today.

To take one important example: Catholic social doctrine proposes a "dignitarian" view of the human person, and challenges certain biotechological procedures, including cloning, on the moral ground that they violate the innate "human dignity" of persons. What, precisely, is the content of that human dignity? What are its component parts? How is it violated by certain practices? What are the consequences for democracy of these violations? John Paul II gave us a supple, rigorous framework for reflection on these questions. It is imperative that the next generation of Catholic social ethicists begins to fill in that framework in order to shift the terms of the public moral debate.

For more than two decades now, the Catholic Church has argued that abortion is not a question of sexual morality but of public justice: a question of the fifth commandment, not the sixth. In the decades ahead, and with the biotechnology challenge compounding the challenge of the abortion license and euthanasia, Catholic social doctrine must demonstrate ever more specifically and persuasively how the protection of innocent life is a first principle of justice without which democracy will self-destruct. The Church's social thought must, in other words, demonstrate ever more persuasively that the life issues are public issues with immense public consequences, and not simply matters of individual "choice." Doing that will require a richer, thicker Catholic theory of democracy.

5. The "Priority of Culture" and the Deepening of Civil Society. In one respect, *Centesimus Annus* marked an official recognition by the papal magisterium that the two great structural questions that had agitated the world since the industrial and French revolutions had been settled — by history. If, under the conditions of modernity (urbanization, mass literacy, industrialization, and post-industrialization) one wants a society that protects human rights while advancing the common good and permitting participation in government, one chooses democracy over the *ancien régime,* or its fascist or communist alternatives. If one wants a growing economy that enables the exercise of economic initiative, fosters participation, increases wealth and spreads it widely, one chooses a market-centered economy over a state-centered economy. These mega-questions of political and economic structure have been settled. But while much of the world may have thought that these were the only real questions at issue, John Paul II and the social doctrine of the Church read the present and the future more insightfully. What remains, the Pope proposed in *Centesimus Annus,* are the truly urgent questions: the questions of public moral culture and civil society, which will determine whether those well-designed machines, democracy and the market, function well.

The formation of men and women capable of leading free political communities and managing free economies so that freedom serves human flourishing is thus another urgent question for the social doctrine of the Church in the decades immediately ahead. Catholic democratic theory has, in the main, focused on structural questions of participation, representation, voting rights, the rights of association, and so forth. With these questions largely resolved, the focus must now be on the priority of culture: on the institutions of civil society and their capacity to form genuine democrats. As indicated above, this will require urgent attention in the immediate future to the problem of corruption and the essentials of integrity in public life. John Paul II's suggestive phrase, the "subjectivity of society," must be filled in with a more thorough analysis of the institutions of civil society and their relationship to the structures of the democratic state and the free economy.

This discussion should include a re-examination of the way in which many trade unions currently function. There is no question that the right of worker-association is well-established in Catholic social doctrine and will remain so. It is also indisputable that in certain advanced societies, unions are now a reactionary economic and political force, impeding necessary economic change and functioning as narrow interest groups rather than as elements of the "subjectivity of society" marked by a profound concern for the common good. The fierce resistance of American teachers' unions to any notion of empowering poor children through the provision of vouchers or tax credits, enabling them to escape failing public (and union-dominated) government-run schools in order to attend independent (often Catholic) schools, is a case in point. Examples of similar union-based resistance to economic change in Europe could be multiplied exponentially. That a union must defend its own goes without saying; when a union defends only its own, to the detriment of the rest of society (and especially the poor), something is seriously awry. Catholic social doctrine needs to rethink the nature and role of unions in the post-industrial economy and in modern democracy.

The political theorist Francis Fukuyama once discerned a paradox at the heart of modern society, a paradox that touches directly on the challenge of "the priority of culture" to Catholic social doctrine:

> If the institutions of democracy and capitalism are to work properly, they must co-exist with certain premodern cultural habits that ensure their proper functioning. Law, contract, and economic rationality provide a necessary but not sufficient basis for both the stability and prosperity of postindustrial societies; they must as well be leavened with reciprocity, moral obligation, duty toward community, and trust, which are based in habit rather than rational calculation. The latter are not anachronisms in a modern society but rather the *sine qua non* of the latter's success.[30]

A Church that recognizes the "priority of culture" in the postmodern circumstances of the 21st century, and whose social doctrine addresses postmodern society at this depth level of its self-understanding, is positioned squarely on the leading edge of the debate over the future of freedom. Far from being left on the margins, such a Church may find itself, at times, disturbingly relevant. But that, too, is one of the challenges facing Catholic social doctrine in the decades ahead.

Chapter Two

The Sovereignty of Christ
and the Public Church

The Institute on Religion and Democracy was founded in the early
1980s by a group of Protestant and Catholic intellectuals, pastors,
and activists who were concerned about the drift in their vari-
ous Christian communities toward an unthinking acceptance of
liberation theology and a tacit acquiescence to Marxist-inspired
forms of government, especially in Latin America. While IRD's
religious and political critics accused it of being a partisan tool
of Reagan-era U.S. foreign policy — a falsehood still circulating
on some of the woolier-minded "progressive" Web sites — the fact
of the matter is that the primary aims of IRD's founders were to
restore the integrity of the social witness of American Christianity
by tying it once again to basic Christian doctrinal commitments,
to defend the religious freedom of all as the first of human rights,
to offer a robust theological and political critique of Marxism and
its sundry political expressions, and to provide a critical Christian
affirmation of democracy as the form of government most congru-
ent with Christian understandings of the dignity of the human
person. These may seem unexceptionable goals now, in the early

21st century, but they caused fierce controversy in the early 1980s, a period when "progressive" Christianity was riding high—and, in the view of IRD's founders, riding roughshod over some classic and foundational Christian truth claims.

This essay, which reflects some of IRD's founding themes, grew out of discussions I had with fellow-members of the Institute's board of directors as we prepared a statement to mark the Institute's tenth anniversary in 1992. In this essay, I have taken the liberty of adopting that statement's basic framework while extending its theological analysis of the distinctive role of Christian witness in the world of politics.

"**J**ESUS CHRIST is Lord." That classic Christological confession in Philippians 2:11 is the most important thing Christians say about everything, including public life. Christians believe that what we now proclaim through grace by faith — that Jesus is indeed Lord — will be revealed to everyone in the fullness of time. And in the revelation of the Lordship of Christ, it will be made clear to all (as it should be clear to Christians now) that every earthly power and every earthly sovereignty is subordinate to the power and the sovereignty of Christ.

That affirmation, "Jesus Christ is Lord," certainly tells us something about Jesus, the incarnate Word of God. But the Christian confession of the Lordship of Christ also tells us something important about ourselves, and about our societies. For as Christian orthodoxy has insisted from apostolic times onward, Jesus Christ reveals, not only the love of God and the glory of God, but also the full meaning of humanness and the ultimate destiny of human beings. What we see in the risen and glorified Christ is the destiny that a God of infinite mercy and compassion has intended for human beings from the first moment of creation. What we see and love in Christ is what we are empowered by the Holy Spirit to hope we shall become: "They shall see his face, and his name shall be on their foreheads. And night shall be no more; they need no light of lamp or sun, for the Lord God will be their light, and they shall reign for ever and ever" (Rev. 22:4–5).

On a certain secular reading of its message, Christianity is alienating, off-putting, incapable of giving a satisfactory account of the heights, depths, and quotidian plains of the human experience. Yet that is to get the matter precisely backward. For the problem with the Christian claim is not that it demeans human freedom or diminishes the struggles and the glories of the human condition; the problem, rather, is that the Christian claim can seem too good to be true. No less an exponent of Christian orthodoxy than Pope John Paul II articulated that claim, and its radical implications for human self-understanding, with unambiguous boldness in his inaugural encyclical, *Redemptor Hominis* [The Redeemer of Man]. In that personal letter to the Church, in which he laid out the basic themes of his papal ministry, John Paul wrote as follows:

> Through the Incarnation, God gave human life the dimension that he intended man to have from his first beginning; he has granted that dimension definitively... and he has granted it also with the bounty that enables us, in considering the original sin and the whole history of the sins of humanity, and in considering the errors of the human intellect, will, and heart, to repeat with amazement the words of the Sacred Liturgy: "O happy fault... which gained us so great a Redeemer!..."
>
> The Redeemer of the world! In him has been revealed in a new and more wonderful way the fundamental truth concerning creation to which the Book of Genesis gives witness when it repeats several times: "God saw that it was good" (Gen. 1, *passim*).[1]

To put it a slightly different way, to confess the Lordship of Christ is to proclaim to the world that, in and through Jesus Christ, God finally and definitively achieved what he had intended for human beings from the beginning: glorification as companions of God within the light and love of the Trinity. Thus Christianity exalts the human person and the human race almost beyond the point of human comprehension, for the Christian claim is that the divinely willed destiny of every human being is, in the startling term of the Eastern Fathers of the Church, nothing less than θέωσις [theosis] or "deification."[2] "God was made man so that man might become God" is the characteristic patristic formulation of this dramatic assertion.

Incorporation into Christ is thus the very opposite of "alienation," as that charge has been laid against Christianity for two centuries. For, on the orthodox Christian understanding of these things, the closer we come to God and the more dependent we are upon him, the freer we are as human beings. As Dorothy L. Sayers once put it, God's "love is anxiously directed to confirm each individual soul in its own identity, so that the nearer it draws to Him, the more truly it becomes its unique and personal self."[3] Jesus of Nazareth, the man most radically and unsurpassably open to the God he called "Father," was, in his complete human dependence on the Father and his total abandonment of self to the Father's will, the incarnate Son of God. Thus the *Logos*, the Word of God, comes into history, not to fetch us out of our humanity, but to redeem us in and through our humanness, and by doing so, to transform us into the glorified condition that God has intended for us from the beginning. "God is not beggarly," wrote the 3rd-century theologian Hippolytus, "and for the sake of his own glory he has given us a share in his divinity."[4]

The Gospel episode that most dramatically captures this central truth of Christianity is the story of the Transfiguration of Jesus.[5] There, on Mt. Tabor, Peter, James, and John were given, not only a vision of the glorified Christ, but also a glimpse of their own future glorification. And as it was for them, so it is for us. Although we see only with the eyes of faith, we have Christ's pledge that "blessed are those who have not seen and yet believe" (Jn. 20:29). Seeing Christ, who is one like us, transfigured, we can know our own destiny. Or, as the apostle Paul put it to the early Christians of Corinth, we can understand that in Christ we are being transformed "from one degree of glory to another" (2 Cor. 3:18). All of this is the furthest thing imaginable from "alienation."

This is emphatically not to say, however, that Christianity is simply a religious variant on the secular myth of progress. For at the heart of the Christian claim is the cross: *the* great confrontation with the alternative claims of the principalities and powers of this world. In the eyes of the world, of course, Jesus is the ultimate victim, and perhaps even the ultimate fool. But to the eyes of faith, the way of the cross — the mystery of the redemptive death of Jesus Christ — is the necessary path to the resurrection, and thus to eternal life in the light and love of the Trinity.

From the Christian point of view, then, all of reality is "cruciform" in its basic configuration, its "form," its *Gestalt*. As the Swiss theologian Hans Urs von Balthasar put it, the "historical event of Christ's redemption of mankind" cuts through the entire cosmos in "longitudinal section," leaving no person, and indeed no aspect of creation, untouched.[6] Thus the cross of Christ, and God's triumphant vindication of Christ's sacrifice on the cross, is the ultimate Christian answer to the claims of the world and all its sovereignties.

Witnesses Past and Present

Christians (and those of their persecutors who defend an ultimate earthly sovereignty — which is to say, a false god) have always understood that the Christian claim engages issues of ultimate consequence. Thus the prototype of the Christian witness is the martyr. Indeed, the original Greek word simply meant "witness." Its usage was not confined to those who had died for the faith; rather, all who had suffered persecution "for the sake of the Name" (Acts 5:41) were witnesses, "martyrs." And their witness was not simply to their own convictions, powerful as they were, but to the demands of living in the truth as these witnesses had been grasped by that truth in the person of the Risen Christ.

We may find it hard to imagine, these days, the conviction of being "grasped by the truth" that animated the martyrs of the Roman arena. They lived not merely in a different time and place but in a dramatically different intellectual and imaginative environment, one in which the border between the transcendent and the mundane was far more permeable than it has been in post-Enlightenment modernity.[7] Martyrdom, however, is not something confined to the Christian past. Among our own contemporaries we have Christian witnesses whose decision to "live in the truth," as they put it, cost them dearly and yet finally proved its transformative power: the brave men and women of the resistance Church in central and eastern Europe during the communist period; the persecuted Christians of China, Vietnam, North Korea, and large parts of the Arab Islamic world in the first decades of the 21st century. Millions of Christians died "for the sake of the Name" under communist persecution, the greatest since Diocletian. And among the living "confessors" of the faith must also be counted those further hundreds of thousands of Christians whose participation in the human-rights movements in central and eastern Europe during the 1980s helped overthrow European communism in the nonviolent Revolution of 1989.[8]

Christians in the West should not have been surprised that these contemporary martyr-confessors based their resistance to an evil political system on a theory of the "power of the powerless," a power derived from the individual conscientious decision to "live in the truth," to live "as if" one were a free person.[9] That, after all, is what Christian witnesses had been doing for two thousand years. And that is what Christians are destined to do, in the face of the dehumanizing claims of those who would absolutize worldly sovereignties, until the end of time.

The Body

What is the Church? The Church is the community of believers, gathered and sustained in the power of the Holy Spirit, who proclaim to all the world's peoples and cultures the truth of the Lordship of Christ in history. Thus the community (the *communio* or "communion") of the Church continues to preach the Good News of God's redeeming love first enunciated by Jesus of Nazareth some two millennia ago. The Lord's promise to his disciples that he would not leave them orphans but would beseech the Father to "give you another Counselor, to be with you forever, even the Spirit of truth . . . [who] will teach you all things, and bring to your remembrance all that I have said to you" (Jn. 14:16–17, 26) is fulfilled in the *communio* of the Church, the communion formed by the Spirit at Pentecost[10] and sustained by the same Spirit until the end of time (Rev. 22:17).

The Church is not accidental or peripheral to the saving event that is the life, death, resurrection, and glorification of Jesus Christ. To affirm one's belief in "the holy catholic Church," as Christians do in the ancient Roman baptismal formula we know as the Apostles' Creed, is to affirm that the Church is no mere human invention.[11] Rather, the Church is of the will of Christ. The Church is a dominically ordered community, and incorporation into the Church is part of one's incorporation into Christ. Indeed, we are incorporated into, or grafted onto, Christ by being incorporated into and grafted onto the Church through the Church's proclamation of the Word and the action of the Church's ministry in baptism. Thus the Church is, in another ancient image, the "body of Christ" (Eph. 4:12), and we "put on the Lord Jesus Christ" (Rom. 13:14) by putting on the Church — by living in the *communio* of the faithful, in whose prayer and praise of God we experience a foretaste of the glory that is to be ours in the fullness of time.

Christians have long debated the specific doctrinal weight to be given to the Church, and two thousand years of Christian history have not resolved the divisions that exist on many questions of ecclesiology. It may be that some will remain unresolved until the Lord returns in glory. But all orthodox Christians, whether "high church" or "low church" in their ecclesial sensibility, affirm that there is only one Church of Christ, because there is only one Christ and the Church is his Body.[12] Moreover, one of the more intriguing signs of these times is a new consciousness among traditionally "low church" evangelical Protestants of the importance of the Church in God's plan for the salvation of the world. Thus the evangelical leader Charles Colson has argued that "the Body" is no mere sociological phenomenon, but rather a *communio sanctorum,* a "communion of saints" that makes manifest God's saving work to the world "by gathering into confessing communities to fulfill His mission — that is, to administer the sacraments, preach the Word, and make disciples."[13]

The Church is not incidental to the Gospel. Rather, the Church is the *scola sanctorum,* the school in which we saints learn our true nature and destiny as revealed by Christ. Some Christians believe that the Church is an integral part of the Gospel; others believe that the Church is a communal consequence of the Gospel. But all Christians believe that the Gospel and the Church are inextricably related.

For any Christian, then, the Church is the first community of commitment, the privileged community of identity and allegiance. Because our first allegiance is to the Christ who has saved us, our first institutional or corporate commitment is to his Body, the Church. For it is in the Church that we "live to the Lord"; it is in the Church that we "die to the Lord"; and it is in the Church, the "Bride . . . of the Lamb," that we shall reign with Christ forever (Rom. 14:8; Rev. 21:9).

Christians assert the priority of the Church, not to demean other human commitments, but to place those commitments in their proper context, within the cruciform configuration of all reality. Or, to vary the imagery, Christians believe that through the cruciform grammar of the Christian claim, all the other stories of our lives — the covenantal commitments of husband and wife, the deep bonds between parents and children, the civic friendships within a democratic political community, the responsibilities of citizenship, the various obligations we assume in our work — find their true meaning and value. To put it most simply, Christians believe that they are better husbands, wives, children, parents, friends, colleagues, and citizens precisely because their commitments to wives, husbands, parents, children, friends, co-workers, fellow citizens, and country reflect their fundamental commitment to live in imitation of Christ, within the Body of Christ that is the Church.

The priority of the Church requires that Christians maintain a certain critical distance from all other earthly sovereignties. Jesus himself put the matter dramatically when he said that "if anyone comes to me and does not hate his own father and mother and wife and children and brothers and sisters, yes, and even his own life, he cannot be my disciple" (Lk. 14:26). The point is not, of course, that the love of Christ obliges us to loathe our closest relatives. But the radical demands of the Gospel require that we subordinate even our most intimate and cherished human relationships to the cruciform pattern of the Christian life, such that every aspect of our lives is lived within the grammar of the cross; for, as Jesus continues, "whoever does not bear his own cross and come after me, cannot be my disciple" (Lk. 14:27). No human commitment, not the most solemn covenantal bond of marriage, nor the self-giving love of parent for child, nor the most noble patriotism, can take precedence over the Christian's commitment to Christ. But in that prior commitment, Christians believe, we find the ultimate affirmation and true "location" of every other commitment, relationship, and obligation of our lives. Thus in the Gospel of Luke, the Lord's first articulation of the demands of discipleship — "If any man would come after me, let him deny himself and take up his cross daily and follow me. For whoever would save his life will lose it; and whoever loses his life for my sake, he will save it" (Lk. 9:23–24) — is immediately followed by the Transfiguration, the revelation of future glory (Lk. 9:28–36).

Citizens and Aliens

All this gives "Christian citizenship" a distinctive character. The Christian is always a "resident alien" in the world, because the Christian insists on the singular priority of his commitment to Christ and to the Church. At times, when the surrounding culture is more compatible with the way of life that Christians are obliged to embody, the stress can be on "resident." Then the Church is truly a leaven in society, as the Second Vatican Council taught in 1965.[14] At other times, the stress will be on the Christian as "alien."[15] In such circumstances (recall the Confessing Church in Germany during the Nazi period), what is often dismissed as "sectarianism" is exactly what is required of the Church: for in cultures that deny the basic truths about the human person that Christians must affirm, to be sectarian is simply to be faithful. As Richard John Neuhaus has written:

> Any discussion of Church and society that is not marked by a sympathetic awareness of the sectarian option is not to be fully trusted. In Catholicism, the monastic tradition keeps alive the awareness that there is a radically "other way," and that, in some circumstances of cultural disintegration and hostility to the Gospel, it may be the best way, indeed the normative way. No matter how impressive its institutions or how large its numbers or how palpable its cultural influence, the Church must never forget that it is, in the final analysis, the "little flock" completely dependent upon the promise of its Lord.[16]

Most Christians in established and new democracies today do not seem to feel obliged to take a radically "over-against" or sectarian stance. But the possibility remains that they might, as the experience of Christians who have lived under totalitarianism should remind us. In moments of extreme cultural decadence, for example, Christians will be obliged to speak and act as a distinctively countercultural community. In any event, Christian public life will always be lived in the tension between being residents and being aliens. That this unavoidable tension can be creative is a lesson to be drawn from the history of Christian political thought.

The Body of Christ is thus a *communio,* a communion, of people who are obliged to live ahead of time. Because we have seen, in the resurrection of the Church's Lord, the "grace of God [which] has appeared for the salvation of all men" (Tit. 2:11), and because we have seen the "glory of God" shining on "the face of Christ" (2 Cor. 4:6), we believe, with Paul, that in the fullness of time God will "unite all things in him" (Eph. 1:10). Thus the end of the story, to be finally accomplished in God's good time, in the time beyond time, will be the fulfillment of the vision of Isaiah: "Every valley shall be lifted up, and every mountain and hill made low; the uneven ground shall become level, and the rough places a plain. And the glory of the Lord shall be revealed, and all flesh shall see it together" (Is. 40:4–5).

It is precisely as a people ahead-of-time that Christians live their public lives as resident aliens, without insouciance (for whatever is in the world is, in the final analysis, an object of God's salvific purposes), but also without *Angst.* Because Christians know how the story is going to turn out, and because they know that the worst that could happen in history has already happened — on Good Friday — Christians can live within the unfolding of the world and its story at a critical distance. That critical distance allows Christians both to affirm the world as the arena of God's saving acts and to challenge the temptation of the world's sovereignties to assume an ultimacy that is not theirs.

Public Truth, Public Consequences

From the world's point of view, Christians have always been a maddeningly public people. On the birthday of the Church, Pentecost, Peter simply couldn't contain himself. Not for him a quiet, private celebration of the gift of the Spirit with his fellow Christians; no, Peter had to go charging out into the middle of one of the great festivals of the Jewish year and start proclaiming all manner of things, such that some of his hearers at first thought he was drunk.[17] And ever since, Christians have declined to shut up, so to speak. The people who are ahead of time can't stop talking about the good news that has been entrusted to them. The Gospel they preach is inescapably public in character.

That preaching has had worldly (indeed, political), as well as ecclesial, consequences. The first object of the Church's preaching is, of course, the missionary proclamation of "Jesus Christ our Lord, through whom we have received grace and apostleship to bring about the obedience of faith for the sake of his name among all the nations" (Rom. 1:5). But the nations themselves have not been unaffected by the Church's insistent preaching of "Christ crucified...the power of God and the wisdom of God" (1 Cor. 1:23–24). Indeed, that preaching has had a profoundly formative effect on the political history of the West — and through that, upon the political history of the world.

For the Christian proclamation of the Lordship of Christ and the Fatherhood of God is, at the same time, a tacit refutation of the claims to godliness, to ultimacy, that might be made by any other power. Because God is God, Caesar is not God. And because Caesar is not God, Caesar's reach into our lives is limited. Indeed, because God is God and Caesar is not God, Caesar cannot reach into that part of us that is most deeply and definingly human, the part in which we encounter our Creator, of whom we say, "I believe in God, the Father Almighty, Creator of heaven and earth. . . . " According to the classic teaching of the Church, it is only in the Spirit that we are empowered to say, "Abba, Father!" (Rom. 8:15). That affirmation and that acclamation imply that within every human person there is a privileged sanctuary of conscience (of personhood, if you will) into which the state's writ does not reach.[18]

Because God is God, no other power is God, and no other commitment of the Christian's life can be so life-forming as the confession of the Fatherhood of God and Lordship of Christ. At the same time, commitment to Christ empowers Christians to fulfill the obligations implicit in the other loyalties of their lives in a way that locates those loyalties within a horizon of ultimate consequence, yet avoids absolutizing (and thus distorting, and possibly destroying) the goods of this world.

Christianity, then, is fundamentally anti-totalitarian: which is to say, Christianity implies pluralism. The radical demands of the Christian claim disclose a world in which our absolute obligation is to one final sovereignty; and the communal expression of that obligation in the Body that is the-Church-in-the-world creates the personal and social space in which we can fulfill our duties to the many other lesser sovereignties (family, friendship, profession, voluntary association, country) with legitimate claims upon us, and do so without absolutizing any of them. Thus the Church's commitment to a God beyond history helps make pluralism possible in history. And pluralism is a condition for the possibility of civil society, the tensile strength of which is a barrier to the temptation of all states to enlarge the scope of their power.

This anti-totalitarian — or, put positively, pluralistic — public trajectory of Christianity's basic claim is a truth with serious consequences, not least under the conditions of modernity (and given the technological means of coercive social control that modernity has made possible). We live in an age in which worldly sovereignties have frequently demanded incense and have tried to enforce that demand at the cost of unspeakable human suffering. Nazi racial ideology and the class idol of Marxism-Leninism were the two most murderous examples of Caesars-who-would-be-gods in the 20th century; they were, mercifully, defeated, if at great cost. Yet other idolatrous commitments have threatened the human project since the defeat of the 20th-century totalitarians. Radical claims of nationalism and ethnicity wrought havoc in Europe, the heartland of Western civilization, in the 1990s. Racial and tribal hatreds — idols — continue to make social progress difficult, if not in some cases impossible, in Africa. The god of consumption has proven attractive throughout the world as material wealth has increased exponentially. (And then there is the challenge posed by a jihadism bent on imposing a global caliphate on the world.)

Americans should not think themselves immune to the temptation to make Caesar into God. When the Supreme Court of the United States suggests that the aggrandizement of the imperial autonomous Self is the be-all and end-all of the American democratic experiment (as it did in deciding *Casey v. Planned Parenthood of Southeastern Pennsylvania* in 1992), the principalities and powers are demanding that incense be offered to what is unworthy of our worship. Various campaigns for gender- or race-based political correctness are additional evidence of the American susceptibility to the veneration of idols. Given the fantastic imagination that the human race has exhibited throughout recorded history, the words "never" and "every," should be deployed with great circumspection. Yet it does seem that every human society is tempted to absolutize itself, or some aspect of itself, so that we can speak of a perennial human temptation to idolatry. And idolatry enforced by the coercive power of the state is very bad news for human freedom.

Thus the dual Christian insistence that God is God and that Caesar is not God has had, is having, and will continue to have great public consequences. It influenced the fate of the Roman

Empire (if not quite the way Edward Gibbon imagined). It profoundly shaped one of the great civilizations of the world, that of the Christian Middle Ages, the richly textured social pluralism of which was a kind of preschool for democracy. It contributed to the evolution of modern democratic political theory, through the influence of Calvinism on the Scottish Enlightenment (and thence on the American Founding), and through the development of the social doctrine of the Catholic Church from Pope Leo XIII through Pope John Paul II.[19] In our own time, the Christian refusal to burn incense to a modern idol helped to bring about the collapse of European communism and the demise of the most far-flung continental empire since the days of the Romans.

Christians are, in this sense, dangerous people. But the threat they pose is to those who would make for themselves (or of themselves) a molten calf and demand that others worship it. Thus the public danger of Christianity is its most basic contribution to the preservation of human freedom and to the structuring of a public life conducive to the exercise of that freedom. The fact that their commitment to the world is mediated through their eschatological distance from the world makes Christians good citizens of any state that does not fancy itself God.

The Temptation of the Church

The Church has not, of course, always lived up to the majesty of its mission. The Church is a gathering of sinners. It is through the "earthen vessels" of our humanity (2 Cor. 4:7) that the *communio* of the Church proclaims the Good News of Jesus Christ and attempts to discern the public implications of that Gospel in different cultures and circumstances. Sometimes the Church fails in its discernment.

The classic literary meditation on this failure is Dostoevsky's "Legend of the Grand Inquisitor" in *The Brothers Karamazov*. The chief inquisitor, a prince of the Church, interrogates Christ, who has suddenly returned to Earth. And the cardinal inquisitor berates Christ...for what? For his proclamation of human freedom:

I tell you that Man has no more tormenting care than to find someone to whom he can hand over as quickly as possible that gift of freedom with which the miserable creature is born. But he alone can take over the freedom of men who appeases their conscience...instead of taking over men's freedom, you increased it still more for them! Did you forget that peace and even death are dearer to man than free choice in the knowledge of good and evil? There is nothing more seductive for man than the freedom of his conscience, but there is nothing more tormenting, either. And so, instead of a firm foundation for appeasing human conscience once and for all, you chose everything that was unusual, enigmatic, and indefinite, you chose everything that was beyond men's strength, and thereby acted as if you did not love them at all — and who did this? He who came to give his life for them! Instead of taking over men's freedom, you increased it and forever burdened the kingdom of the human soul with its torments....

Is it the fault of the weak soul that it is unable to contain such terrible gifts? Can it be that you indeed came only to the chosen ones and for the chosen ones? But if so, there is a mystery here, and we cannot understand it. And if it is a mystery then we, too, had the right to preach mystery and to teach them that it is not the free choice of the heart that matters, and not love, but the mystery which they must blindly obey, even setting aside their own conscience. And so we did. We corrected your deed....And mankind rejoiced that they were once more led like sheep, and that at last such a terrible gift, which had brought them so much suffering, had been taken from their hearts. Tell me, were we right in teaching and doing this? Have we not, indeed, loved mankind, in so humbly recognizing their impotence, in so lovingly alleviating their burden and allowing their feeble nature to sin, even with our permission? Why have you come to interfere with it now? And why are you looking at me so silently and understandingly with your meek eyes?[20]

The enduring temptation of the Church is to substitute itself and its authority for the freedom of human beings. As Dostoevsky suggests, the Church can do this out of misplaced compassion as well as for institutional self-aggrandizement; indeed, the Grand Inquisitor's whole defense of ecclesiastical and political authoritarianism is that it lifts from men the burden of freedom. And freedom is indeed a fearsome thing.

But it is in overcoming our fear of freedom, and in bending freedom to ends worthy of human beings made in the image of God, that we live out our vocation as creatures endowed with intelligence and free will. Thus the Church violates human dignity, as well as the explicit mandate of its Lord, when it denies men and women the freedom that is their birthright as sons and daughters of God. "For freedom Christ has set us free; stand fast therefore, and do not submit again to a yoke of slavery" (Gal. 5:1).

The typical way in which the Church has succumbed to the temptation embodied in the legend of the Grand Inquisitor is by forging inappropriate alliances between altar and throne, so that the coercive power of the state is put behind the truth claims of the Church. This is bad for both the Church and the state.

It is bad for the Church because coerced faith is no faith. In 1774, in his *Summary View of the Rights of British America,* Thomas Jefferson wrote that "the God who gave us life gave us liberty, at the same time."[21] Two centuries later, in 1986, Cardinal Joseph Ratzinger and the Congregation for the Doctrine of the Faith affirmed that "God wishes to be adored by people who are free."[22] These

two striking declarations, born of very different philosophical positions, nonetheless touch on a single great truth: that God created
us for freedom, the freedom to assent freely to the truth about ourselves (which includes the truth about the right ordering of our
communities). Christians believe that the core of that truth — that
we come from God and are destined for God — is definitively revealed in Jesus Christ. The Christian claim that God takes our lives
seriously is embodied in the Christian affirmation that the assent
of faith, to be genuine, must be freely given.

Coercion is bad for individuals within the Church or contem-
plating entry into the Church. It is also bad for the public witness
of the Church. A community gathered or maintained by coercive
state power cannot give full and effective witness to the liberating
love of God in Christ. A Church dependent (or even heavily re-
liant) on the sword (or purse) of the state has misplaced the trust
it ought to place in God alone. Americans, in particular, are wary
about the excessive entanglement of Church and state because of
what that entanglement can do to the state and to civil society. But
for Christians, the first reason for the Church to eschew any excessive reliance on the state is our overriding concern for the integrity
of the Church. The Gospel has its own power, and the Church must
bear witness to that. Moreover, a Church dependent on state authority is open to forms of manipulation that are incongruent with
the Gospel and that dangerously narrow the Church's necessary
critical distance from all worldly sovereignties.

God has not ordained any single pattern of relationship between
Church and state, between the *communio* of the Body of Christ and
the *civitas* of public life. Nor need we think that the right ordering
of the relationship between the Church and civil public authority
requires what Richard John Neuhaus has termed the "naked public square."[23] Neither Christian orthodoxy nor democratic theory
demands that public life be denuded of a people's religious convictions. Indeed, both would seem to require that the public discourse

engage the citizenry's deepest convictions as they bear on determining and advancing the common good. And those convictions,
in American democracy and in several of the new democracies
of central and eastern Europe, are religious convictions. (Perhaps
more precisely, and in terms of public policy, they are religiously
grounded moral convictions.) But how the relationship between
the Church and the polity is ordered will necessarily vary according to historical circumstances and differences among cultures. The
two extremes to be avoided are the sacralization of the state and the
consequent subordination of the Church, and the politicization of
the Church with a consequent deterioration of the state's (and the
citizenry's) legitimate prerogatives. Between these extremes there
is considerable room for both Christian orthodoxy and political
science to maneuver.

Adopting the World's Agenda?

The dramatically coercive authoritarianism of the Grand Inquisitor
is not the only mode in which the Church betrays its evangelical birthright and corrupts its distinctive integrity. The Church
can succumb to worldly temptation in more subtle ways that also
diminish both Christian witness and human freedom. Take, for example, a World Council of Churches mantra that was popular in
the 1960s and 1970s: "The World Sets the Agenda for the Church."
   The best possible construction of this aphorism is that it sought
to capture in a catchy phrase the Church's enduring commitment
to be a servant of humankind. Yet in principle, and indeed as things
worked out in practice, that slogan meant that the Church had
abandoned its critical distance; in the name of being prophetic,
the Church lost its prophetic edge. As expressed in the programs
of the WCC, "the world sets the agenda for the Church" meant
that the Church adopted a certain politics and economics as the final
index of Christian orthodoxy. (The politics and economics were, in

this case, leftist, but that is not what really mattered; the problem had arisen earlier in untoward Christian alliances with political forces on the right.) Christians who could not, in conscience, agree that the politics and economics in question best contributed to human flourishing were, so to speak, excommunicated. To claim that "the world" (or any partisan agenda in it) "sets the agenda for the Church" (understood both as the Mystical Body of Christ and as an institutional reality in society) is to subordinate the sovereignty of Christ to a worldly sovereignty, to subordinate the mission of the Church to a political agenda, and to subordinate the unity of the Church to a partisan definition of *communio*. Such subordinations cannot fail to corrupt the Church and to diminish its evangelical witness.

The temptation to subordinate the Gospel to politics may have been tempered over two millennia, but it has not completely abated. Thus the Rev. Joan Brown Campbell, the general secretary of the National Council of Churches of Christ in the U.S.A., proposed in early 1993 that President Bill Clinton occupied "the ultimate pulpit in this country." This was a curious affirmation for a minister of the Gospel to make. The freely elected president of the world's leading democracy surely occupies a powerful position, and the presidency can indeed be a powerful instrument for moral, and even religious, persuasion. As Robert Bellah and others have noted, the American presidency, by combining the offices of chief of state and head of government in one person, has inevitably acquired a certain sacerdotal dimension in terms of what Bellah termed American civil religion: no other public official can "speak for America" (and speak to America) as the president can.[24]

But to suggest that the bully pulpit of the presidency is the country's ultimate pulpit is to demean the power of the Gospel and to reverence the presidency in ways that can damage both Church and state. It is also to suggest that the most important decisions Americans make are political decisions, and that society's gravest problems are susceptible to a political solution. Neither of these suggestions sits easily with Christian orthodoxy or with sound democratic theory.

That the Church is the prior community of Christian commitment is, to repeat, a fundamental Christian doctrine. But that prior community has not received detailed instructions from its Lord on a myriad of questions about the right ordering of social and political life. To suggest that it has cheapens revelation and demeans the legitimate autonomy and authority of the civil community. The Church, in other words, has limited competence. Because its competence engages the most urgent questions of human life, however, it can help to orient the public discussion of less urgent issues toward ends worthy of human beings.

In other words, it is by being the evangelist of the Gospel that the Church is most truthfully and effectively the servant of the world. This is increasingly understood throughout the global Christian communion, and it would seem to be no accident that the churches that are vigorously advancing the Church's primary mission of evangelization are those showing the greatest vitality at the beginning of the third Christian millennium. Further, the highest teaching authority of the Catholic Church (Dostoevsky's model of coercive authoritarianism) has flatly rejected any coercion, ecclesiastical or political, in its missionary and public activity. As Pope John Paul II put it in his 1990 encyclical *Redemptoris Missio* [The Mission of the Redeemer], "The Church proposes; she imposes nothing."[25] The days of altar-and-throne are, for Catholics at least, a thing of the past, and for the weightiest of reasons: altar-and-throne arrangements are bad for the Church and its evangelical mission.

The Public Church Today:
In Defense of the Human

The 21st-century world badly needs a vital Christianity that proclaims the sovereignty of God and bears witness to human freedom.

Totalitarianism — the radical subordination of the individual and his personhood to the claims of the worldly sovereignty of the state, legitimated by ideology and enforced by draconian means of social control — may not be implied by the logic of modernity, as some conservatives have sometimes suggested. But totalitarianism in either its fascist or communist form is quite probably implied by some accounts of modernity (not least, by those dependent for their ideological impetus on the Jacobin radicalism of the French Revolution); and in any case, totalitarianism is a distinctively modern form of political organization. The scars of the 20th century's totalitarian experiments run deep, and not only in countries that have lived under the totalitarian jackboot.

It would be the height of folly to think that totalitarianism can happen only to other people, indeed to inferior other people. The Nazi horror took place in what was arguably the most cultured nation in Europe. Recall also the approbation that far, far too many men and women of intellectual and artistic accomplishment gave, serially, to Lenin, Stalin, and Mao, not to mention smaller fry such as Fidel Castro. For totalitarianism is, on one reading, the modern, technological solution to the ancient human problem of freedom. As the thirst for freedom is universal, so is the fear of freedom. And the fear of freedom can lead people, even very intelligent people, to reach for chains.

Nor should we think that only people addicted to ideology are vulnerable to the totalitarian temptation. Totalitarianism — or some variant that involves extremely unpleasant forms of social control — can arise as a response to chaos and the breakdown of social order. And that precipitating breakdown need not happen only under conditions of general economic disaster, as in Weimar Germany during the Great Depression. It could happen under conditions of relative prosperity.

For if freedom is decisively severed from the truth about the human person (not that difficult to imagine in a cultural climate it which the very notion of such a truth is regarded as impossibly *outré* — which is to say, a cultural climate like that of North America and western Europe) we will likely be reminded of a hard fact of public life: that a free-standing and merely instrumental freedom inevitably degenerates into license. License, the distorted diminishment of freedom, then becomes freedom's undoing. For as Nietzsche discerned a century ago, social life in which freedom is not tethered to moral truth reduces down to the assertion of power, and power is corrupted into my capacity to impose my will on you.[26] The contest between conflicting wills-to-power then yields social chaos. And as the Grand Inquisitor knew so well, men cannot live without order. They may fear freedom, but they absolutely abhor chaos; rather than endure chaos, they will ask, even demand, to be chained.

During the great struggle against totalitarianism that occupied fifty-five years in the middle of the 20th century, Christianity played a crucial public role (sometimes more adequately, sometimes less) as a lobe of humanity's conscience on questions fundamental to the dignity of the human person. As the Second Vatican Council put it in the midst of that struggle, the Church is "the sign and the safeguard of the transcendence of the human person."[27] And the Church is that sign and safeguard precisely because it discerns in every person the God-given capacity for final communion with the Creator. The Church is the *defensor hominis,* the defender of man and the promoter of what is authentically human, because the Church is the Bride of the Lamb who "redeemed us to God by his blood" (Rev. 5:9).

At the beginning of a century pockmarked by the scars of the previous century's tyrannies, at a time when the human capacity for self-governance is justifiably regarded with a measure of skepticism even among free peoples, and at a historic moment when proponents of a religious tradition with a very different view of the human future are assertively (and sometimes murderously) making the claim that they have solved the problem of freedom, one crucial public task of the Church in the 21st century is to bear witness to the enduring truths about the human person that we learn from the biblical tradition. These truths about humanity are what make free government possible. The first, which harkens back to Genesis 1–3, is that we are creatures of intelligence and free will, capable of rational reflection and decision-making. The second, a specification of the first (and a truth in which Christian tradition is complemented by classical philosophy), is that we are capable of discerning the truth of things by reflecting on the structure of the world and discovering the moral logic built into the human person and the human condition. And the third truth is the public implication of the first two: that we are creatures capable of ordering social and political life so that they serve the ends of human flourishing.

The Church best witnesses to these truths, and thereby serves the cause of human freedom, when it is the Church: a universal, inclusive *communio* of faith, hope, and love with a special care for the marginal and the dispossessed. To put it another way, the first public task of the Church is neither policy analysis nor policy prescription; it is to be the Church. In so doing, the Church reminds society of the destiny for which God created the world. And by reminding society of that destiny, the Church best helps society resist the totalitarian temptation, which is another form of the temptation to idolatry.

First Things First

This is not to say that all the Church has to offer to the debate over the right ordering of our freedom is a general doctrine of humanity's origin and goal. For well over fifteen hundred years, Christians have drawn out the implications of the Gospel vision of the dignity and end of the human person in a second-order reflection on freedom and justice in society. In other words, Christians have engaged, as Christians, in political philosophy. More recently, Christian social ethicists and political theorists have focused on specific matters of public policy, from issues of war and peace to the regulation of medical research. At all these levels of public engagement, though, the Church is giving witness to the self-understanding of its public mission proclaimed by the Second Vatican Council in 1965:

> The joy and hope, the grief and anguish of the men of our time, especially of those who are poor or afflicted in any way, are the joy and hope, the grief and anguish of the followers of Christ as well. Nothing that is genuinely human fails to find an echo in their hearts. For theirs is a community composed of men who, united in Christ and guided by the Holy Spirit, press on towards the kingdom of the Father and are bearers of a message of salvation intended for all men. That is why Christians cherish a feeling of deep solidarity with the human race and its history.[28]

The question, finally, comes down to putting first things first. There are three of these "first things": the Lordship of Christ; the *communio* of the Body of Christ, the Church; and the Church's proclamation, through the power of the Holy Spirit, of the saving action of God in Christ, in which the world learns its destiny and all men and women discover their true dignity as human beings.

When these priorities shape the Church's witness to the world, the Church's evangelical mission and its sacramental celebration of the mystery of God's redemptive love disclose certain basic truths about the right ordering of society. The Church's self-understanding as a *communio* both in and beyond time also clarifies the distinctive autonomy and dignity of the institutions of governance in the world. The Church must have no desire to be Caesar, and Caesar must not pretend to be God. The cause of human freedom and dignity is best served when Church and state acknowledge, freely and respectfully, each other's spheres of competence. While the Church knows that its competence is in matters of ultimate consequence, this is no barrier to its acknowledgment of the state's authority in those things that pertain "to Caesar" (Lk. 20:25).

The implications of all this? No partisan Church, but rather a public Church. No sacred state, but a limited state at the service of human dignity and the common good. In short: a *public Church* in a *civil society* served by a *limited state*. Or, in the American shorthand, a free people under a limited government.

This is not, to be sure, the Kingdom of God, which is a reality of God's making. But it is a form of governance that has shown itself compatible with the truth about the human person that is at the heart of the Gospel message. That compatibility is the basic point of tangency between Christianity and democracy.

Chapter Three

Diognetus Revisited, or, What the Church Asks of the World

In its original form, this essay was commissioned by the Center for Catholic and Evangelical Theology for a conference entitled "The Left Hand of God," held at Grace Lutheran Church in Lancaster, Pennsylvania, in October 1995. The essay was later published in a collection of conference papers edited by Carl Braaten and Robert Jenson, The Two Cities of God: The Church's Responsibility for the Earthly City. *It marked one of my first attempts to incorporate themes from the theology of Hans Urs von Balthasar into my thinking about political theology, and while the reception of that incorporation among some Balthasarians was notably chilly, others in that complex tribe happily took a more positive view.*

The anonymous, sub-apostolic Letter to Diognetus has played an important role in modern Catholic social thought since the Second Vatican Council, which cited it on several occasions. For the past three decades, the Letter has also been a basic text for Christian pro-life work. In addition to exploring the implications of the

Letter's image of the Christian as a "resident alien" in the world, the essay challenges the notion (prominent among both Catholics and Protestants, and at various points along the spectrum of political opinion) that the Church has a well-defined agenda for the world. The essay also explores briefly the bottom-line obligations of Christian social witness and action: the defense of religious freedom; the promotion of pluralism, understood as the public debate about public goods, ordered and disciplined by the canons of moral reason; and the defense of the possibility of participation in public life by citizens whose vocations call them to witness and action in that sphere.

N THE SUMMER of 1994 I was invited to address a retreat at-
tended by most of the Catholic bishops of the United States.
The retreat's theme (which embodied the deplorable tendency
in contemporary AmChurchSpeak to turn a fine noun into a grating participle) was "Shepherding a Future of Hope"; my assigned
topic was "Hope in Society." Some of the bishops were, I expect,
anticipating a bit of social justice shoptalk, leavened with perhaps
a few lurid political tales from the Potomac fever swamps, where
I work. But then as now, I began my thinking about the Church's
hopes for the world, and the Church's demands on the world, by
looking back to the second Christian century, the time of "the
churches the apostles left behind."[1]

My text is the *Epistula ad Diognetum,* the *Letter to Diognetus,*
which has become an important patristic reference point for contemporary Roman Catholic social thought.[2] We don't know who
Diognetus was, nor do we know who wrote him this letter. But the
anonymous Christian apologist who wrote to Diognetus created
an image of the-Church-in-the-world that has had a powerful influence on Christian reflection ever since, proposing as he did that
"what the soul is to the body, Christians are to the world."[3]

To be the soul of the world: the image carries with it paradoxical (some would say, dialectical) connotations of distance and
intimacy, the present and the future, the mundane and the transcendent. Those varied connotations were made a bit more precise
when the author of the *Letter to Diognetus* described Christians-in-
the-world in these terms:

> ... Christians are not distinguished from the rest of human-
> ity by country, language, or custom. For nowhere do they live
> in cities of their own, nor do they speak some unusual di-
> alect, nor do they practice an eccentric life-style.... But while
> they live in both Greek and barbarian cities, as each one's lot
> was cast, and follow the local customs in dress and food and

other aspects of life, at the same time they demonstrate the remarkable and admittedly unusual character of their own citizenship. They live in their own countries, but only as aliens; they participate in everything as citizens, and endure everything as foreigners. Every foreign country is their fatherland, and every fatherland is foreign. They marry like everyone else, and have children, but they do not expose their offspring. They share their food but not their wives. They are "in the flesh," but they do not live "according to the flesh." They live on earth but their citizenship is in heaven. They obey the established laws; indeed in their private lives they transcend the laws.[4]

Resident Aliens, Ahead of Time

This image of the "resident alien" nicely captures the worldly position of Christians, which is distinctive because it is always in the mode of an experiment. There is one Christian orthodoxy; there is no single way of Christian being-in-the-world. Sometimes Christians will be more comfortably "resident"; at other times, the wickedness of the principalities and powers will require them to be more defiantly "alien," even "sectarian" (which can, under certain circumstances, be a synonym for "faithful"). At all times, though, Christians live in the world in a somewhat unsettled condition. For the world, in Christian perspective, is both the arena of God's action in history and the antechamber to our true home, which is "the city of the living God" (Heb. 12:22).

Through the image of the resident alien, the *Letter to Diognetus* also reminds us that the Church's basic Christological confession — "Jesus Christ is Lord" (Phil. 2:11) — is the only secure ground for Christian hope. Anything else is simply optimism, and optimism is a fragile commodity, especially in that part of "the world" that is politics. In contrast, Christian hope, built on the transformative conviction that Jesus is Lord, is the sturdy, enduring theological virtue that, as the *Catechism of the Catholic Church* teaches, "responds to the aspiration to happiness which God has placed in the heart of every man," an aspiration Christians pursue by "placing our trust in Christ's promises and relying not on our own strength, but on the help of the grace of the Holy Spirit."[5] Hope is built on faith, not on a calculus of probabilities.

Lived out in the world amidst the agitations of the politics of the world, Christian hope should reflect the temporal paradox of Christian life: that Christians are a people both in and ahead of time. Christians are the people who know, and who ought to live as if they knew, that the Lord of history is in charge of history. Christians are the people who know how the story is going to turn out, and that puts Christians in a unique position vis-à-vis the flow of history. As Hans Urs von Balthasar has put it, Christians are the people who, amidst the world's accelerating development, "can confront [that development] with a divine plan of salvation that is coextensive with it, indeed that always runs ahead of it because it is eschatological."[6]

Christians know how the story is going to turn out. It is in this sense of making sense of the world that the *Letter to Diognetus* develops the image of Christians as the "soul of the world," claiming that, while "Christians are detained in the world as if in a prison, they in fact hold the world together."[7] Christians know and bear witness to the fact that, in the power of the Spirit, God and his Christ will be vindicated. Or, to recall a phrase that caused a stir in 1989, Christians know all about the "end of history."[8] Christians know that at the end of history, the world's story, which is anticipated in the Church's story, will be consummated in the Supper of the Lamb, in the New Jerusalem whose "temple is the Lord God the Almighty and the Lamb" (Rev. 21:22). Christians know that the world's story will be fulfilled beyond the world, in that true city, the "dwelling of God . . . with men," where God will "wipe away every tear from their eyes, and death shall be no more, neither shall there be mourning nor crying nor pain any more, for the former things have passed away" (Rev. 21:3a, 4).

Now if that is what you know — if that is the conviction on which your life is built, if that is the perception that orients reality for you — well, that gives you a rather distinctive angle on the world and its politics. The further paradox is that it is precisely this eschatological dimension of Christian hope that helps Christians create the moral and cultural conditions in which it is possible to build a pluralist democracy whose public life contributes to genuine human flourishing. More will be said about this in a moment. For now, suffice it to say that Christian hope as lived in the world must be a reflection of the Christian conviction that the end of the story — the end of our personal stories, and the end of the world's story — has already been disclosed in the resurrection of Jesus Christ and his ascension to the right hand of the Father in glory.

Eschatological Hope and Worldly Courage

Formed by that truth (which is the central truth of history), and within those aforementioned dialectics of intimacy and distance, present and future, the mundane and the transcendent, Christian resident aliens can tackle their tasks as citizens without attempting to force the Kingdom into history here and now.[9] A popular contemporary Catholic hymn bids us to "build the City of God." Sorry, but I must decline. Christians who think themselves obliged to build the City of God suffer from a theological misapprehension whose political consequences, history has taught us, can range from the picaresque through the foolish to the grotesque.

No, that fevered urgency for a political construction of the Kingdom is not the way Christians ought to think of their worldly obligations. Knowing that the Son, the "first-born among many brethren" (Rom. 8:29), has been raised to glory, and knowing that he, not we, will build the City of God, Christians can relax a bit about the world and its politics: not to the point of indifference or insouciance or irresponsibility, but in the firm conviction that, at the extremity of the world's agony and at the summit of its glories, Jesus remains Lord. The primary responsibility of Christian disciples is to remain faithful to the bold proclamation of that great truth, which is the truth that the world most urgently needs to hear.

Moreover, it is in pondering that salvific truth that Christians discover the courage to live out the "hope that is within" us (1 Pet. 3:15). The world, to put it candidly, can be a pain in the neck, and the politics of the world even more so: which means that the frenzied "politics of the Kingdom" of late-20th-century progressive Christianity is not the only temptation set before Christians-in-the-world. The temptation to a kind of eschatological indifference that leads to an abrogation of social responsibility is at least as old as Paul's second letter to the Thessalonians; the temptation to cynicism also has a venerable pedigree. From where, then, do Christians draw the courage to engage the world and its politics, in a manner befitting those "born of water and the Spirit" (Jn. 3:5)? Hans Urs von Balthasar finds the source of what he calls "the courage to pursue the path of history"[10] in the conviction that "the Word became flesh and dwelt among us, full of grace and truth" (Jn. 1:14):

> Only Christianity has the courage to affirm the present, because God has affirmed it. He became a man like ourselves. He lived in our alienation and died in our God-forsakenness. He imparted the "fullness of grace and truth..." to our here and now. He filled our present with his presence. But since the divine presence embraces all "past" and all "future" in itself, he has opened up to us all the dimensions of time. The Word that became flesh is the "Word in the beginning"; in him we have been "chosen before the foundation of the world." It is also the "final word," in which everything in heaven and on earth shall

be caught up together: Alpha and Omega.... [Thus] it is not possession, but a being-possessed, that lends wings to Christian hope. It vibrates with the thought that the earth should reply to heaven in the way that heaven has addressed earth. It is not in his own strength that the Christian wants to change the earth, but with the power of grace of him who — transforming all things — committed his whole self for him.[11]

Because the world was formed by the Word — the *Logos,* the Reason of God — the world, even in the grasp of sin, has an innate intelligibility; it is not the arena of absurdity, or meaninglessness, or madness, or incoherence (*pace* the postmodernists). Because the world has been transformed by the incarnate Word who dwelt among us, the Christian disciple cannot despise the world or despair of it. For the world has been impressed with "a new spiritual form, chiseled on the very stone of existence": the form of the Incarnate and Crucified One, who is also and forever the Risen One.[12]

The worldly vocation of a Christian can take the form of a contemplative withdrawal from the world, in which the contemplative dies to worldly things as a sacrificial offering for the salvation of the world. For most Christians, however, the obligation to engage the world in which the Word dwelt, "full of grace and truth," will be fulfilled in the form of action informed by contemplative prayer and reflection.[13] And so we come to the question of the Church's hope for the world.

The Public Difference the Church Makes

"The Church's hope for the world": to put it another way, what does that Church ask of the world? And does that asking suggest certain hopes — or, perhaps better, prudential judgments — about the right ordering of that part of the world that is the *polis,* the political community, society organized politically for common, purposeful action?

Here, it might seem, is where we discover the "Church's agenda for the world." But there is no such agenda. Or at least there is no agenda such as that suggested by Christian Coalition congressional scorecards, U.S. Conference of Catholic Bishops political responsibility statements, "JustLife" candidate-evaluation criteria, or the sundry public-policy pronouncements of the mainline/old-line Protestant justice-and-peace curias or the Sojourners community. These artifacts may be interesting or boring, enlightening or obfuscating, wise or stupid. But they are not, in the strict sense of the term, ecclesial statements. They may be statements from the Church, or from some faction within the Church; but they are not statements of the Church. The Church is not one political possibility, one political ideology, among many thousands of such possible contestants in the public arena.[14] If the Church is to become, in its presentation of itself to the world, what it "already is and is to be, namely, the leaven that facilitates the ultimate unification of the world in its totality, the enzyme and organism of the eschatological salvation that has appeared in Christ";[15] if, in other words, the Church is to be faithful to its origin in Christ, in the blood and water that flowed from the side of the Crucified One (Jn. 19:34) — then the Church cannot have an agenda commensurate with other political agendas.

But that does not mean that the Church has nothing to ask of the world. And what it asks of the world implies certain things about the right ordering of the political community.

The first thing the Church asks of the world is the space — social, legal, political, even psychological — in which to carry out its distinctive ministry of word, sacrament, and charity.

The Church asks the world to let the Church be the Church. Put more sharply, the Church expects and, if circumstances warrant, the Church demands that it be allowed to be what it is: a reality "in the nature of a sacrament—a sign and instrument...of communion with God and unity among all men."[16] The first thing the Church asks the world is that the Church be allowed to be itself.

This is, to be sure, no small thing. Nor is it a private matter. For the first thing the Church asks of the world has serious implications for the world, especially for that part of the world we call the state, which is the juridical embodiment of the political community. The state that can grant the Church the space it requires is a state that neither claims nor seeks any final authority over the Church's ministry of word, sacrament, and charity. This requires a limited state, one whose powers are circumscribed by custom (i.e., by moral-cultural habit) and by law. Thus the first thing the Church asks of the world is that that part of the world called the "state" adopt for itself a self-limiting ordinance.

This first request implies a deep critique of the totalitarian temptation, in both its hard (fascist or communist) and its softer (modern bureaucratic) embodiments. The latter is worth dwelling on for just a moment.

We all understand that something was fundamentally wrong when Nazi Germany attempted to co-opt the Church for political ends, or when the Soviet Union under Lenin, Stalin, and their heirs tried to obliterate the Church, and to co-opt, suborn, and manipulate what was not obliterated. We understand also that the persecution of the Church in China, North Korea, Vietnam, Sudan, Cuba, and Saudi Arabia in the early 21st century is an evil that bespeaks a fundamentally disordered political community. But we should also realize that the modern bureaucratic state's temptation to expand the reach of its regulatory power can, even in established democracies, constitute a denial of the first thing the Church asks of the world. The state's disinclination to grant the first request the Church makes of the world implies a disinclination to recognize the limits of its own competence and power. And that is bad news for democracy, as well as for the mission of the Church.

By being itself, the Church serves a critical demythologizing function in a democracy. That the Church's hope is focused on Christ and his Kingdom relativizes all worldly expectations and sovereignties, thus erecting a barrier against the coercive politics of worldly utopianism. Rousseau had it backward when he argued that a certain form of Christian conviction "made any reasonable civil order impossible."[17] The true relationship is this: by locating the finality of our hope (and thus the object of our highest sovereign allegiance) in the time beyond time, the Church helps create the space for a free, vigorous, and civil interplay of a variety of proposals for ordering public life in the here-and-now, none of which is invested with ultimate authority. Democracy is impossible when politics is absolutized, for absolutized politics must necessarily be the politics of coercion. Christian eschatology and its crucial capacity to demythologize and debunk the pretensions of the political helps to make democracy and the politics of persuasion possible.

If a limited state is one implication of the first thing the Church asks of the world, then the second implication is pluralism. The two are closely related. For the limited state is one that recognizes that the political community is not the only community to which human beings owe allegiance.

The Church's claim for open space for its mission and ministry implies the possibility of a plurality of communities within society to which men and women are bound with strong ties of commitment and affection. Moreover, the Christian believes that, in a rightly ordered polity, there is no essential contradiction (although there will always be tensions) between the obligations of discipleship and the obligations of citizenship. Thus the community of the Church helps demonstrate that genuine pluralism, far from leading to social chaos, contributes to the public order that every just state is obliged to promote. The Christian claim for free or open space is not simply anti-totalitarian in its public implications; to

put the matter more positively, the Church is bullish on pluralism — on orderly conversation among the many communities of
our lives. Pluralism is essential for the Church's public functioning;
pluralism is also essential for any political community that aspires
to freedom. For there can be no freedom without the free mediating
institutions of civil society. These are, as Alexis de Tocqueville recognized, the first "political institutions" of a democracy, precisely
because they establish the crucial distinction between society and
the state, and society's moral priority over the state.[18] Through the
plural free associations of civil society we know that the state exists
to serve society, not vice versa. The Church's claim for free space
within society helps keep society open, and the state limited.

*The second thing the Church asks of the world is that the world
consider the possibility of its redemption.*

As we know from the martyrologies, the world does not always
take kindly to the Church's proposal that it might need redemption, and that the redemption it needs has been effected in Christ.
Indeed, this was an exceptionally costly proposal to make in the
20th century, the greatest century of martyrdom in the history of
the Church. That fact barely registers on the consciousness of most
Christians in the West. Yet the late Pope John Paul II saw in the
20th-century rebirth of a "Church of martyrs" both a preparation
for the springtime of evangelization that should characterize the
21st century, and the fulfillment of the Church's longing for unity.
The "most convincing form of ecumenism," John Paul wrote in
1994, "is the ecumenism of the saints and of the martyrs. The
communio sanctorum speaks louder than the things that divide
us."[19] In their common shedding of blood for the cause of Christ,
Protestants, Orthodox, Anglicans, and Catholics have achieved a
Christian unity that still eludes the Church in the world.[20]

All Christians are called to be martyrs, not necessarily to the
shedding of blood, but in the original Greek sense of the martyr as
"witness."[21] That to which the Christian bears witness is the truth

about God and man revealed in the life, death, and resurrection of Jesus Christ. And that is the truth the Church asks the world to consider: Jesus Christ, who "fully reveals man to himself and brings to light his most high calling";[22] Jesus Christ, the "answer to the question that is every human life."[23]

In the postmodern 21st-century West, the Church's proclamation of this truth and the Church's invitation to the world to consider the possibility of its redemption meet less with a direct refusal than with a kind of societal indifference. God, Christ, redemption, sanctification: surely all these are beyond the pale for serious, mature, modern adults, concerned with authenticity and autonomy. The Christian claim may be a useful myth, capable of producing citizens (especially lower-class citizens) with desirable behavioral characteristics. But that the Christian claim poses the issue involved in understanding the truth of the world: well, excuse us, we have other things to do.

Even worse than indifference is the calculated insouciance toward the Christian proposal common among a certain sort of intellectual in affluent societies today. This insouciance is rooted in a cavalier attitude toward the very possibility that human beings can know the truth of things.[24] Despite its self-conscious worldliness, this epistemological flippancy constitutes a real and present danger to the world. For its public expression is the decadence of what the late Alan Bloom called debonair nihilism, and debonair nihilism has awful public consequences: it creates a toxic social and cultural environment, the primary victims of which are not the well-off but those on the margins of society, who have far less room for error in the conduct of their lives. As we have seen in our inner urban communities, one result of principled skepticism and debonair nihilism among the chattering classes and the wealthy is a vast breakdown of social order among the poor. If this chaos were to spread beyond the communities to which it is now largely confined, the further result would almost certainly be a breakdown of democratic order, as the state reached for an authoritarian solution to an intolerable problem.

Thus in challenging the world to remain open to the possibility of its redemption, the Church is helping to nurture — indeed to revivify — certain moral understandings about the cultural foundations of democracy and the civil liberties we associate with democracy. You cannot have a democracy without a critical mass of democrats, i.e., people who have committed themselves to the ethos of democratic civility and who have learned the moral habits — the virtues — necessary to live civility and tolerance. There is a huge chasm between this ethos and the insouciance of debonair nihilism and principled hedonism.

To put it another way, a world that has preemptively dismissed the question of its possible redemption is unlikely to be able to secure the cultural foundations on which a civil, democratic society can be built and sustained. Perhaps in other times and places, this was not so.[25] But today, the world's premature dismissal of the question of its redemption often results from a deep-rooted skepticism about any matters of truth and falsehood, and thus creates a situation in which citizens cannot give a persuasive account of why the democratic way of doing the public business is morally superior to other arrangements.[26] The principal challenge to this skepticism and its attendant moral confusions (and social pathologies) is the Christian Church, or, more precisely, Christian orthodoxy. The Nicene Creed contains no blueprint for conducting politics. But the Church that can faithfully recite the Nicene Creed and defend its plausibility as The Way Things Are can give a much thicker account of its commitment to the dignity of the human person and to the politics of human freedom than what is on offer in most academic philosophical circles today. The Church that can say that *this* — the claims contained in the Creed — is the truth about the world's story is far more capable of defending its commitments to the rights of all than the radical or insouciant skeptic is capable of defending religious freedom, freedom of speech, and other basic human rights. The Church that can defend the prerogatives of reason can better defend democracy against irrational (and often violent) religion (as in jihadism) than the skeptic for whom the claims of reason are a mere cultural construct.

Eucharistic Church, Public Church

This kind of witness in and for the world requires a particular kind of ecclesial community. The Church capable of claiming its rightful space within society and of proposing that the world consider the possibility of its redemption in Christ is emphatically not a Church conceived in mundane terms as another voluntary organization with a political task. Rather, the Church that can claim room for mission and that can ask the world to consider itself redeemable (and redeemed) is a Church that conceives itself eucharistically, as the Body of Christ. And as Christ's Body, it shares Christ's destiny, which is not a destiny to power but one in which "being given" means being broken and shared out.[27]

This is, to be sure, a post-Christendom Church; but that seems appropriate, in itself as well as in a post-Christendom world. Such a Church is also a Church at risk; but that, as Balthasar reminds us, has always been the Church's situation. For in being broken and shared out for the world,

> ... [the] Church will suffer the loss of its shape as it undergoes a death, and all the more so, the more purely it lives from its source and is consequently less concerned with preserving its shape. In fact, it will not concern itself with affirming its shape but with promoting the world's salvation; as for the shape in which God will raise it from its death to serve the world afresh, it will entrust [that] to the Holy Spirit.[28]

The Acts of the Apostles, the inspired portion of the history of the Church, ends with the account of a shipwreck—the result of which is the furtherance of the Church's evangelical mission to the nations.[29] Reflection on that imagery should be reassuring as the Church considers how it might, today, claim its proper space in society and propose to the world the possibility of its redemption.

A public Church eucharistically conceived also enables us to grasp that the *Letter to Diognetus* was expressing a central Christian truth, not merely a pious sentiment, when its author affirmed that, for Christians, "every foreign country is their fatherland." That is obviously not the case in worldly terms, even for the most assiduous of what we would call "inculturators." But it is certainly true when Christians gather with their fellow believers in a foreign country around the eucharistic table of the Lord. Since 1992, I have been privileged to teach in a seminar on modern Catholic social thought and the democratic prospect, held annually in Poland for students from North America and from the new democracies of central and eastern Europe. Each year I am more and more impressed by the distinctive perspectives these students bring to social and political questions from their different national histories and cultural backgrounds. And yet I am even more struck by our unity in eucharistic fellowship at the altar. On the basis of its eucharistic *communio*, the Church cannot give the unity of an ordered and free political community to the world; if such a *polis* is possible, it will have to be organized in specifically political terms. But the eucharistic community of Christians for whom every foreign country is a homeland is a powerful counter-case to the claims of the radical dividers and multiculturalists, for whom difference has become the first principle of anthropology and "human nature" is a will-o'-the-wisp.

The kind of eucharistically centered Church that can propose to the world the question of its redemption also challenges implicitly (and, at a secondary level of witness, explicitly) a claim variously advanced by Marxists, deconstructionists, authoritarian Confucians, and Islamists: namely, that the notion of universal human rights is a species of Western cultural imperialism, and that there are no universal human rights because there is no universal human nature. This is an important public witness to make today, for if there is no universal human nature and no universal moral law, then there can be no universal conversation about the human future; there can only be Hobbesian world in which all are at war with all.[30]

From a Christian point of view, the unity of the human race will be fully realized only in the Kingdom of God, which is finally a work of God's doing, not ours. Moreover, the human unity that believers experience in the Body of Christ cannot be transferred or copied in one-to-one correspondence to the world. But the fact of our unity in Christ across the barriers of sex, race, ethnicity, and culture is a powerful reminder to a sullen and cynical world that the claims of the dividers — who are all monists, either monists of a single ideology or monists of indifference — are not the only word on the human condition and the human prospect. Much less are they the final word.

The Causes for Which We Must Contend

There is, then, no Christian agenda for the politics of the world. The Church's hope for the world does, however, include a number of causes for which Christians are bound to contend in the world of politics, because of what Christians believe we know about the human person through the revelation of God in Christ.

The most important of these is religious freedom.

Here we return to the first thing the Church asks of the world. The Church cannot be the Church if it attempts to put the coercive power of the state behind its truth claims, or if it acquiesces in the state's assumption of that role. Coerced faith is no faith. As the *Letter to Diognetus* puts it, the God of Christians "saves by persuasion, not compulsion, for compulsion is no attribute of God."[31] The Church's defense of religious freedom is thus not a matter of institutional self-interest. Religious freedom is an acknowledgment, in the juridical order of society, of a basic truth about the human person that is essential for the right ordering of society: a state that claims competence in that interior sanctuary of personhood and conscience where the human person meets God is a state that has refused to adopt the self-limiting ordinance essential to right governance (not to mention democracy). Religious freedom is the first of human rights because it is the juridical acknowledgment (in constitutional and/or statutory law) that within every human person is an inviolable haven, a free space, where state power may not tread — and that acknowledgment is the beginning of limited government. In defending religious freedom, therefore, the Church defends both the truth about the human person and the conditions for the possibility of civil society.[32]

The second cause for which the Church must contend is pluralism. What is often called "pluralism" today is really plurality: the sociological fact of difference. Plurality is a given in the world, and within most modern societies. Pluralism is a signal cultural accomplishment, the transformation of difference and division into an ordered conversation about the greatest of all political questions, first identified as such by Aristotle: "How, then, ought we to live together?"[33] The question has an inescapable moral core, disclosed in the verb "ought." And so in the Aristotelian tradition (later adopted in various forms by various Christian political thinkers), politics is always an extension of ethics. To contend for the creation of a genuine pluralism of participation and engagement is one public face, so to speak, of the Church's challenge to the world in the matter of the world's possible redemption. For to build a genuine pluralism means to reject any monism of indifference or insouciance about the moral-cultural health of the public square.[34]

Finally, the Church must contend for the possibility of participation in public life. Here we return to Christian anthropology. As the *Catechism of the Catholic Church* puts it, "Participation is the voluntary and generous engagement of a person in social interchange. It is necessary that all participate, each according to his own position and role, in promoting the common good. This obligation is inherent in the dignity of the human person."[35]

The Church's defense of participatory democratic freedoms can be justified as a prudential judgment about the relative merits of various political systems. The most secure ground for the Church's defense of democracy, however, is the Church's understanding of the revealed truth about man as the *imago Dei,* the "image of God": a person, not an autonomous Self, with intelligence and free will and thus capable of reflection and decision. The Church certainly does not hold that everyone is obliged to engage in the daily business of politics. But because the Church proposes to the world a vision of the human person in which the defense of individual liberties is intimately related to the responsibility of promoting the common good, the Church must contend for the possibility of active political participation by those who discern a vocational obligation to those tasks. In this respect, the Church is not simply anti-totalitarian and pro-pluralist; the Church is populist.[36]

The Heart of the Matter

This construal of the "public Church" will undoubtedly strike some as terribly minimalist, perhaps even irresponsible. What about the environment, or the status of women, or health care reform, or parental choice in education, or humanitarian intervention in Darfur, or a flat tax, or the National Endowment for the Arts, or abortion, or euthanasia, or the war against terrorism? These are indeed important issues; the life issues bear directly on whether the

American republic will continue to exist in moral-cultural continuity with its Founding, while the war against jihadist terrorism
involves the question of the very future of the West and of democracy. But Christians damage the integrity of the Church and its
public witness when Christians suggest, explicitly or implicitly, that
politics, understood as the contest for power in the world, engages
Christian hope, understood as one of the three theological virtues.
I think I can make a fairly persuasive case for my position on any
of the issues listed just above, and those positions will be informed
by what I understand to be the relevant middle axioms of Christian
social ethics. But the outcome of these questions — which is to say,
the politics of these questions — does not touch, directly, "the hope
that is within" me (to return to St. Peter's first letter). If it did, there
would be something defective about my hope.

The Church that conceives its public witness in these terms is
the most relevant Church imaginable. Political analysts working
strictly within the boundaries of the social sciences are now coming
to understand the truth of Pope John Paul II's assertion that, within
free societies today, the really interesting and urgent questions have
to do with culture, not with the structures of politics and economics.[37] Neither democratic politics nor the market can function
properly absent the tempering and guidance provided by moral
habits, or what an older generation would have called "virtues."
Democracy and the market, in other words, are not machines that
will run of themselves; nor can democracy and the free economy be
sustained on the basis of liberal-individualist principles alone. The
foundations of the house of freedom, to adopt a phrase from the
Catholic bishops of the United States, are built out of the virtues
of citizens — virtues about which the Church has some important
things to say.

A Church that recognizes the priority of culture in the postmodern circumstances of the free society, and whose social witness
addresses that society at the deepest level of its self-understanding,

is thus positioned squarely on the cutting edge of the debate over the future of freedom. Far from being hopelessly out-of-it, such a Church, one whose social witness is drawn from the most profound source of the hope that it bears, may sometimes find itself uncomfortably relevant.

But that, too, can be one of the costs of discipleship.

Chapter Four

The Paradoxes of
Disentanglement

This essay began with an invitation from the University of Chicago's John M. Olin Center for Inquiry into the Theory and Practice of Democracy to deliver a lecture under its auspices in 1995. It was an immensely enjoyable evening, full of sharp questions, which I remember with pleasure and gratitude.

Throughout 2004 and 2005, Cardinal Christoph Schönborn, O.P., and I were in vigorous conversation about the contrasting states of Christianity and democracy in "Old Europe" and America. That conversation eventually led to our organizing an international conference in Vienna in April 2006 on the sometimes-forgotten Christian roots of democracy on both sides of the Atlantic. Cardinal Schönborn invited me to deliver a public lecture in the archiepiscopal palace during that conference, and it struck me as a good moment to revisit, revise, and extend the argument I had made in Chicago, in light of the intense European debate on whether the continent's Christian roots could be publicly acknowledged as a source of 21st-century Europe's commitments to human rights, democracy, and the rule of law.

As several colleagues suggested during the Vienna conference, the Catholic Church's entanglement with state power could be interpreted as a kind of Babylonian captivity from which the Church has finally been liberated. The question I tried to press in Vienna, and which shapes this essay in the form in which I present it here, is whether that disentanglement has been the unmitigated boon to European democracy that the advocates of laïcité *(or, more broadly, a thoroughly secularized and relativist European public square) claim. The question has obvious and urgent implications on the North American side of the Atlantic, too — indeed, it has profound implications throughout the democratic world.*

A CCORDING TO a line of analysis that has taken many forms, ancient and modern, I am a dangerous man, a threat to the public order: not because my political inclinations run to anarchism or to fantasies of dictatorship, but precisely because I am a Catholic committed to the great tradition of Christian orthodoxy.

Let me add, right at the beginning, that this alleged conflict is not how I usually experience the relationship between my Catholicism and my life as a citizen of the United States of America. That relationship is far better, if far more variously, described by words like "energized," "frustrated," "appalled," "comforted," and "bemused." Furthermore, the recording angel, studying the routine patterns of my life, would not be very likely to describe me as someone who is a threat to American democracy: I pay my taxes. I vote. I obey the laws (although I do confess to a propensity to jaywalking, a disdain for the 55-mile-per-hour speed limit, and a disinclination to let the local county government's Department of Ecology define the optimal moment for cutting my lawn). I make arguments about public policy in a civil manner. I work through the normal political processes to help elect candidates I favor, and I accept the results of elections in which candidates I prefer lose (which, in my case, is "frequently"). I present myself for jury duty when I am called. As a speculative matter, I could, I suppose, become a threat to the American constitutional order, in the sense that I would work to overthrow and replace it — but that change in my behavior would be the result of a fundamental change in the character of that constitutional order, not in my religious convictions.

Nevertheless, as a student of the history of Christianity, of Church/state relations in America, and of the theory of democracy, I cannot help but be impressed by the number of intelligent thinkers who were (and, in some cases, are) firmly convinced that people like me are mortal perils in a democracy, and indeed to democracy.

In an important book, *The Christians as the Romans Saw Them,*
the American patristics scholar Robert Louis Wilken explores in
far more detail than we can digest here the nature of the threat that
primitive Christianity and its truth claims seemed to pose to the
guardians of the established order of Rome.[1] Yet these charges are
worth revisiting briefly, if only as a vivid reminder of the truth of
the French aphorism, *plus ça change, plus ça la même chose.*

Pliny the Younger, for example, described Christianity in a letter to Trajan as a "degenerate sort of cult carried to extravagant
lengths." Celsus, the late-second-century philosopher whose critique of Christianity occasioned one of the great works of patristic
apologetics, the *Contra Celsum* of Origen, thought that Christians
were socially down-market, people of limited intelligence whose
faith was the religion of the stupid and indeed of stupidity. Moreover, according to Celsus, Christians were sectarians who privatized
religion and rendered the public square naked by transferring religious convictions to the sphere of private association; to make
matters worse, the Christian doctrine of the Incarnation and the
Christian claim that men were saved only by the name of Christ
constituted denials of the unity of the one God and undermined
the authority of the one emperor. Porphyry, the biographer of Plot-
inus and the editor of his *Enneads,* asked, "How can men not be
impious...who have apostasized from the customs of our fathers,
through which every nation and city is sustained?"

Somewhat closer to our own time, Jean-Jacques Rousseau, in ex-
plicating his theory of civil religion in the concluding chapter of his
Contrat Social, had this to say about Christianity in its "priestly"
form: "Far from winning the hearts of the citizens for the state, it
removes them from it, as from all earthly things. I know of nothing
that is more actively opposed to the social spirit." Priestly Christianity, Rousseau continued, is a purely spiritual religion, "which is
occupied only with heavenly things; the native land of the Christian is not of this world." Moreover, Rousseau argued, the political

defect of this form of Christianity is innate, as it derives explicitly from the founder; as Rousseau put it, "Jesus came in order to set up a spiritual kingdom on earth; thereby the theological system was separated from the political system, and this in turn meant that the state ceased to be *one* state, and that inherent tensions emerged, which have never ceased to agitate the Christian peoples." The result is "a continuous struggle between the jurisdictions…which has made any reasonable civil order impossible in the Christian states." Priestly Christianity, according to Rousseau, has created circumstances in which men have "two legislations, two sovereigns, two native lands," and thus are subjected to "antithetical obligations." And so, Rousseau concludes, the Christian can never be, at one and the same time, a pious believer and a good citizen. Christianity is, in the final analysis, *insociable:* the true Christian cannot, by reason of his Christianity, be integrated into society.[2]

Reading through the *dicta* on religion from the United States Supreme Court over the past sixty years, one finds a strikingly, if disturbingly, similar pattern of critique. For the Supreme Court has not been content to render legal decisions about controverted matters; it has, in the course of that judging, painted a portrait of religious conviction that is quite remarkable. Indeed, if one knew nothing about American religion except what one had read in the decisions of the Supreme Court since the landmark *Everson* case in 1947, one would have to conclude that religious conviction is indeed a danger to the democratic order. For religion, according to the Court, is inherently divisive. Why? Because it is inherently coercive. And why is it inherently coercive? Because it is inherently irrational. Justice Harry Blackmun, author of the notorious *Roe v. Wade* decision, which declared abortion-on-demand a constitutional "right," sharply contrasted "rational debate" and "theological decree" in the 1992 case, *Lee v. Wiseman,* and even suggested that religion is potentially homicidal. On the Supreme Court's understanding of it, religion is something the state can tolerate if consenting adults engage in it behind closed doors. But, as Justice John Paul Stevens suggested in a 1994 decision that restricted the rights of Hasidic Jewish parents to educate their children as they deemed appropriate, it's probably bad for the kids.[3] European instances of an assault on Christian conviction based on its alleged irrationality would not be difficult to find, not least in the 2003–4 debate over the proposed European constitutional treaty. Here, of course, the charge of "irrationality," coming as it does from the partisans of postmodernism, is not without a certain irony.[4]

How should Christians respond to all this? These ancient, Enlightenment, and contemporary objections to Christianity's impact on public life are not adequately met by softening the claims of Christian orthodoxy, thereby turning Christianity into a vaguely agreeable and unexceptionable set of behavioral injunctions, largely having to do with tolerance — and "tolerance" understood according to the rubric, "anything goes, so long as no one else gets hurt." The American Protestant ethicist H. Richard Niebuhr's lampoon of the attempt to retool the Gospel to fit the regnant cultural assumptions of his day — the mid-20th century — remains justly famous for its demolition of the vacuity of a certain modernist Christianity: "A God without wrath brought men without sin into a kingdom without judgment through the ministrations of a Christ without a cross."[5]

No, the only Christianity worth considering, in itself and in relationship to democracy, is the kind of Christianity that, in the playwright Henrik Ibsen's phrase, is far more deep-down-diving and mud-upbringing. A Christianity that takes itself seriously as the bearer of great truths about the human person and human community, human origins and human destiny, is a Christianity to contend with; a Christianity indistinguishable from the editorial page of the *New York Times, Le Monde, Gazeta Wyborcza,* or the *Globe and Mail* is hardly worth anyone's bother.

The question of the relationship between Christianity and democracy has engaged some of the finest theological and philosophical minds of our times: I am thinking, in particular, of Jacques
Maritain, the French neo-Thomist who helped develop the Universal Declaration of Human Rights.[6] I am thinking of Reinhold
Niebuhr, whose Christian defense of democracy in the face of many
liberal churchmen's appeasement of totalitarianism in the 1930s
marked an important point in American religious-intellectual history.[7] I am thinking of Father John Courtney Murray, the American
Jesuit whose reflections on the Catholic experience of the Church-
state issue in the United States helped pave the way for the Second
Vatican Council's landmark Declaration on Religious Freedom.[8]
And I am thinking of Karol Wojtyła, Pope John Paul II, quon-
dam Docent in philosophy at the Catholic University of Lublin,
whose penetrating analysis of democracy in the 1991 encyclical,
Centesimus Annus, drew respectful attention around the world.[9]

I cannot, of course, review in detail the work of these giant figures
here, nor can I settle in any definitive way the controversies over
the relationship between Christian piety and politics, or Christianity and democracy. What I can do is to describe, and defend, what
it is that putatively dangerous folk like me — orthodox Catholics
engaged in ecumenical and interreligious dialogue with Protestant,
Orthodox, and Jewish collaborators — bring to the ongoing experiment in self-governance that is Western democracy. This will not, I
hasten to add, be a utilitarian defense of "useful" religion. Rather, I
want to draw out some of the implications of Catholic truth claims
about human nature, the human person, human community, and
human destiny for the conduct of democratic states. These claims
are, I believe, true. That they have important public implications
is also, I think, true. But their public utility is not the final warrant
of their validity.

Let me suggest that there are at least three important impacts
that Christian orthodoxy, and the behaviors that it warrants, has

on the experiment in self-governance that is Western democracy, European and American.

Making Room for Democracy

The first thing that Christian orthodoxy does for democracy has to do with the problem of what we might call "making room" for democracy."

The words have become so familiar to us that we may have lost an appreciation of their revolutionary import. So let's revisit a key moment in St. Matthew's Gospel:

> ... Then the Pharisees went and took counsel how to entangle him in his talk. And they sent their disciples to him, along with the Herodians, saying, "Teacher, we know that you are true, and teach the way of God truthfully, and care for no man; for you do not regard the position of men. Tell us, then, what you think. Is it lawful to pay taxes to Caesar, or not?" But Jesus, aware of their malice, said, "Why do you put me to the test, you hypocrites? Show me the money for the tax." And they brought him a coin. And Jesus said to them, "Whose likeness and inscription is this?" They said, "Caesar's." Then he said to them, "Render therefore to Caesar the things that are Caesar's, and to God the things that are God's." When they heard it, they marveled; and they left him and went away [Mt. 22:15–22].

Now that is a truly revolutionary text, the public implications of which have been working themselves out for two millennia. During those centuries, Christians have not reached agreement on either the theological nuances of the text or its practical implications. Some see Jesus's injunction as a call to radical withdrawal from contact with the principalities and powers of this, or any other, age. Others find in it a biblical warrant for a "two kingdoms" social ethic. No doubt someone, somewhere, is using Matthew 22 to buttress an argument for the flat-rate income tax. But virtually everyone ought to be able to agree that the story of Caesar's coin teaches two things that have decisively influenced both the Church and the world over the past two thousand years.

The first things to be noted about the text is that Jesus gives Caesar his due. That Caesar has authority is not denied. Nor did the primitive Church deny that authority even after Caesar, in the person of his procurator, Pontius Pilate, had executed the Church's Lord. The New Testament's First Letter of Peter, widely regarded by biblical scholars as being based on an ancient Christian baptismal sermon, enjoined the newly baptized to "Be subject for the Lord's sake to every human institution, whether it be to the emperor as supreme, or to the governors as sent by him to punish those who do wrong and to praise those who do right" (1 Pet. 2:13–14). Similarly, Paul enjoined the Romans to "be subject to the governing authorities. For there is no authority except from God, and those that exist have been instituted by God" (Rom. 13:1). Caesar, in brief, is not to be denied what is rightly his.

But the second crucial aspect of Matthew 22 is that Jesus, by juxtaposing Caesar and God, de-divinizes the emperor, and thereby declares the priority of fidelity to God. As Paul later reminded his Romans, there are no legitimate things of Caesar's that are not Caesar's by reason, ultimately, of God's authority. But Jesus also insists that there are things of God's that are not Caesar's. Because God is God, Caesar is not God. And if Caesar attempts to occupy the ground that properly belongs to God alone, Caesar must be resisted.

This Gospel text has had world-historical impacts for two millennia. It stood behind Pope Gelasius I's 4th-century reflections on the distinction between priestly and royal authority. It stood behind Pope Gregory VII in his controversy with the Emperor Henry IV during the investiture controversy; the Church's defense of its liberties against encroaching political power were both a working-out of Jesus's injunction not to give Caesar what was not legitimately his and a force decisively shaping the social pluralism of the Middle Ages. Matthew 22 stood behind the popes of the 19th century in their resistance to the attempt by several European states to reduce the Church to a sub-division of the state. And it has had echoes down to our own time.

To take but one example: for five years after the accession of the communist government of Poland in 1948, the Polish Church, under the leadership of Cardinal Stefan Wyszyński, tried with great deftness to reach a modus vivendi with the regime that did not involve a fundamental compromise of the *libertas ecclesiae,* the freedom of the Church. But in May 1953, the regime ordered the implementation of a decree giving the state the authority to appoint and remove priests and bishops; all clergy were also to be required to take an oath of loyalty to the Polish People's Republic. Which meant, in practice, that the Church was to become a wholly owned and operated subsidiary of the Polish state, itself a husk owned and operated by the Polish community party and its masters in Moscow.

Cardinal Wyszyński now chose the path of confrontation, and in a historic sermon at Warsaw's St. John's Cathedral, he threw down the gauntlet: "We teach that it is proper to render unto Caesar the things that are Caesar's and to God that which is God's. But when Caesar seats himself on the altar, we respond curtly: he may not." Later, the entire Polish episcopate issued a memorandum which concluded with the memorable words, "We are not allowed to place the things of God on the altar of Caesar. *Non possumus!*" "We cannot!"

That act cost Cardinal Wyszyński three years of imprisonment and internal exile under house arrest; but he eventually won his point. Moreover, a strong case can be made that the *Non possumus!*

of the Polish episcopate was a crucial marker along the road that led, by a long and complex path, from the abrogation of freedom in east central Europe after World War II to the restoration of democracy in those lands in 1989. Wyszyński's successful defense of the independence of the Church made the completion of the totalitarian project in Poland impossible. Because the Church remained free and remained vital, the Polish communist state could not occupy the totality of social space, as its doctrine demanded of it. The resistance Church made possible by Cardinal Wyszyński and the bishops' *Non Possumus!* became, in time, the ground on which the overwhelming majority of the men and women who made the Solidarity revolution of 1980, and later the Revolution of 1989, came to the spiritual maturity that gave them the courage to be nonconformist and to take the risk of freedom.[10]

Much more is involved here than rallying the troops, of course. Because Caesar is not God, the realm of the political is a realm of neither ultimacy nor totality. By "de-divinizing" Caesar, Christianity desacralizes politics. And that is an achievement of great public importance. Why? Because it clears the social space on which a politics of persuasion can form: the social space on which a juridical state with limited and defined legal powers, whose primary function is securing the basic rights of its citizens, can be built. Because Caesar is not God, civil society is possible. Because Caesar is not God, the state is at the service of society, rather than the other way around. Because Caesar is not God, we can be democratic citizens of a limited, constitutional state.

Christianity thus brings what Cardinal Christoph Schönborn, O.P., once described as a "leavening of division" to public life.[11] The desacralization of politics that is implied in the de-divinization of Caesar is, in contemporary terms, a crucial barrier against both the totalitarian temptation and against the tendency of all modern bureaucratic states to extend indefinitely the reach of their coercive power. When a grandmother in the Queens section of New York

City insists that the state cannot mandate teaching of sexual techniques to primary school children, as when Cardinal Wyszyński and the Polish episcopate issued their historic *Non possumus!* as when Gregory VII faced down the Holy Roman Emperor Henry IV in the 11th century, as when German bishops went to jail rather than truckle to Bismarck, as when Thomas More and John Fisher went to the scaffold as the King's good servants but God's first, we are hearing echoes of that confrontation between Jesus and his critics two thousand years ago, on the matter of piety and politics, Caesar and God.

By establishing that politics, while important, is never ultimate, but only penultimate, Christian orthodoxy makes a considerable contribution to the never-ending project of "making space for democracy." Indeed, if, with Aristotle, we mean by "politics" the ongoing and public deliberation of that great question, "How ought we to live together?" then Christianity's insistence on the penultimacy of the political helps make genuine politics possible.

Making Democrats

The second impact that Christian orthodoxy and the behaviors it warrants has had, and continues to have, on the Western democratic experiment has to do with the kind of a people we are, and the kind of people that we aspire to be, as citizens of democratic states.

Throughout the West, we have been powerfully reminded in recent years that you cannot have a democracy without a sufficient number of democrats: without a critical mass of men and women who have internalized the habits of the heart and the habits of the mind — the virtues — that are essential to the conduct of an experiment in democratic self-governance. Contrary to the expectations of some Enlightenment political theorists, democracy (as John Paul II insisted in *Centesimus Annus*) is not a machine that can run by itself. If the machinery of democracy is well designed, the machine can, for a time, compensate for the inadequacies of the citizenry. But over the long haul, the machine needs mechanics — and mechanics of a certain cast of mind and soul — to make it work, such that the machinery serves the ends of human flourishing. The machine needs mechanics who will continue to affirm the superiority of this kind of machine over others, and who will do that precisely because of how they conceive their own human dignity and that of their neighbors.

Every two-year-old ever born is a natural tyrant: a beautiful bundle of willfulness and self-centeredness who must, in our societies, be transformed, somehow, into a democratic citizen, a member of a civil society. I would not presume to suggest, because I do not believe, that Christian orthodoxy constitutes the only possible set of religious and moral warrants capable of making tyrants, which is what all of us are at birth, into democrats. But I do know that democrats — like Christians — are made, not born. And I believe that Christian personalism and a Christian optic on the human condition can be a powerful and positive influence in shaping the attitudes toward "the other" that are essential to the democratic experiment.

C. S. Lewis was a talented novelist and a brilliant literary critic who also happens to have been the most successful Christian apologist of the 20th century, a man whose books continue to sell literally millions of copies every year. On June 8, 1941, Lewis, a layman with no formal theological training, preached a sermon in Oxford's University Church of St. Mary the Virgin, the former pulpit of John Henry Newman and Edward Pusey. Lewis's sermon, entitled "The Weight of Glory," ended like this:

There are no *ordinary* people. You have never talked to a mere mortal. Nations, cultures, arts, civilizations — these are mortal, and their life is to ours as the life of a gnat. But it is immortals whom we joke with, work with, marry, snub, and exploit — immortal horrors or everlasting splendors. This does not mean that we are to be perpetually solemn. We must play. But our merriment must be of that kind (and it is, in fact, the merriest kind) which exists between people who have, from the outset, taken each other seriously — no flippancy, no superiority, no presumption. And our charity must be a real and costly love, with deep feeling for the sins in spite of which we love the sinner — no mere tolerance, or indulgence which parodies love as flippancy parodies merriment. Next to the Blessed Sacrament itself, your neighbor is the holiest object presented to your senses.[12]

As it happens, Lewis was a man deeply skeptical about modernity, who never read newspapers, took no part in politics, and would probably have been far more comfortable living in the 13th century than in the 20th. But in "The Weight of Glory," he described rather precisely some of the core qualities we should want to see embodied in democratic citizens today: a commitment to democratic equality that is sustainable in and out of season, because it is grounded in something far deeper than a pragmatic or utilitarian calculus and is thus able to discriminate between serious and spurious claims of inequality; a willingness to engage the "other" seriously, across the many barriers of difference that separate us in societies characterized by increasing cultural and social plurality; a commitment to truth-seeking and truth-telling, regardless of the consequences ("living in the truth," as the human rights resistance in Czechoslovakia put it in the 1980s); a certain seriousness about life, but without the kind of bogus solemnity that characterized the public ceremonial of totalitarian states; a respect for the legitimately private space of others; a charity that displaces naked ambition as the motive for public service.

In the midst of the Second World War, Lewis challenged the congregation at St. Mary the Virgin to live their Christianity seriously for its own sake. At the same time, that basic Christian stance of reverence toward others who are never, ever "mere mortals" can also help form the kind of political community in which people "have, from the outset, taken each other seriously" — seriously enough to engage in the public discourse that is the lifeblood of democracy; seriously enough to engage a real argument around the question, "How *ought* we to live together?"

Put another way, and to adopt a formulation from the Protestant theologian Paul Tillich, democratic politics requires a democratic political culture: and culture is formed by cult, by religion, by what we honor, cherish, and worship — by that which binds us together, in the root sense of the Latin *religio*. The question is not, then, whether piety has much to do with politics; the real questions are, what kind of piety, informing what kind of politics? Christian orthodoxy is in this sense a "piety" that, by engendering reverence toward the neighbor, the "other," as a unique subject who is also the object of the salvific will of God, helps form precisely the kind of citizens who can make a democracy work — particularly under conditions of plurality, which is to say, amidst racial, ethnic, and religious difference.

This latter point is worth pausing on for a moment. One of the not-so-subtle fears at work in contemporary debates about the public role of Christianity in democracies is the fear that vibrant religious conviction, publicly expressed in debates over public policy, inevitably leads to religious intolerance and thence to civic strife. No doubt that has happened; and it continues to happen in other venues with which we are all familiar from the newspapers. But surely the more interesting datum to be drawn from the American experience is that in the United States today — in that vibrantly, maddeningly, diversely, and, it appears, incorrigibly religious society — religious tolerance is religiously warranted.

The roots of religious tolerance in contemporary America are found neither in pragmatism nor in a utilitarian calculus; rather, those roots are religious roots. Tens of millions of Americans believe it to be the will of God that we not kill each other over our differences as to what constitutes the will of God.[13] And that conviction is strongest among those whose Christian conviction is most robust. Religious tolerance in America— the management of plurality, if you will, — is, in the main, a religious accomplishment. And while that accomplishment has been shaped by important interreligious encounters, especially between Christianity and Judaism, the basic demographics of the situation tells us that the religious accomplishment of religious tolerance in America is, in the main, a Christian accomplishment.

That accomplishment is, to be sure, never secure, nor is it unique to the United States. As the legal scholar Joseph Weiler, an orthodox Jew, has reminded Europeans during the early years of the 21st century, the social doctrine of the Catholic Church offers a far thicker set of warrants for genuine tolerance — differences engaged with respect and charity— than anything else on tap in contemporary European high culture.[14] Moreover, genuine religious toleration is always an accomplishment to be deepened, never an achievement to be taken for granted. Further, I would suggest that the religious accomplishment of religious tolerance is set firmly on the path to a secure future only when it has begun to build a genuine pluralism out of what today passes for pluralism, which is really, and too often, a monism of indifference.

We are used to thinking of "pluralism" as a sociological fact. But the sociological fact is *plurality*. As Father John Courtney Murray taught us, genuine pluralism is never a mere sociological fact: it is, rather, a great moral-cultural accomplishment, "creeds intelligibly in conflict" in the give-and-take of democratic deliberation. Thus true pluralism is an exercise in tolerance; and true tolerance, as Father Richard John Neuhaus has written, is not the avoidance of differences, or an indifference to differences, but the thoughtful engagement of differences within the bonds of civility.[15] Pluralism is an achievement: the achievement, Murray put it, of an orderly conversation, which is another way of saying a "civil society."

As Murray nicely put it in the 1950s, what is it that impels us to "lay down our arms . . . and . . . take up argument?"[16] Again, there are many possible ways to build the kind of character that allows one to "take up argument," and thereby become a democratic citizen. But surely one reasonable way is via the Christian claim that we are called into argument, and called out of barbarism, by the grace of Christ, the *Logos* of God, who is the guarantor of the intelligibility and ultimate benignity of the created order. "Next to the Blessed Sacrament itself, your neighbor is the holiest object presented to your senses." Not a bad aphorism for a democrat amidst plurality, seeking to help turn that plurality into pluralism.

Giving an Account

In the third place, Christian conviction makes an important contribution to the legitimation of democracy, in that Christian religious convictions and moral norms enable Christians to give an account of their democratic convictions.

In the American Declaration of Independence, Thomas Jefferson prefaced the moral case for American independence by bowing toward a "decent respect to the opinions of mankind." Serious political action is political action undertaken after serious moral reflection and with serious moral justification. Jefferson's determination that an account be given — and indeed that a moral account be given — was not only admirable in its own time. This willingness to give an account, or as Jefferson put it, this commitment to "declare the causes" of our actions, ought to characterize the democratic citizen making the case for democracy in any age.

Why? Because democracies, as we have seen, are not machines that can run by themselves. Democracies are what we might call "proposition regimes," for democracy is a distinctive mode of political community formed and sustained by certain intellectual and moral convictions, and certain habits of virtue. Genuine democrats are the bearers of a proposition, and that proposition is itself the product of moral convictions. To be able to give an account of those convictions is no small part of the responsibility of citizenship, at least in democratic countries.

What is a good citizen? Richard John Neuhaus once put the matter succinctly, in these terms:

> A good citizen does more than abide by the laws. A good citizen is able to give an account, a morally compelling account, of the regime of which he is part. He is able to justify its defense against its enemies, and to convincingly recommend its virtues to the next generation so that they, in turn, can transmit the regime to citizens yet unborn. This regime of liberal democracy, of republican self-governance, is not self-evidently good and just. An account must be given. Reasons must be given. They must be reasons that draw authority from that which is higher than the self, from that which is external to the self, from that to which the self is ultimately obliged.[17]

Father Neuhaus went on to ask, provocatively, whether an atheist could meet this test of good citizenship. Now there are many ways of being an atheist, and it is not without interest to recall that atheism — being *a-theos,* without God, or more precisely, the gods — was the charge leveled against Christians who were thereby regarded as subversives in times of Roman persecution. Neuhaus, however, was particularly concerned about the distinctive modern form of being *a-theos,* "without God," which he styled the "atheism of unreason": a way of being *a-theos* that "denies not only the possibility of truth claims about God but the possibility of claims to truth at all."[18]

In this conceptual world, if such it may be called, to deny God is as nonsensical as affirming God. There is no "truth" per se; there is only the truth that the relevant "community of discourse" agrees to take as true. One has to wonder, Neuhaus concluded, whether it is at all possible for someone who is *a-theos* in this fashion to be a good citizen, in the full sense of the term. For the atheist of unreason cannot, by his or her own self-understanding, give a morally persuasive or compelling account of the democratic regime that has a public grip beyond the community of selves that just happens to find it true.

This judgment provoked an interesting response from a more old-fashioned-style atheist, Paul Kurtz, former professor of philosophy at the State University of New York at Buffalo and author of *Humanist Manifesto II.* Kurtz rumbled, in response to Neuhaus's argument, "Is this the opening salvo of a campaign to deny atheists their rights?" To which Father Neuhaus responded, "Relax, Mr. Kurtz. Your rights are secured by my understanding of the truth, even if mine are not by yours."[19]

In an intellectual and cultural climate in which, as the philosopher Alasdair MacIntyre argued years ago, it is extraordinarily difficult to say, "You ought to do this," but only, "I'd prefer that you do this," we seem to be stymied by Pontius Pilate's famous question to Jesus in the Gospel of John: "Truth? What is truth?" Pilate believed, perhaps cynically, perhaps sincerely, that that question, "What is truth?" was a real conversation-stopper. So do many of those who occupy the commanding heights of culture on both sides of the Atlantic in the early 21st century. In fact, though, for a democracy which must give an account — to itself, to its competitors and enemies, and to succeeding generations — of the truths about the human person and human community on which it was founded, Pilate's question ought to be the conversation-starter, not the conversation-stopper.[20]

In his 1993 encyclical letter, *Veritatis Splendor* [The Splendor of Truth], Pope John Paul II had some interesting things to say about the relationship between truth and freedom. Contrary to a media caricature of John Paul that lingered for more than two decades, the Polish pope in fact celebrated and championed the modern world's emphasis on freedom. (As a man who spent the first forty years of his adulthood living under, and struggling against, Nazis and communists, how could he not?) But what happens, the Pope asked, when freedom gets untethered from truth; can freedom stand by itself, without decomposing into license? For if freedom becomes license, then freedom becomes its own undoing, as every aspect of personal and social life becomes, as Friedrich Nietzsche understood, simply the assertion of power. And that means, among many other things, the death of democracy. For when truth is democratized — which is to say, when the truth is no more than the will of each one of us or a majority of us — then democracy, unable to give a finally compelling account of its own truth, is exposed, naked, before its enemies.[21] Democracy is not, to repeat, a machine that will run of itself.

Americans whose political history as an independent nation began with the assertion of certain self-evident truths shouldn't find the late Pope's reassertion of a relationship between freedom and truth all that foreign. Neither should Europeans, heirs of a civilization that gave the world the very idea of moral reason. And in considering whether religiously informed moral truths constitute some sort of threat to democracy, we might well revisit James Madison's famous *Memorial and Remonstrance,* one of the key 18th-century texts that shaped the American constitutional tradition of religious freedom. Throughout the Western world, we have become accustomed to the notion of "rights" as trumps, free-floating claims sundered from any sense of duties; so it is instructive to return to Madison's understanding of religious freedom as an inalienable right that is ordered to a prior and supervening duty. Here is what the chief conceptual architect of the U.S. Constitution wrote in *Memorial and Remonstrance:*

> It is the duty of every man to render to the Creator such homage and such only as he believes to be acceptable to him. This duty is precedent, both in order of time and in degree of obligation, to the claims of Civil Society. Before any man can be considered as a member of Civil Society, he must be considered as a subject of the Governor of the Universe: And if a member of Civil Society, who enters into any subordinate Association, must always do it with a reservation of his duty to the General Authority; much more must every man who becomes a member of any particular Civil Society, do it with a saving of his allegiance to the Universal Sovereign.[22]

Christians are not the only people capable of "giving an account" of their democratic commitments. Other accounts are given, and some of them have considerable public purchase; still other accounts are thin indeed, and one fears for the future of the West if these thin accounts — and especially those accounts that are essentially utilitarian in nature — were to become the only accounts publicly available in Western democracies. But the Christian claim that we can give such an account, a defense, of the democratic proposition and experiment, based on biblically and theologically warranted moral understandings, puts Christians in a position to offer a more robust legitimation of democratic regimes than some, and perhaps many, others. And that is a matter of no small public consequence in an age when aggressive alternative conceptions of the just and virtuous society are advancing their case in the world, often through violence.

A Great Paradox

A great paradox has been cast up by the past two hundred years or so of Western history: the years in which Christendom has come to an end.

While the situation is obviously a complex one, I believe it to be very good for the Church throughout the world that Christendom — the Constantinian alliance of the Church with state power — is over and done with. The end of Christendom has freed the Church for its essential, constitutive tasks of evangelization, worship, and charity, and its public task of culture-formation. Moreover, the end of Christendom gets the Church out of the coercion business, which was one of the great blots on the Church's record of which Pope John Paul called Christians to repent publicly in preparation for the Great Jubilee of 2000.[23]

That same pope, in his 1990 encyclical letter on Christian mission, flatly rejected coercion in evangelization, writing that "the Church proposes; she imposes nothing." Now, as the late Holy Father knew, that has not always been the case. But that it now is the case for more than a billion Catholics is very good news for both the Church and the world in the 21st century and the third millennium. The Church has no business putting the coercive power of the state behind its truth claims; nor does the Church have any business re-sacralizing politics, of any ideological hue. The end of Christendom is, to repeat, a very, very good thing for the Church.

On the other hand, and here is our paradox, I am not at all convinced that this disentanglement that we call "the end of Christendom" has been an undifferentiated blessing for those persons and institutions charged with the tasks of governance — despite the claims of atheists old and new. The democratic machine, to repeat it one last time, cannot and will not run of itself. Democracy must tend to the safe maintenance and moral health of that social space we call "civil society," lest skepticism and moral relativism create new forms of dictatorship (aimed at the coercion of consciences), and in order to keep the encroachments of the bureaucratic state under control. Democracy needs a critical mass of democrats, and democrats are made, not born: how shall we "grow" the democrats that we need to sustain our democracy? And democracy must be able to render an account of itself, to offer a persuasive and compelling moral justification for this strange, sloppy, confused, maddening, exhilarating, tawdry, and glorious way of doing the public business. It is good, indeed it is essential, for the democratic state that it not be a sacred state. But the democratic state needs the disentangled Church — the post-Christendom Church — in order to remain a law-governed democracy in which freedom serves the ends of genuine human flourishing.

Why? Perhaps it could be different, as a matter of abstract speculation. But we live in a real world, not an abstract world. And in this real world, the world in which the atheism of unreason and the moral relativism that is its natural child have had a profound impact on our culture and our civil society, democracy is in serious trouble. When three justices of the Supreme Court of the United States can reduce the meaning of freedom to each individual's capacity to determine "the concept of existence, of meaning, of the universe, and of the mystery of human life," we are in trouble.[24] When members of the European Parliament declare religious freedom a "source of discrimination," we are in trouble.

See, then, how far we have come. At least some members of the U.S. Supreme Court and the European Parliament seem to believe that all moral judgments are, somehow, sectarian religious judgments; and since those kinds of judgments are, as American jurists and European parliamentarians have described them, inherently private and un-public, they cannot be in play in the public square. So the result is not only a religiously naked public square, but a morally denuded public square in which, by definition, there can be no account given in the defense of democracy.

On this thin understanding of democracy, there can be no community of genuine democratic discourse. There can be no civil society, no "creeds intelligibly in conflict." Here, rather, is a congeries of monads, who can hardly be considered citizens of a political community, since they are related and mutually engaged only by their capacity to contest each other's "concept of existence" by lawsuit. Here, there is but the state, and the individual. And we ought to know, from the history of the most sanguinary of centuries, the 20th, where that can eventually lead—just as we ought to recognize that a community unable to give an authoritative and reasonable moral account of its commitments to civility and tolerance is disarmed in the face of religiously warranted assaults on civility and tolerance from jihadists.

There is no resolution, then, of the paradox of disentanglement. In pondering that paradox, though, the thought occurs that the far greater burden of the end of Christendom is born by the democratic state than by the Church. The Church, now, can give a carefully and deeply argued account of why it supports and defends the democratic project in history. But can democracy, and can democrats, on either side of the Atlantic?

Chapter Five

Is Political Theology
Safe for Democracy?

The beginning of the contemporary American religion-and-politics debate, at least in its most developed intellectual form, can be dated precisely: it began in earnest with the publication in 1984 of Richard John Neuhaus's book The Naked Public Square. *In the years that followed, the religion-and-politics debate (which could also be styled the Christianity-and-democracy debate) intersected with several other contentions: the ongoing struggle to secure the inalienable right to life, and the related arguments set in motion by the new genetic knowledge and the attendant revolution in biotechnology; the dissatisfaction among liberal political theorists with the thinness of John Rawls's account of democracy and the subsequent effort on the American Left to define a viable set of moral warrants for the philosophical defense of democracy; the ongoing debates over the origins and resolution of the Cold War; the intellectual challenges posed by the Chinese model of authoritarian capitalism and by Islamist jihadism. Each of these debates in turn engaged questions of political theology.*

Then, in the mid-years of the first decade of the 21st century, a new phenomenon arose: a "new atheism" that, while a bit thin on both data and serious arguments, was rich with black legends — and thus became a roaring success commercially, thereby grabbing the attention of the mass media. As the flame of the new atheism was burning bright, an attempt to seize the intellectual high ground while nonetheless advancing the new atheists' political agenda emerged when Mark Lilla, a veteran combatant in the wars of American political theory, published The Stillborn God: Religion, Politics, and the Modern West. *Stripped to essentials, Professor Lilla's argument came down to this: political theology, however construed, is, was, and always will be a mortal threat to democracy. As I did not perceive myself or my colleagues in those draconian terms, it seemed that a counterargument ought to be mustered.*

The occasion for that came when the editors of Commentary *asked me to review Lilla's book. As it happened, I had just read Rémi Brague's study* The Law of God: The Philosophical History of an Idea, *and it struck me that Brague's work gave us useful analytic tools with which to dissect Professor Lilla's reading of the modern history of Western political thought. By extension, Brague's work underscored the grave limitations of the new atheists' approach to thinking about the sources of the Western freedom project. A slightly shorter version of the essay that ensued appeared in* Commentary *in November 2007; the full version of the essay, slightly modified, is reproduced here.*

S INCE THE RISE of the Religious New Right two generations ago, the religion-and-politics battle in the American culture war has been fought on many, often interactive, fronts.

As Richard John Neuhaus argued in *Commentary* in 1985, the new political activism of evangelical and fundamentalist Protestants in the 1970s began, not as a political offensive intended to convert America, but as a defensive reaction.[1] In the wake of the cultural meltdown of the 1960s, evangelicals and fundamentalists had largely retreated into their own enclaves, content to live their lives and raise their children as they saw fit without engaging the larger political culture. However, attempts by the Carter administration to bring federal regulatory pressure to bear on religious schools, coupled with the rise of evangelical theologians who pressed the case for Christian responsibility in shaping politics and culture, compelled the evangelicals to re-engage. What began as self-defense — "Leave us alone" — eventually became a significant political movement promoting traditional morality in public life.

Viewed through a wider historical lens, the revolt of the evangelicals was but the latest episode in an ongoing struggle over the meaning of the First Amendment's religion clause. For the first century and a half of the Republic, the First Amendment religion clause was a backwater of constitutional jurisprudence. That began to change, rapidly, with a series of Supreme Court decisions sprung from the *Everson* case in 1947. As post-*Everson* federal jurisprudence began to suggest, ever more aggressively, that religion was something that must be reluctantly permitted to consenting adults behind closed doors, but that was certainly bad for the kids, constitutional scholars and legal activists took to the academic, journalistic, and political barricades to challenge what seemed to be the Court's attempt to effect three drastic changes in American public life: to drive confessionally serious Christianity from the public square, to establish secularism as a quasi-official national creed, and to define the imperial autonomous Self as the end-all and be-all of the Constitution's "more perfect Union." On those barricades, they were joined by religious intellectuals and activists representing a wide variety of theological and denominational positions.

Still, if the religion-and-politics wars have been about politics (electoral politics, and the politics of constitutional interpretation, which in turn shaped each other), they have also been about ideas — very basic ideas.

The very fact that American public life and American electoral politics were both roiled by debates over the proper place of religious conviction and religiously informed moral argument in the public square was a de facto challenge to the secularization hypothesis, which held that modernization inevitably led to secularization, understood as a dramatic decline in religious conviction and a drastic weakening of the culture-forming effects of religion. The American religion-and-politics wars were also, if perhaps less obviously, a challenge to the late-20th-century Jacobin or secularist version of the Whig theory of history, which had come to posit the evolution of Western democracy as a development against Christianity — a hypothesis in sharp contrast to the historiography of the likes of Christopher Dawson, who argued that the Enlightenment origins of modern political theory and democratic political institutions should not blind us to the deeper roots of the Western democratic project in the fruitful interaction of Athens, Jerusalem, and Rome: philosophical rationality, biblical religion, and law. So an argument about the intellectual and cultural roots of democracy was engaged.

Then, in the 2004 electoral cycle, the American religion-and-politics wars turned into a challenge to the self-understanding of the Catholic Church as a self-disciplining community with the capacity to define — and defend — its own doctrinal and moral boundaries. For the first time since the election of John F. Kennedy in 1960 had seemingly settled the "Catholic question" in American public life, critics of the nation's largest denomination (now largely secularist rather than Protestant, but including more than a few deracinated Catholics) suggested that there was something un-American about the Catholic Church. Meanwhile, inside the Church, a fierce controversy unfolded over what a given politician's stand on certain issues dictated about his or her status in the household of faith. All of this spilled over into the 2006 and 2008 campaigns, and indeed seemed likely to remain a fixed point of contention in Catholic America for decades.

The next turn of the wheel — ironic, in that it displayed certain parallels to the revolt of the Religious New Right a generation and a half ago — was the rise of what one of its paladins, Christopher Hitchens, dubbed the "new atheism." The commercial success of Hitchens's *God Is Not Great,* following on the heels of similar bestsellers by Richard Dawkins (*The God Delusion*), Daniel Dennett (*Breaking the Spell: Religion as a Natural Phenomenon*), and Sam Harris (*Letter to a Christian Nation*), may not have added very much to the sum total of our knowledge about religion, or about the impact of religious conviction on public life. But these bestsellers kept the polemical pot boiling, and that in turn sharpened the question of what role — if any — religious conviction, or even religiously informed moral argument, should play in American public life.

Then, in the fall of 2007, came Mark Lilla, formerly of the University of Chicago's famed Committee on Social Thought and recently appointed professor of humanities at Columbia University. Lilla's book, *The Stillborn God: Religion, Politics, and the Modern West,*[2] was given a rollout for which authors and publishers alike yearn: a cover story in the *New York Times Magazine* — which in turn confirmed the reader's hunch that *The Stillborn God* was intended to be an unavoidable reference point, and perhaps even a turning point, in the American religion-and-politics wars.

With some reservations, Christopher Hitchens quickly claimed Professor Lilla for the new atheist camp in a *Slate* column. But even considering Hitchens's reservations, this wasn't really fair to Lilla, whose mind and style are of an entirely different caliber from the likes of Dawkins, Dennett, Harris, and Hitchens. *The Stillborn God* is marked by impressive learning, and by the author's gift for translating some of the more stylistically challenged among the philosophers (Hobbes, Kant, and Hegel, for example) into language accessible to the non-specialist. *The Stillborn God* is also a useful reminder that the reduction of our politics to the broadcast manipulation of consumer tastes and emotions is — or ought to be — an embarrassment. As Lilla reminds us, we stand on the shoulders of intellectual giants, and our public discourse (to use the vastly overused noun du jour) ought to reflect that, at least minimally.

On the other hand, *The Stillborn God* has many grave flaws, such that its far-more-sophisticated and nuanced analysis ends up giving aid and comfort to the new atheists while underwriting their program of advancing an American public square scoured of religiously informed moral argument — a point one suspects was not lost on the editors of the *New York Times Magazine,* not generally known for giving marquee treatment to authors whose views do not coincide with the *Times's* devout secularism. Happily, another learned and literarily gifted scholar of the history of ideas, France's Rémi Brague, had just gone over a lot of the same intellectual-historical terrain as Mark Lilla, with dramatically different results. Thus Brague's book, *The Law of God: The Philosophical History of an Idea,*[3] offers, if unintentionally, a serious challenge to Lilla's thesis (not to mention that of the new atheists).

In the 17th century, Mark Lilla argues, "a Great Separation took place, severing Western political philosophy decisively from cosmology and theology. It remains the most distinctive feature of the modern West to this day."[4] Lilla applauds the Great Separation.

Brague agrees that, in the early phases of philosophical modernity, a serious and consequential attempt was made to sunder political thinking from a general theory of the universe and from ideas about God; but he raises grave questions about the results. So an important argument about the history of ideas and the impact of ideas on history is joined.

The Threat That Is Political Theology

Mark Lilla defines "political theology" as "discourse about political authority based on a revealed divine nexus," the nexus in question involving God, us, and the world.[5] It seems a rather constrained definition: Is "political theology" only about questions of authority, or does it also engage questions of the nature of man-as-citizen, the definition of public goods (such as justice, order, peace, security), and the identification of the appropriate means to attain those goods?[6] Be that as it may, Lilla is surely right in arguing that the evolving and sometimes sharply contested debate involving Christian political theology and issues of governance in the West took many history-shaping twists and turns between the Constantinian settlement and the end of the Middle Ages. Then, on Lilla's account, a fierce battle among Western Christians (the Reformation) intersected with this ongoing dispute between the champions of divine revelation and those charged with the tasks of governance; the lethal result was the European wars of religion in the 16th and 17th centuries. Those wars were, indeed, a very bad business, which more or less derailed the advance of European civilization for the better part of a century. Yet, on Lilla's reading of this awfulness, the bloodletting between and among Catholic and Protestants did have one positive consequence: by demonstrating the real-world effects of "divinely revealed" ideas of right-governance, the European wars of religion triggered the Great Separation of "political theology" and political philosophy, a severance first effected by the English thinker Thomas Hobbes.

Mark Lilla is an unabashed, albeit not uncritical, admirer of Hobbes. And that in itself is something of a feat, for Hobbes is rather easy to dislike, with his draconian view of the fear-driven human person (I fear, therefore I am; I fear, and that fear defines my interaction with all others), and his preference for absolutism in politics (because only an all-powerful tyrant can control a society composed of fear-driven individuals). Lilla, however, tries to disentangle Hobbes's taste for the leviathan state from his prior intellectual achievement, which was to change the question in a definitive way: Hobbes changed the question of politics from a question about God and his will to a question about man and his nature. As Lilla put it in his *Times Magazine* article:

> Hobbes planted a seed, a thought that it might be possible to build legitimate political institutions without grounding them on divine revelation. He knew it was impossible to refute belief in divine revelation; the most one can hope for is [to] cast suspicion on prophets claiming to speak about politics in God's name. This new political thinking would no longer concern itself with God's politics; it would concentrate on men as believers in God and try to keep them from harming one another. It would set its sights lower than Christian political theology had, but secure what mattered most, which was peace.[7]

Whatever Hobbes's achievement in creating modern political philosophy, though, his bleak view of the human condition and his prescription for the leviathan state were not terribly attractive. Thus, Lilla argues, it was John Locke who, in effect, "humanized" and sold Hobbes, in the sense of making a Hobbesian, man-centered approach to thinking about politics more palatable. Locke agreed with changing the subject, from God to man. But he had a rather less dyspeptic view of the human condition than Hobbes, and he didn't much like the idea of tyranny, so he "began to imagine a new kind of political order in which power would be limited, divided, and widely shared; in which those in power at one moment would relinquish it peacefully at another, without fear of retribution; in which public law would govern relations among citizens and institutions; in which many different religions would be allowed to flourish, free from state interference; and in which individuals would have inalienable rights to protect them from government and their fellows." This "liberal-democratic order," Lilla continues, is "the only one we in the West recognize as legitimate today, and we owe it primarily to Hobbes."[8] Why? Because Hobbes had effected, at least intellectually, the Great Separation. And a liberal-democratic order is impossible to imagine — at least for Professor Lilla — without the displacement and exile of political theology for the sake of political philosophy: without banishing God-talk from public life.

On this account, we in the West are the political heirs of the good Hobbes: the Hobbes who (as Lilla writes) "levels . . . the Christian conception of man," thereby completing "the most devastating attack on Christian political theology ever undertaken," the net effect of which was to enable post-Hobbesian moderns the possibility of "escape" from their intellectually barren, social disruptive, and ultimately lethal theological patrimony.[9] By killing the political relevance of the idea of man made in the image of God (which Lilla curiously attributes to Christian political theology, not to Genesis), Thomas Hobbes, via the intellectual ministrations of the kinder, gentler John Locke, made democracy, the rule of law, the constitutional defense of human rights, and religious freedom possible.

This historic changing-of-the-subject might have been expected to have settled things, and Mark Lilla rather wishes that it had. But then the French philosopher Jean-Jacques Rousseau intervened, and set in motion what became a rather nasty—indeed, extremely nasty—mess. For while Rousseau shared Hobbes's caustic criticism of clerical ignorance and theocratic authoritarianism, he was, on Lilla's reading of him, a friend of religion. And thus he insisted, in his romantic way, on honoring the seemingly ineradicable human religious impulse, rather than bracketing it when the subject turned to public life and politics. Even more consequentially, Rousseau identified that impulse with an "inner light" that shapes our moral intuitions, including our moral intuitions about society, our obligations to others, our philanthropy, and indeed every other aspect of our public lives. Religion could not, as Hobbes would have wished, be hermetically sealed off in some private sphere or preserve without violating the authenticity of that "inner light" and its intuitions. True, some religion was bad, but that was "priestly" religion (read: Catholicism); it could be controlled and contained while the "inner light" helped society "usefully." Or as Rousseau's Savoyard vicar puts it in *Emile* (a novel which Lilla exegetes at some length), "I believe all particular religions are good when one serves God usefully in them." The religious camel's nose was, once again, under the flap of the political tent.

Immanuel Kant and Georg Wilhelm Friedrich Hegel then followed Rousseau rather than Hobbes, much to Professor Lilla's chagrin. The Sage of Königsberg, while attempting to salvage universal and rationally defensible principles of morality by appeals to a "categorical imperative," also argued for a kind of universalized Protestantism as the apex of human religious development. Hegel, for his part, took an even more dangerous turn by promoting religious conviction as the vital core of any authentic *Volksgeist* (national spirit or national "idea"). Where that could lead was demonstrated, and the real-world trouble began, when the liberal Protestant theology of the 19th-century German academy (influenced by the philosophy of Schelling and defined by Adolf Harnack and Ernst Troeltsch) so identified itself with the Wilhelmine *Volks-geist* that it vigorously defended German aggression in World War I and, almost until the very end, the slaughter in the trenches: a civilizational catastrophe far worse than, if weirdly reminiscent of, the earlier wars of religion.

This liberal Protestant cave-in to Prussian militarism and German nationalism in turn triggered a messianic or apocalyptic reaction among religious thinkers in the 20th-century inter-war period, which was deeply marked, as Lilla reminds us, by a thoroughgoing disgust with modernity and a new quest for authenticity among many European intellectuals. Some of those religious intellectuals pulled up on the reins before they came to the political brink, like the Jewish thinkers Martin Buber and Franz Rosenszweig, and the Christian theologians Karl Barth and Dietrich Bonhoeffer. But others soon found a vessel for their fantasies in the man Churchill once described as "a maniac of ferocious genius, the repository and expression of the most virulent hatreds that have ever corroded the human breast—Corporal Hitler."[10]

All of which, Lilla concludes, "served to confirm Hobbes's iron law: Messianic theology eventually breeds messianic politics."[11] The Great Separation, then, can never be taken for granted; and neither can the liberal-democratic order which, according to Mark Lilla, requires that thorough separation between theology and political theory. The Great Separation must constantly be willed. Or, as Lilla puts it, in a way that challenges the secularization-is-inevitable certainties of the new atheists while tacitly affirming their public agenda:

> Rousseau was on to something: we seem to be theotropic creatures, yearning to connect our mundane lives, in some way, to the beyond. That urge can be suppressed, new habits learned, but the challenge of political theology will never fully disappear as long as the urge to connect survives.

So we are heirs to the Great Separation only if we wish to be, if we make a conscious effort to separate basic principles of political legitimacy from divine revelation. Yet more is required still. Since the challenge of political theology is enduring, we need to remain aware of its logic and the threat it poses. This means vigilance, but even more it means self-awareness. We must never forget that there was nothing inevitable about our Great Separation, that it was and remains an experiment.[12]

Where does this leave us today? *The Stillborn God* does not advance a practical agenda of action, but in his *Times Magazine* piece, Mark Lilla did address the most urgent question of religion-and-politics today, which is of course the threat of global Islamist jihadism. And here, too, Lilla distinguished himself from the new atheists and from those in the U.S. foreign policy establishment who imagine that the answer to jihadism is to convert 1.2 billion Muslims into good secular liberals who take their religion from Muhammad and their politics from John Rawls. Whether jihadist ideology is in fact "political theology" in any serious sense of "theology" is not a question over which Lilla lingers; still, he was surely right to remind the readers of the *Times Magazine* that many Westerners "find ourselves in an intellectual bind when we encounter genuine political theology today: either we assume that modernization and secularization will eventually extinguish it, or we treat it as an incomprehensible existential threat.... Neither response takes us a step closer to understanding the world we now live in." Lilla then suggests, rather tentatively, a dialogue with "liberal" Islamic thinkers like Khaled Abou El Fadl of UCLA and the Swiss professor Tariq Ramadan, even though he recognizes that this Islamic reformism can, while promoting the beginnings of an Islamic case for what we know as "civil society," also "foster dreams of returning to a more primitive faith, through violence if necessary."[13]

As for the United States and the American religion-and-politics wars, well, we must constantly remind ourselves, Lilla writes, that "it's a miracle" that Americans manage to settle, within constitutional bounds, their deeply felt differences over a host of issues, especially the life issues of abortion, euthanasia, and bio-technological research. And "miracles can't be willed." Thus we must continually choose — a telling word, in this context — "to keep our politics unilluminated by divine revelation," relying on "our own lucidity," which we must deploy in a world, and a country, "where faith still inflames the minds of men."[14]

A Richer Account of an Argument

Thus, Mark Lilla. In *The Law of God,* Rémi Brague, a distinguished scholar of Plato, Aristotle, and medieval Jewish and Islamic philosophy who divides his time between the Sorbonne and the University of Munich, agrees with Lilla to this extent: contemporary thinking on religion-and-politics is "dominated" by "one of the grand narratives in which modernity tries to explain itself: an escape of the political from the domain of theology." This master narrative, in turn, contains several sub-plots: "the secularization of a world supposed to have been 'enchanted'; the laicization of a supposedly clerical society; the separation of church and state, supposed to have been originally one."[15]

None of this, Brague argues, holds up under close examination. The so-called "altar-and-throne" alliance "goes back no further than the Restoration in France." The "divine right of kings had barely been formulated before the seventeenth century" and is thus a modern, not medieval, idea. The "laicization" of politics, which is another way of describing what Mark Lilla calls the Great Separation, is an odd turn of phrase masking a conceptual confusion, for "lay" is in fact a Christian notion, indeed a liberal notion, originally meant to describe man as possessed of a dignity that makes him capable-of-citizenship. As for "secularization," well, "the term hints at what it is supposed to explain, namely, that there exists something like a 'secular' domain distinct from the religious domain; a 'pro-fane' that defines its position at the temple parvis (*fanum*)."[16]

Things, in other words, are a lot more complex than they are made to seem in the modern grand narrative. Brague does not, of course, deny that there have been, are, and always will be "disturbing" issues involved in "the divine's claim to strike the field of the political with full force...."[17] But rather than approach those issues by means of a quarantine — preemptively refusing theology any encounter with political thinking, as if Athens *really* had nothing to do with Jerusalem — Brague prefers to speak of a "theio-political" problem: the question of the divine, however construed, in its interaction with our ideas about the right-ordering of society.[18] That problem is an enduring feature of the human condition, and the purpose of scholarly inquiry into the history of ideas is to understand how Judaism, Christianity, and Islam have addressed the problem over the past three millennia or more.

There is no room here to do justice to the intellectual richness of Brague's narrative, or to honor the breadth of his research. His survey of classical, biblical, Christian, Talmudic, Byzantine, and Islamic efforts to deal with the "theio-political problem" occupies several engaging chapters. In the course of these, Brague illustrates some of the deep theological and philosophical reasons why Islam has had difficulties finding intra-Islamic warrants for what we would now call "pluralism" and "civil society." Among Islam's difficulties here, Brague suggests, is its lack of a natural law tradition, of the sort that Christianity borrowed from the Greeks: a way of thinking and arguing based on rational moral analysis that, at its best, can serve as a kind of general public grammar and vocabulary through which peoples of diverse religious convictions (and no religious convictions) can debate how we ought to live together.

Brague then turns to the Middle Ages, where he finds important Jewish thinking (Jehuda Halevi and Maimonides) and a Christian approach to the religion-and-politics question that stresses that law, even divine law, must be both rational and intelligible. Brague's paladin here is Thomas Aquinas. For Aquinas, the divine law and its relationship to our public affairs cannot be understood as something utterly external to man and to the human experience; nor is divine law to be construed primarily as a matter of a restraint on human freedom. As Brague writes, "Thomas considers the law [including divine law, manifest in revelation] to be a gift of God to a rational and free creature. Law is the form that providence takes in relation to a free being: the law is to the rational creature what instinct is to the irrational one. Thomas defines law as the way we act when in full possession of our freedom."[19]

Nothing in Thomas Aquinas, Brague insists, supports the "divine right of kings," for kings, too, are subject to a divine law aimed at "liberating reason and permitting it to be itself" — that is, permitting reason, including reasoning about politics, to contribute to human flourishing.[20] Thus in Aquinas (and in sharp contrast to that other Thomas, Hobbes), there is no zero-sum game between God and man, revelation and reason, faith and politics. Aquinas's concept of law and its relationship to human freedom also challenges those heralds of the contemporary autonomy project and modern legal positivism, the late medieval philosophers Duns Scotus and William of Ockham, who emphasized the centrality of will — God's will, and our wills — in understanding the moral life. Scotus and Ockham turned Aquinas inside out and upside down, such that, in their work, "the divine law was understood above all as the expression of the will of God imposed on things already created, and no longer as the impression of divine wisdom on the very nature of the created."[21] Substitute "the leviathan state" for "God" in this formula, and suddenly Hobbes looks less like a brilliantly innovative thinker responding to the awfulness of the European wars of religion and more like the heir of an unfortunate tendency in one stream of late medieval Christian thought.

According to Rémi Brague, a decisive turn toward our current difficulties in understanding the complex relationships among freedom, law, and the divine (however we conceive it or deny it) came, not with the wars of religion, but with the rise of modern mathematical physics and its distinctive concept of "laws of nature." The founding father here was, of course, Descartes. By asserting that God established eternal mathematical truths that are the "law of nature," Descartes opened the door to the positivism of August Comte, to the abandonment of any search for causation and meaning in nature, and to Comte's definition of the "laws of nature" as merely "the constant relations that exist between observable phenomena."[22] The intellectual power of the scientific method then spilled over into other areas of life and thought, with a perhaps inevitable result: modern legal positivism, which claims that "law" is whatever-we-say-law-is, period.

Brague is critical of this entire trajectory, suggesting that the "law" of gravity or the second "law" of thermodynamics are not really "laws," because nature cannot choose to disobey them. Rather these "laws" are the descriptions we give to Comte's "constant relations" among the things we can see and measure. That may seem a merely semantic quarrel, but in fact it cuts to the heart of the problem both Lilla and Brague address: for if the "laws of nature" as modern mathematical physics understands them are the paradigm for all "law," and if, in consequence, the "law" is whatever we say it is, then the fundamental "laws" on which free societies are based rest on rather shaky foundations. To invoke yet another Thomas — Jefferson — and his appeal to the "laws of Nature" in the Declaration of Independence: if the laws we make to govern ourselves rest on the "laws of nature" that are merely descriptive, and if nature is understood as random and purposeless, then the laws we make in reference to those "laws of nature" could be very different from those enumerated in the Bill of Rights.

Rémi Brague's description of our current situation might be, in certain respects, reasonably agreeable to Mark Lilla:

> Today there is constant talk about the distinction between the political and the religious. Some boast of living in a culture in which such a distinction has occurred, and they advocate carrying it through to the point of eliminating all influence of the religious in public life. Other congratulate themselves for living in a culture in which that same distinction is not always irreversible, or else they dream of mending the tear threatening the fine wholeness of the community. Both camps invoke this distinction to reproach the other for having abandoned (or for not having abandoned) what they both suppose to be a primeval indistinction. This mirror symmetry creates distortions in the way that cultures view one another: Europe perceives that separation as progress; Islam, as a sign of decadence.[23]

But Brague immediately distinguishes his view — historically, philosophically, and prudentially, in terms of contemporary politics — from Lilla's:

> One might well wonder, however, whether that separation, which has received so much praise, and its concrete translations in the "separation of church and state," ever actually took place. Moreover, that pat phrase is deceptive. For one thing, it suggests the existence of an initial union; for another, it supposes that the state and the church are institutions that have always existed. Neither hypothesis has much of a foundation. We would do better to speak of a parallel development of two institutions that never formed a unit. The political and the religious are two independent sources of authority; they have

crossed one another's paths more than once, but they never have merged in spite of efforts to fit them together, sometimes to the advantage of one, sometimes to that of the other. Although there has been cooperation between the two, there has never been confusion about which is which.[24]

Like Mark Lilla, Rémi Brague is concerned about the fragility of our present political arrangements, about the protection of basic human rights, and about the future of the rule of law, democratically deliberated. But he will not concede that an effective defense of the Western democratic project requires the canonization of Thomas Hobbes and his Great Separation. The key to the disjunction between these two formidable intellectual historians — Lilla, promoter of Hobbes, and Brague, sympathetic analyst of Aquinas — is both theological and anthropological. Lilla and Brague have very different ideas of God and his revelation, and very different ideas of us, ideas that are inextricably intertwined. Lilla urges unending vigilance in public life against the religious fevers that still inflame and infect our minds. Brague, at the end of *The Law of God,* suggests the theological conditions for the possibility of a very different approach to the "theio-political problem," an approach more philosophically (and theologically) modest than the banishment of theology and indeed all God-talk into an outer darkness beyond the democratic pale:

> In the Bible and in Christianity... the presence of the divine does not comport an immediate demand for obedience. A space opens up in which God manifests himself, thus offering himself to a gaze that might risk something like a description. The divine shows itself, or rather gives itself, before asking anything of us and *instead* of asking. Not only is it true that "God owes us nothing" (Leszek Kolakowski), but he does not *ask* anything of us. Although God does indeed *expect* something of his creatures (that we develop according to our own

logic), he does not, in fact, *demand* anything, or rather, he asks nothing more than his gift already asks, thanks to the simple fact that it is given: to be received. In the case of man, that reception does not require anything but humanity. As magnificently stated by a somewhat surprising author [Montesquieu], "God wants nothing from us but ourselves." That claim is addressed to all aspects of the human, the intelligence among them.[25]

Including, it hardly seems necessary to add, the intelligence that informs both political philosophy and theology: two intellectual disciplines which, sharing a concern for how we best live together, ought to be in dialogue.

A Choice between Thomases?

The Stillborn God has its commendable moments. Mark Lilla asks the right questions: "If there are varieties of religious experience, how do they each affect public life? . . . What might they contribute to a healthy public life even in liberal democracies? Is there a way of recognizing that contribution without raising the specters of political theology and political messianism?"[26] Lilla's demolition of the fatuities of 19th-century liberal Protestantism (admittedly a fat target) is masterful. Lilla also raises an appropriate caution-flag to the more exuberant secularists, like Christopher Hitchens, when he writes that the story of political theology "is the transcript of an argument conducted over four centuries by serious men who understood what was at stake in their quarrel and offered reasons for their positions."[27]

Yet reading Mark Lilla in tandem with Rémi Brague suggests, forcefully, just how much of that transcript Lilla has left out or underplayed. Thus Brague's telling of the tale of religion-and-politics

serves to highlight the many historical and philosophical problems with Lilla's storyline: Lilla's insistence that "Christian political
theology" inevitably leads to tyranny and despotism; his false picture of medieval Christendom, which completely ignores the rich
social pluralism of the Middle Ages; his failure to grasp how the
Catholic Church's successful insistence on the freedom to order its
own internal life according to its own criteria (as, for example, in
the famous "investiture controversy" that pitted Pope Gregory VII
against the Holy Roman Emperor Henry IV) created essential historical conditions for the possibility of that pluralism; his insistence
on the wars of religion as being exclusively theological, when in fact
these horrors had a lot to do with political ambitions, economic interests, and the bloody birth-pains of the modern nation-state. By
widening the historical lens, Brague also reminds us that the Western accomplishment of distinguishing in both theory and practice
between *sacerdotium* and *regnum,* between religious authority and
political authority, was in fact a Christian accomplishment, which
in turn found their deepest religious and theological roots in ancient Jewish convictions about the dangers inherent in the idolatry
of the political. The European wars of religion, and the Enlightenment, certainly played crucial roles in creating the modern political
forms by which we acknowledge the distinction between religious
and political authority; but the arguments for such a distinction
had been made long before, and in explicitly theological terms,
by Augustine, Aquinas, and many others standing in the biblical
tradition.

The Stillborn God avoided direct commentary on the present
state of the religion-and-politics argument in America. Professor
Lilla was not so reticent in his *New York Times Magazine* summary of his book, however; and in what amounted to a throw-away
line, he showed rather more of his political hand than he had exposed in his book. Arguing that the American experience of the
religion-and-politics question is "utterly exceptional," and that the

fact that our deep differences over a host of bitterly contested issues are settled peaceably and legally is due to the happy combination of "a strong constitutional structure and various lucky breaks," Lilla concludes that, well, "It's a miracle."[28]

No, it isn't. And it never was. It was, and is, an accomplishment. And no matter how we weigh the various influences — some manifestly secular, others clearly religious — that shaped the First Amendment religion clause and the culture that crafted it, accepted it, and lived its provisions, it is a simple demographic fact that respect for religious freedom and commitments to religious toleration are, in the main, a religious accomplishment in the United States today; how could they be otherwise, given the vibrant, confusing, sometimes maddening, but impossible-to-ignore religiosity of the American people? Does Professor Lilla really believe that the social, cultural, and moral consensus that keeps America from reprising the wars of religion is based on a national devotion to the political philosophy of Thomas Hobbes? The overwhelming majority of Americans accept the really Great Separation — of religious authority and political authority, not of religion and public life — because they believe themselves religiously obliged to do so, and because there is (just?) enough of the old natural law grammar and vocabulary left in our public life so that we can conduct the debate over the oughts of public life in a genuinely ecumenical and interreligious fashion, rather than by playing denominational trump cards or by claiming direct guidance from divine revelation.

There is another issue here, which Lilla's image of a "miracle" doesn't acknowledge and which his book does not address: and that is the question of warrants — of how we defend what is ours, and what is right. How, today, do we defend the American commitment to religious freedom, civility in public life, and tolerance of those with whom we disagree? Through the pragmatic or utilitarian argument that, well, it's just less messy to be tolerant and civil? That won't hold up long under pressure; moreover, the pragmatic "answer" risks dubious concessions to the salami tactics of the Islamists, which have already distorted democratic public life in western Europe.[29] By a tacit agreement (perhaps enforced by a radically secularist Supreme Court) that religiously grounded public moral argument is out-of-bounds in the American public square? That may work in certain Manhattan zip codes, but it won't work in most of America.

However ironic it may seem to Mark Lilla (much less Christopher Hitchens), the fact is that Protestant evangelicals and fundamentalists who believe that God wants them to be tolerant of, and civil to, people who have a different idea, or no idea, of what God wants have a thicker, more personally demanding, and thus more publicly resilient set of arguments in defense of religious freedom and the civil society than the pragmatists and utilitarians. So do those Catholics who take seriously the teaching of the Second Vatican Council and Pope John Paul II on religious freedom as the first of human rights — a claim the Catholic Church argues on genuinely public, not sectarian, grounds.[30] There's no miracle, here. But there is political theology at work, and at work in defense of the democratic common good.

There is a sense, then, in which the argument over religion-and-politics offers us a choice between two Thomases, Hobbes and Aquinas, their radically different views of human nature and the human prospect, and thus their deeply divergent understanding of politics, its pitfalls and its possibilities. Mark Lilla wants his Hobbes without the English philosopher's dark view of man. Rémi Brague, I suspect, knows that there is no such thing as Hobbes Lite, and that a thoroughly grim view of the human condition runs the very real risk of underwriting an ignoble politics. Those who wish to put the ongoing religion-and-politics debate — in America, throughout the West, and between the West and the rest — on a more secure intellectual foundation had better figure out the same thing.

Chapter Six

Popes, Power, and Politics

In Witness to Hope: The Biography of Pope John Paul II, *I was able to explore at some length the late Pope's public impact as an expression of Karol Wojtyła's distinctive personal story, his convictions about the influence of culture on history, and his evangelical understanding of the papacy. The invitation to deliver the 2000 Erasmus Lecture for the New York–based Institute on Religion and Public Life gave me the opportunity to shift the focus a bit and examine the ways in which John Paul II's reshaping of the history of his times, which is now broadly conceded, had enduring impacts on the institution of the papacy and on the diplomacy of the Holy See.*

The Holy See is called "the Vatican" in common parlance and journalistic shorthand, But in fact "the Holy See" is not identical with Vatican City State. Rather, the Holy See is the juridical embodiment, recognized in international law and practice, of the global ministry of the Bishop of Rome as head of the Catholic Church. To illustrate the point from modern history: "the Holy See" functioned diplomatically between 1870 and 1929, between the seizure of the Papal States and the creation of Vatican City

State by the Lateran Treaty, even though the popes of that period controlled no sovereign territory.

Both the new role of the papacy as an office of global moral witness and the diplomacy of this unique non-state actor called "the Holy See" teach important lessons about world politics, I suggested in the Erasmus Lecture. Those lessons, and the challenges they present to the diplomacy of the Holy See, have been confirmed by the impact of John Paul's successor, Pope Benedict XVI. Originally published in the February 2001 issue of First Things, *the journal of the Institute on Religion and Public Life, the essay has been revised to take account of developments during the last years of John Paul II and the first years of Benedict XVI, and in light of November 2006 discussions with the grand strategy seminar of Yale University's international security studies program.*

POPE JOHN PAUL II's decisive impact on the history of the late 20th century is acknowledged across the spectrum of opinion, from American Cold War historians like John Lewis Gaddis to Russian Cold War actors like Mikhail Gorbachev. At his death, even those critical of John Paul's magisterium (which they somehow misconceived as "conservative" or "not in the spirit of Vatican II") managed to concede that John Paul II's human rights activism had helped bring down the Berlin Wall. Yet the imprint of the shoes of this fisherman could be found far beyond the new democracies in his native east central Europe. They could be found in Latin America and in east Asia. They could be found in Africa, which John Paul refused to consign to historical oblivion. They could be found wherever thoughtful men and women debate the circumstances of real existing democracy in the early 21st century, for John Paul II did much to define the key moral issues of public life in the democracies and in the politics of international institutions.

Some sober analysts of papal history argue that one must return to the early 13th century and Pope Innocent III to find a pontificate with such a marked influence on the public life of its time. Even measured by such a yardstick, however, John Paul's historical footprint looms large. For Innocent III's impact, serious as it was, was on one part of a small peninsula jutting out into the Atlantic from the Eurasian landmass. John Paul II's impact was genuinely global.

Yet there is another, and more important, difference here. For the "political" impact of John Paul II, unlike that of Innocent III, did not come from deploying what political realists recognize as the instruments of political power. Rather, John Paul's capacity to shape history was exercised through a different set of levers.

As Bishop of Rome and sovereign of the Vatican City microstate, John Paul II had no military or economic power at his disposal. True, the Holy See maintains an extensive network of diplomatic relations and holds Permanent Observer status at the United Nations. But whatever influence John Paul had through these channels simply underscored the fact that the power of his papacy lay in a finely honed gift of moral persuasion that was capable of being translated into political effectiveness.

This "John Paul II difference" — political effectiveness achieved without the normal instruments of political power — is interesting in itself. It also has heuristic value.

It tells us something about the nature of politics at the beginning of the third millennium of the Christian era. Contrary to notions widely accepted in the last two centuries of the second millennium, the public impact of John Paul II suggests that politics (understood as the contest for power), or economics (understood as the quest for wealth), or some combination of politics and economics, is not the only, or perhaps even the primary, engine of history. The revolution of conscience that John Paul ignited in June 1979 in Poland — the moral revolution that made the Revolution of 1989 possible — is simply not explicable in conventional political-economic categories. Thus John Paul's public accomplishment provided empirical ballast for intellectual and moral challenges to several potent modern theories of politics, including French revolutionary Jacobinism, Marxism-Leninism, and utilitarianism. The political world just doesn't work the way the materialists claim.

At the end of a 20th century in which too many people believed, with Mao Zedong, that power comes out of the barrel of a gun, the paradoxical public impact of John Paul II also reminded the world (and the Church) of five other truths: that the power of the human spirit can ignite world-historical change; that tradition can be as potent a force for social transformation as a self-consciously radical rupture with the past; that moral conviction can be an Archimedean lever for moving the world; that "public life" and "politics" are not synonymous; and that a genuinely humanistic politics always depends upon a more fundamental constellation of free associations and social institutions in which we learn the truth about ourselves as individuals and as members of communities.

In sum, and precisely because it was not mediated through the conventional instruments of political power, the political accomplishment of John Paul II helped free the 20th century from the tyranny of politics, a tyranny that reached a particularly malign expression in 1917 when the Bosheviks began the first sustained modern experiment in totalitarianism. By demonstrating in action the linkage between profound moral conviction and effective political power, the public accomplishments of John Paul II helped restore politics to its true dignity while keeping politics within its proper sphere.

In retrospect, the distinctive modus operandi of this politically potent Pope also suggests the necessity of a reflection on the future of the papacy, the world's oldest institutional office, and on the future of institutional Catholicism in the third millennium of its history.

It was, and still is, tempting to see John Paul's public accomplishment as the expression of his singular personal experience. John Paul II's "culture-first" view of history and his bold confidence in the political efficacy of moral truth were indeed deeply influenced by his unique *curriculum vitae.* His Slavic sensitivity to spiritual power in history (prefigured in Soloviev and paralleled in Solzhenitsyn); his Polish convictions about the cultural foundations of nationhood (shaped by a lifelong immersion in the literary works of Adam Mickiewicz, Cyprian Kamil Norwid, and Juliusz Słowacki); his experience in the underground resistance during World War II and his leadership in a culturally based resistance to communism from 1947 to 1978 — all of these are, if you will, distinctively "Wojtyłan" experiences. As Rocco Buttiglione insightfully suggested, history viewed from the Vistula River basin does indeed look different than history viewed from Berlin, Paris, London, or Washington, D.C.[1] And there can be little doubt that this difference decisively shaped the potent public presence of the first Slavic and Polish pope.

On the other hand, John Paul II always insisted that he was not a "singularity," to adapt a term from astrophysics. Rather, as he understood it, he and his pontificate were the products of the contemporary Catholic Church, as the Church has been shaped by the Second Vatican Council — which Karol Wojtyła always understood as a great, Spirit-led effort to renew Catholicism as an evangelical movement in history. I would press this further, though. In the paradoxical public potency of John Paul II, the world saw played out, in dramatic form, trends that had been under way in Catholicism for two centuries: trends that were waiting, so to speak, for a new kind of pope to forge a new kind of interaction between the papacy and the world of power.

Lessons from an Entanglement

That popes have been players in the world of power since at least the 5th-century pontificate of Pope Leo the Great is a well-known fact of Western history (if there are "well-known facts of Western history" these days). So is the fact that, from 756 until 1870, the popes were temporal rulers of a large part of central Italy, the Papal States. The details of that millennium-long history of temporal power are beyond our scope here. Suffice it to say that it is a tale in which the student of history will find goodness and wickedness, justice and injustice, civility and incivility, ecclesiastical interference in civil affairs and political interference in internal Church affairs.[2] But from this vastly complex story, in which the popes were civilizers as well as temporal rulers, and political leaders on more than one occasion because of the default of those who ought to have taken political responsibility, three key points may be drawn.

The first involves the pope's unique position as universal pastor of a global Church. From at least the late 4th century, when

Pope Gelasius I distinguished between "the consecrated authority of the priesthood" and the "royal power" as two distinct modes of authority "by which this world is ruled on title of original and sovereign right," it has been understood that the pope cannot be the subject of any other sovereignty. He must himself be a sovereign, in the specific, technical sense that the free exercise of his universal ministry cannot be subject to any higher earthly power. Indeed, as Father Robert Graham, S.J., wrote in the 1950s, "The papacy was exercising a form of sovereignty long before that word took on the clear-cut political and juridical meaning it was later to have."[3] That is why papal diplomacy, today as ever, is not conducted by the pope as head of Vatican City State, but as an expression of the sovereignty of the "Holy See" — the juridical embodiment of the universal pastoral ministry of the Bishop of Rome. The recognition of this papal sovereignty in the exchange of ambassadors between the Holy See and sovereign states, and in the Holy See's representation in international organizations, tells us something about the world as well as about the papacy: it is a tacit recognition that moral norms are relevant in international public life, and that there are actors in the drama of world politics other than states.

The second lesson to be drawn from the papacy's entanglement with temporal power involves the Church's role in the creation of civil society. The *libertas ecclesiae,* the "freedom of the Church," has been a check on the pretensions of state power for centuries, whether that be the power of feudal lords, absolutist monarchs, or the modern secular state. Where the Church retains the capacity to preach the Gospel openly, to order its life and ministry according to its own criteria, and to offer various ministries of charity to the wider society, that very fact constitutes an anti-totalitarian, or, to put it positively, a pluralist principle in society. According to that principle, there are spheres of conviction and action where state power does not, or ought not try to, reach.

However confusedly the various popes may have sought to assert this principle theologically or to secure it practically, the fact remains that the *libertas ecclesiae* was a crucial factor in creating the social space on which other free institutions could form over the centuries; the controversies between Thomas Becket and King Henry II, or between Pope Gregory VII and Emperor Henry IV, were about more than the relative positions of these men in the societies of their time. No matter how tyrannically some of its occupants behaved on occasion, the institutional fact of the papacy has been a barrier to the tyranny of the political for a millennium and a half or more. And if the institutions of civil society are schools for learning the proper exercise of political freedom, then the papacy's defense of the *libertas ecclesiae* helped, through a complex historical and social process, to lay the foundations of modern democracy.

In many instances, however, the papacy's involvement with temporal power involved a tacit commitment to play the political game by the accepted realist conventions. And therein lies the third lesson for the future: that this kind of entanglement, the agreement to play by others' rules, can lead to difficulties and betrayals. The worst of these were in the realm of the human spirit and involved attempts to coerce consciences (as Pope John Paul II acknowledged on the First Sunday of Lent, 2000, when he asked God's forgiveness for the times in which the Church had used coercive state power to enforce its truth claims). Yet there was another, perhaps less familiar, dimension to this aspect of the problematic of entanglement: the fact of the Papal States and the pope's position as a temporal sovereign could lead the papacy into alliance politics that set the shepherd against part of the flock. In 1830–31, for example, Pope Gregory XVI sided with Czarist Russia as it suppressed a rebellion of independence-minded Poles, because of the complex web of European alliance politics and then-regnant Catholic theories of the rights of constituted sovereigns.

There are multiple ambiguities surrounding the term "Constantinian," but neither "Carolingian" nor "Gregorian" quite captures the phenomenon I am trying to describe here. So permit me to call the deep entanglement of the Church and the papacy with state power, and the papacy's tacit acceptance of criteria for political judgment that were sometimes incompatible with the Church's evangelical mission and the papacy's evangelical function, the "Constantinian arrangement" — and to note that this state of affairs was the product of both a distinctive history and a strategic judgment: that the Church's truth claims and public position required the buttressing of something like "Christendom." This Constantinian arrangement had multiple theological and practical tensions built into it from the outset. With the Second Vatican Council and the pontificate of John Paul II, a renewed ecclesial self-understanding and different historical circumstances have created a new model of engagement between the papacy and power. With Vatican II and John Paul II, the Constantinian arrangement has been quietly buried.

The beginnings of a new form of papal engagement with the world of power date to the mid-19th century. At that point, the Papal States had been under continuous political and military pressure for forty years, first from revolutionary France and Napoleon, later from Italian nationalism. The popes resisted the loss of their temporal sovereignty to the bitter end. Yet even as the old edifice of papal temporal power was crumbling, the first probes toward a papacy of witness and moral suasion could be detected.

Cambridge historian Owen Chadwick locates the first of these probes in 1839, when Pope Gregory XVI condemned the slave trade. It was a condemnation he had no capacity to enforce; Gregory XVI couldn't even get the Portuguese government, the chief offender on this score, to pay him any attention. But he did it anyway, in an effort at moral persuasion. A new method of papal engagement with the world of power could also be detected in the mid-19th-century popes' struggles with European governments, defending local bishops and local churches on contested questions such as local episcopal authority and marriage law. Here, for the first time, the popes brought into play the levers of international public opinion and the international press. During this period, the popes gained more effective control over local churches; but this trend, often deplored as "centralization," also meant that the popes could help local churches against various governmental pressures. Because of this, Chadwick concludes, Catholics in Germany, France, the United Kingdom (and even Spain and Austria) came to think of papal power as "indispensable to their freedoms."[4]

In 1854, 1862, 1867, and 1869–70, large numbers of bishops came to Rome from all over the world for the doctrinal definition of Mary's immaculate conception, for a protest against encroachments on the temporal power, to celebrate the jubilee of the martyrdoms of Peter and Paul, and to participate in the First Vatican Council. These bishops' presence in Rome demonstrated to the European powers that the Church had a life of its own, independent of the assertive modern state and its tendency to occupy every nook and cranny of social space. The largest of these gatherings, Vatican I, was, among many other things, a pivotal moment in the emergence of a new form of papal engagement with the world of power. The Council's declaration that the pope enjoyed a universal pastoral jurisdiction denied, as a matter of principle, that the modern state had any role in the Church's internal governance; this in turn began a process in which the authority of local bishops (5/6 of whom were appointed by governments in the early 19th century) was once again tied to their communion with the Bishop of Rome, rather than to their "communion" with their temporal rulers. Against European anti-clericals and secularists, the large representation of Catholic bishops from outside Europe at the First Vatican Council demonstrated that the Catholic Church was not simply a department of the European *ancien régime*.[5] And the immense personal popularity of Pope Pius IX, widely perceived throughout the Catholic world as a victim of unscrupulous men of power after the loss of the Papal States in 1870, bound individual Catholics to the papacy while creating the modern model of the pope as a charismatic public personality.

The demise of the Papal States was, in fact, the crucial change creating the conditions for the possibility of a papacy that engaged world politics with its own evangelical instruments. This first became evident in the pontificate of Leo XIII, "the first Pope since Charlemagne not to inherit a state to govern."[6] Leo's 1879 encyclical on the reform of Thomism, *Aeterni Patris*, suggested that the Church had a distinctive way of engaging the intellectual life, as well as a spiritual life independent of modern state politics. *Rerum Novarum*, Leo's 1891 encyclical "on the condition of the working class" and the Magna Carta of Catholic social doctrine, became a powerful instrument in the hands of a papacy seeking to teach the nations, not rule them — a papacy exerting its influence by argument. (Could such a statement of social doctrine have been issued if the popes had remained temporal rulers of the Papal States, burdened with the notion that they possessed plenipotentiary power in social, economic, and political life? It seems unlikely, perhaps even impossible.)

As with any historical process involving a venerable institution, though, the evolution of the post-Constantinian papacy from Pius IX to John Paul II was complex and uneven. At the same time as the popes were exploring new modes of engagement with politics and the world of power, the Holy See sought to restore itself as a player in international affairs after the loss of the Papal States. The 1929 Lateran Treaty between the Holy See and the Kingdom of Italy settled one problem: as sovereign of Vatican City State (all 108.7 acres of it), the pope would not be subject to any higher temporal authority. Throughout the turbulent middle decades of the 20th century, the Holy See tenaciously sought to rebuild its diplomatic relations, to secure the Catholic Church's legal standing in modern states, and to give the Holy See a place at the table in international forums. The table was not always welcoming. In 1919, the Holy See had diplomatic relations with only twenty-six states, principally from Latin America, and Pope Benedict XV was blocked from participating in the Versailles peace conference by Clause 15 of the secret accord that bound Italy to the Allies in 1915.

Papal and Vatican analysis of the politics of the mid-20th century was sometimes remarkably prescient, and sometimes not-so-prescient. Pope Benedict XV saw more clearly than most European statesmen that World War I was an act of civilizational suicide. (Benedict also bankrupted the Holy See in caring for those displaced by the war, such that the Cardinal Camerlengo, Pietro Gasparri, had to borrow money from the Rothschilds in order to pay for the papal conclave of 1922.) Yet conventional ways of thinking about international affairs could lead to myopia at the Vatican at times when clarity of evangelical and moral insight would have been welcome. No serious student of these matters believes that Pope Pius XII was an anti-Semite or that Pius welcomed the prospect of a Nazi-dominated Europe.[7] Indeed, serious students of this period know that Pius XII took heroic actions on behalf of European Jews and other victim of Nazism, to the point of acting as a middleman in a plot to overthrow Hitler by force.[8] At the same time, senior diplomatic figures in the Holy See may have been so conditioned by realist modes of analysis that they missed the totalitarian difference in German National Socialism, thinking it rather a particularly ugly form of classic German nationalism.[9] If this is true, it must be noted that the Holy See's diplomats were not alone in this misreading. But it must also must be said that one expects more in terms of moral clarity from the Holy See than from Number Ten Downing Street or the Quai d'Orsay.

In any event, by the 20th anniversary of the conclusion of the Second World War, the Holy See's quest for a place at the table of international political life had been vindicated. The Holy See had full diplomatic relations with fifty-two countries in 1965 and since 1964 has had a settled place as a Permanent Observer at the United Nations. In the aftermath of World War II, Pius XII and John XXIII developed the model of the pope as a charismatic public figure with international moral authority. Then came the crucial moment: the Second Vatican Council, whose teaching on both Church and state accelerated Catholicism's post-Constantinian transformation and made possible the re-constitution of the papacy as a primarily evangelical institution.

Rather than conceiving the Church by analogy to the state, as both theology and canon law had done for centuries, *Lumen Gentium,* Vatican II's Dogmatic Constitution on the Church, described the Church as an evangelical movement with a global mission, a movement in which the purpose of office (including the Office of Peter) is to facilitate the response of all the baptized to the universal call to holiness. According to *Lumen Gentium,* every other function of the Church, including its relationship to the worlds of power, must serve these primary purposes of evangelization and sanctification.

Dignitatis Humanae, the Council's Declaration on Religious Freedom, taught that the state was incompetent in theological questions and declared that the Church would no longer put coercive state power behind its truth claims. In doing so, *Dignitatis Humanae* made possible the emergence of the Catholic Church as an assertive, effective proponent of basic human rights.

Gaudium et Spes, Vatican II's Pastoral Constitution on the Church in the Modern World, portrayed the free and virtuous society in pluralistic terms, as created by the interaction of a political system, an economic system, and a cultural system. In doing so, *Gaudium et Spes* suggested an image of the Church as the teacher and evangelist of culture, rather than a political player in the conventional sense.

And *Christus Dominus,* the Council's Declaration on the Pastoral Office of Bishops in the Church, drew a bright line between the Church and the world of power by teaching that, in the future, governments would not be allowed "rights or privileges" in the nomination of bishops.[10]

On the other hand, and as if to underline the unevenness of evolutionary change in large institutions and the complexity of the issues involved in the encounter between the papacy and power, the immediate post–Vatican II period witnessed what may have been the last significant initiative in the 1,650-year history of the Constantinian papacy: the *Ostpolitik* of Pope Paul VI (the former Giovanni Battista Montini) and his "foreign minister," Archbishop Agostino Casaroli.

The Montini/Casaroli *Ostpolitik* was a fourteen-year-long attempt to achieve, through classic bilateral diplomacy, a *modus non moriendi* (a "way of not dying," in Casaroli's phrase) with the communist states of central and eastern Europe. The *Ostpolitik* included both a tacit papal commitment to avoid a public moral critique of Marxist-Leninist systems, and efforts by the Holy See to curb the activities of clandestinely ordained underground priests and bishops in Warsaw Pact countries. This diplomatic strategy of *salvare il salvabile* ("saving what could be saved," as Casaroli often described it) was informed by two realist political assumptions: that the Yalta division of Europe was a fact of international life for the foreseeable future, and that the breach marked by the iron curtain would be closed only by a gradual convergence, in which a slowly liberalizing East eventually met an increasingly social-democratic West. During that glacial process, Paul VI and Casaroli agreed, the Church had to make provision for the appointment of bishops and the continuity of the Church's sacramental life by reaching agreements with existing governments, even if such agreements were deplored (as they usually were) by the local underground Church.[11]

In electing a Polish pope in 1978, the College of Cardinals did not consciously reject this strategy of accommodation (which Paul VI, who was characteristically ambivalent about it, described privately as "not a policy of glory"). Some of those who promoted Cardinal Karol Wojtyła's candidacy were advocates of the *Ostpolitik*, and one, Cardinal Franz König of Vienna, was an architect of it and a significant diplomatic agent in it. In the first year of his pontificate, however, John Paul II made clear that he intended to pursue, personally, a different tack — a post-Constantinian strategy of resistance through moral revolution.

Three times in the first four days of his pontificate, John Paul vigorously defended religious freedom as the first of human rights and the non-negotiable litmus test of a just society; it was a theme that had been muted under the *Ostpolitik* of Paul VI and Archbishop Casaroli. His contacts with the exiled Cardinal Iosyf Slipyi and his defense of the religious and cultural freedom of the persecuted Greek Catholic Church in Ukraine (then the Ukrainian Soviet Socialist Republic) hit a particularly sensitive nerve in the Soviet system, as did the new Pope's capacity to inspire and strengthen the resistance Church in Soviet Lithuania. Then, during his epic first pilgrimage to Poland in June 1979, John Paul comprehensively unveiled his strategy of political change through moral revolution — the revolution of aroused consciences. By returning to the people of Poland their authentic history and culture and thus giving them a form of power that the regime's truncheons could not reach, the Pope demonstrated that the communist emperor had far fewer clothes than realist analysts (including both Western political leaders and Vatican diplomats) suspected. In doing so, he opened the path to the emergence of Solidarity. The rest, as they say, is history.

In his posthumously published memoirs, *Il martirio della pazienza* [The Martyrdom of Patience], the late Cardinal Casaroli, whom John Paul II appointed his secretary of state in April 1979, suggested that there were no substantive differences between his

Ostpolitik and the "eastern politics" of John Paul, only a difference of "phases." This is not a claim that will withstand close scrutiny, as two examples will illustrate. Just before John Paul's address to the United Nations in October 1979, Cardinal Casaroli systematically went through the draft text of the speech, eliminating references to religious freedom and other human rights issues the Soviet Union and its satellites might find offensive; John Paul just as systematically restored the cuts.[12] Then in 1983, shortly after the Pope had had what diplomats refer to as a "frank exchange of views" over martial law with General Wojciech Jaruzelski (those outside the door heard fists being pounded on desks inside), John Paul, standing at the window of the dining room of the archbishop's residence in Kraków, engaged in some banter with students clamoring outside, while several guests, including Cardinal Casaroli, tried to continue their dinner. Finally, according to another eminent guest who was present, Cardinal Casaroli exploded, saying to the startled dinner table, "What does he want? Does he want bloodshed? Does he want war? Does he want to overthrow the government? Every day I have to explain to the authorities that there is nothing to this!"[13] That does not sound like the reaction of a man whose differences with his superior were merely matters of tactics or timing.

The more plausible explanation of the relationship between Pope John Paul II and Cardinal Casaroli — an explanation that illustrates the complex dynamics of the relationship of the papacy to power at this transitional moment in papal history — is that, in appointing this diplomatically skilled churchman, the principal architect and agent of Paul VI's *Ostpolitik,* as his own secretary of state, John Paul was deliberately adopting a dual strategy. Remnants of a Constantinian approach to playing by the rules-of-the-game would be deployed for whatever they might achieve; the diplomatic dialogues initiated by Casaroli over the previous fourteen years would continue, and the communist regimes in question could not charge the Vatican with reversing course or reneging on formal agreements. Meanwhile, the Pope himself would pursue a post-Constantinian strategy of appealing directly to peoples who could be aroused to new, nonviolent forms of resistance — and thence to self-liberation — through a call to moral arms and a revival of Christian humanism.[14]

The *Ostpolitik* of John Paul II is the clearest example to date of the effective deployment of a post-Constantinian model of engagement between the papacy and the world of power. It was unmistakably different from the Montini/Casaroli *Ostpolitik*, ecclesiologically, strategically, and tactically. It marked a decisive break-point with the Constantinian arrangement of the past, even as it set the stage for further post-Constantinian papal forays into the worlds of power.

Unavoidable Tensions

What does all this mean for the future? An answer may begin to come into focus via a tale of two journalists.

One of them, a distinguished American columnist and a Jew who has been known to say, "I don't know whether I believe in God but I sure fear Him," asked me, on May 16, 2000, who the next pope would be. I said I hadn't the faintest idea, to which he replied, "Well, will he be like John Paul?" Yes, I replied, I thought the next pope would continue the evangelical style of John Paul II, including the papal role as global defender of basic human rights. Good, my friend said — and then laughed. When I asked what was so funny he said, "You know, in 1978, I couldn't have cared less who the next pope would be. Now it's something important to me." My friend has no personal religious investment in the papacy. But he recognized that there was something good for the world in the fact of a universal moral reference point embodied in an ancient office, the occupant of which acted in world affairs according to the logic of biblical truth claims about the dignity of man, rather than according to the realist rules-of-the-game.

Three days later, Vittorio Messori, a prominent Italian journalist who had been John Paul II's interlocutor in the international bestseller *Crossing the Threshold of Hope,* wrote a column in Turin's *La Stampa* arguing that twenty-two years of Slavic exceptionalism and "agitation" had been enough for the Church, and that a return to "normality" was called for — by which Messori meant a return to the Italian papacy. Italians, Messori argued, had a native disposition for the papal office and for maneuvering deftly through the rocks and shoals of history.

The American Jewish agnostic, it seems to me, had a clearer insight into what the papacy of John Paul II meant for the Church and the world than the Italian Catholic journalist. And while he would obviously not put it in these terms, my agnostic friend also had a firmer grasp on the fact that the Church, while a "resident alien" in the world, always exists *for* the world, for the world's salvation, than the Catholic commentator for whom the Church remains primarily an institution to be managed.

In the locks along the ship canal that divides Seattle north and south, salmon swimming home to spawn pass through a series of "trapgates," beyond which there is no possibility of return. With the Second Vatican Council as authoritatively interpreted and embodied by John Paul II, the Catholic Church has passed through a trapgate in history from which there is no turning back. The popes of the 21st century may not bring such distinctive gifts of spirit and intellect to the Office of Peter as John Paul II. We don't know. But Karol Wojtyła's achievement in recasting the papacy was not Wojtyła's alone. There was a logic — a *theo-logic,* if you will — in the evangelical/pastoral model of the papacy Wojtyła so brilliantly embodied; and that logic suggests that the model of the papacy he created will have long-term staying power.

There is no one image of Peter in the New Testament, but rather a tapestry of images: Peter the fisherman-disciple, who "left everything" to follow Jesus (Lk. 5:10–11); Peter the witness to great moments in the ministry of Jesus, including the raising of Jairus's daughter (Mk. 5:37) and the Transfiguration (Mk. 9:2); Peter the shepherd, entrusted with the keys to the kingdom of heaven (Mt. 6:19) and enjoined to feed the Lord's lambs (Jn. 21:15–17); Peter the first confessor of the faith, whose sermon on Pentecost after the outpouring of the Spirit marks the beginning of Christian mission (Acts 2:14–41); Peter the visionary who is given supernatural guidance as he baptizes the Gentile centurion Cornelius and his family (Acts 10:9–16); Peter the Christian martyr, whose ministry means being led, finally, "where you do not wish to go" (Jn. 21:8). But the "figure in the tapestry," to adapt an image from Henry James, the thread that ties these multiple images together, is Peter's distinctive mission to "strengthen the brethren" (Luke 22:32) — a dominical injunction frequently cited by John Paul II.[15]

John Paul II revitalized the papacy for the 21st century by retrieving the Office of Peter's deepest roots, which lie in the New Testament's portrait of Peter's unique role as the apostle who "strengthens the brethren," and renewing the papacy through those recovered roots. In doing so, John Paul aligned the exercise of the Office of Peter with the Second Vatican Council's teaching on the nature of the office of bishop in the Catholic Church, an office in which, the Council Fathers write, "preaching the Gospel has pride of place."[16] Bishops are, first and foremost, evangelists, not managers. As John Paul has demonstrated with effect, that is as true for the Bishop of Rome as it is for the bishop of the smallest missionary diocese.

That this process of retrieval and renewal will continue long beyond John Paul II is also likely because the structure of expectations surrounding the papacy has changed. Now more than ever, both the Church and the world expect the Bishop of Rome to be a global witness to moral truths about the dignity of the human person. Nor has John Paul's immediate successor disappointed those expectations. For in his September 2006 Regensburg Lecture, Pope Benedict XVI demonstrated that he, too, understood the papacy's new role in international public life, as he put two questions on the global agenda — the dangers posed to the human future by irrational faith, and the dangers posed by a loss-of-faith in reason — that could not have been articulated by any other world leader in precisely that way.

To argue that the pontificate of John Paul II constituted a decisive moment of development in the Office of Peter in the Church is not to say, however, that the post-Constantinian papacy will be without its own ambiguities and tensions.

There are built-in ecumenical tensions in the exercise of a global papal ministry of moral witness and persuasion. More than a few evangelical Protestants found this one of the most compelling features of John Paul II's papacy. But the development of this model in the 21st century may cause further difficulties with Orthodox Christians, some of whom will see in it a claim of universal jurisdiction they cannot abide. I think they will be mistaken in this, for, as John Paul II suggested in the 1995 encyclical *Ut Unum Sint* [That They May Be One], the papacy's universal ministry of witness need not include a jurisdictional role in the East of the sort the Bishop of Rome exercises in the West. But psychology can be as determinative as theology in these matters, and Catholics must frankly face the fact that the emergence of an evangelical/pastoral papacy with universal reach has added another item to the rather lengthy list of problems to be sorted out between the Catholic Church and the complex and often conflicted worlds of Orthodoxy.

There are also tensions between the evangelical/pastoral or "witness" model of the papacy and the current diplomatic position of the Holy See. Despite a bizarre and doomed effort to strip the Vatican of its Permanent Observer status at the U.N. in the late 1990s, the issue here is not whether the Holy See can act as a diplomatic agent with international legal personality; that is a long-settled issue in international law and diplomatic practice. The question is, should it?

In the beginning of the 21st century, the Holy See enjoys full diplomatic exchange at the ambassadorial level with more than 170 countries. In developed democracies in which the Church's legal position is secure, this diplomatic representation has little to do with public affairs, and the papal nuncio functions almost exclusively as the papal representative to the Catholic Church in a given country, a representation that has to do primarily with the selection of bishops. In new democracies, papal diplomacy has helped secure free space for the Church to function, through concordats and other legal instruments. In places where Catholics are under pressure or persecuted, the papal nuncio can function as a safeguard for local Catholics — a lifeline to Rome, and to the capacity of popes to focus the spotlight of international public attention on things that authoritarian regimes would rather keep hidden. The fact that the Holy See is a recognized international diplomatic and legal actor also gives the Church and the pope a means of engaging totalitarian regimes with whom the Holy See does not have diplomatic relations, which are usually countries in which the local Church is too weak to defend itself effectively.

On the international plane, where issues of grave moral import are now regularly being decided, the diplomatic *quiddity*, so to speak, of the Holy See can make a significant difference.[17] John Paul II's defense of the universality of basic human rights at the United Nations in 1979 was a factor in the collapse of communism, as it was in 1995 in meeting the challenge of those who claimed that the very idea of "universal human rights" was Western cultural imperialism. The Pope's personal campaign prior to the

1994 Cairo World Conference on Population and Development, and adroit Holy See diplomacy in Cairo itself, frustrated the efforts of the Clinton administration and its European and NGO allies to have abortion-on-demand declared a fundamental human right under international law. Holy See diplomacy since 1994 has been important in rallying opposition to the new totalitarianism of lifestyle libertinism in regional and international forums, on issues of the family, homosexuality, etc. There are undoubtedly ambiguities in aspects of this kind of papal engagement with the world of power; in trying to accomplish certain moral ends (e.g., to secure universal access to education and parental rights in education) the Holy See may find itself acceding to declarations full of other dubious matter (e.g., the international Convention on the Rights of the Child). But it is also true that something important would have been lost, these past two decades, had the Holy See and the papacy not been diplomatically engaged on the international plane.

It is extremely unlikely that any pope in the foreseeable future will dismantle the Holy See's diplomatic network, notwithstanding the likely permanence of this post-Constantinian moment in the history of the papacy. In some instances, this would damage the position of hard-pressed local churches. Internationally, it would mean abandoning a modest but real leverage that, in itself, is arguably good for the international system: the leverage of moral suasion, which reminds the world of power that the world of power is not all there is.

But try, for a moment, a thought-experiment: From the Church's distinctively evangelical point of view, would the abandonment of international legal and diplomatic linkages between the Office of Peter and the world of power be desirable? Is this engagement not in deep tension with the notion of the Church as an evangelical movement in history? Can popes be moral witnesses and "players" at the same time? Wouldn't it be simpler, cleaner, purer if the papacy abandoned all formal linkages to the structures of worldly power and acted as an agency of moral witness alone?

It depends on what you mean by "Church," and what you mean by "politics."

The Church, according to Vatican II, is an evangelical movement in history. To be such a movement in history means to have a concrete institutional form and to deal with other institutions through the best means that human beings have developed for ordering our common life: politics and law. The Church is not a state and must carefully avoid acting like a state. But the Catholic Church is more than a voluntary association with a cause. It is the institutional embodiment of truth claims, and according to its own self-understanding, the basic forms of that institutionalization are of the will of God: the Church as a *communio* of believers; the episcopate, the priesthood, and the Office of Peter as servants of that *communio* and its service to the world.

However ambiguously — and the ambiguities will be lessened if the Church of the third millennium further develops the post-Constantinian model of engagement with power — the fact of the papacy's formal entanglement with national and international political structures is an expression of the Church's reality as a sovereign community: a community that fully possesses the means to achieve its spiritual ends, and is therefore neither dependent on, nor subject to, other sovereignties in the pursuit of those ends. That expression is important, for the Church to be what she is.

The reality of the papacy's formal entanglement with politics is also important for politics, however. If by "politics" we mean the will-to-power and my capacity to impose my will on you, then it would be unseemly, even self-contradictory, for an evangelical movement committed to the method of persuasion to be a "player" in that game. But if by "politics," even international politics, we mean both the quest for power and mutual deliberation about the public goods of our common life — if in politics, even the politics of nations, we understand ourselves to be engaged in the sphere of ethics — then things look different. A global evangelical movement constituted as a sovereign institution for its own spiritual ends has a place at the table in the deliberation about those public goods. That place-at-the-table is both a reminder of the ethical dimension of the exercise of power and a check on the absolutist tendency built into all modern politics. By reminding the world of power that it is not sovereign over all aspects of life, the papacy, engaged diplomatically, performs an invaluable service to the world of power. It is not the power to bring princes to confession on their knees in the snow. It is more important than that.

The Holy See in the 21st century plays a large role in mounting certain crucial moral arguments — arguments rooted in the inalienable dignity of the human person — in an international political environment in which multiple other claims are in play, including the defective morality of utilitarianism and its reduction of the human person to an object fit for manipulation. For the papacy to withdraw from formal involvement in international political life would be to concede a considerable part of the terrain of moral argument to the new Benthamites and their plans for remaking the human condition by remanufacturing human beings. The Holy See is not the only actor engaged in moral and political combat with the new utilitarians; but as the Cairo population conference demonstrated, it is the most potent and effective defender of the dignity of the human person as the foundation of rightly ordered thinking about politics.

Thus, precisely for the world's sake, the Church must continue to run the risks of ambiguity in its engagement with worldly power, even as the papacy of the 21st century is transformed in the image of John Paul II, the heir and legatee of the Second Vatican Council.

Chapter Seven

Two Ideas of Freedom

In 2001, the William E. Simon Foundation created an annual lectureship at the Ethics and Public Policy Center in honor of the late Secretary of the Treasury. It was my honor to deliver the inaugural William E. Simon Lecture on December 5, 2001, which by happy coincidence marked the twenty-fifth anniversary of the Ethics and Public Policy Center. That date, of course, fell less than three months after 9/11. Yet it seemed to me that the topic I had chosen for the first Simon Lecture prior to the attacks on New York and Washington — the deficiencies in Sir Isaiah Berlin's famous "two concepts of liberty" — was of even more urgent interest after 9/11 than when I was pondering it during the summer of 2001, in those last moments of what has rightly been called America's post–Cold War "holiday from history."

In addition to analyzing why Berlin's "two concepts" just didn't work, the first Simon Lecture was intended to challenge the widespread notion that serious reflection on the problem of freedom in its many dimensions is a distinctly modern preoccupation. In fact, many of the 21st-century problems we have with living freedom nobly — or even arguing about freedom sensibly — derive from a defective idea of freedom that first burst onto the scene seven hundred years ago, in the early 14th century. That defective idea also had an important (and generally deleterious) influence on the evolution of moral theology in the Catholic Church. So it was with an eye to both Church and state that I proposed to deepen the critique others had made of Berlin's work by revisiting the argument between Thomas Aquinas and William of Ockham on the nature of freedom. That argument, it turns out, has important implications for thinking through the freedom that must be defended in light of the new world disorder post-9/11.

In a slightly different form, this first Simon Lecture appeared as "A Better Concept of Freedom" in the March 2002 issue of First Things. *The argument of the essay was further refined when it was the basis for my Alexis de Tocqueville Lecture at the Catholic University of Portugal in June 2002.*

O N OCTOBER 31, 1958, Isaiah Berlin delivered his inaugural lecture as Chichele Professor of Social and Political Theory at Oxford. Entitled "Two Concepts of Liberty," it was, according to Berlin's authorized biographer, "the most influential lecture he ever delivered."[1] Indeed, one can argue that Berlin's "Two Concepts of Liberty" was one of the most important political essays of the 20th century, for it clarified an important element in the forty-five-year-long contest between the imperfect democracies of the West and the pluperfect tyranny of the Soviet Union. Moreover, Berlin's essay defended the liberal democratic project in such a way as to reinforce the liberal anti-communist consensus that historians still associate with men like President Harry Truman, Secretary of State Dean Acheson, Presidents John F. Kennedy and Lyndon Johnson, and Senators Hubert H. Humphrey and Henry M. Jackson. As things turned out, that consensus held just long enough so that, deepened intellectually and reinforced politically by conservative and neoconservative thinkers and political leaders in the 1970s and 1980s, freedom's cause finally won out over Marxist-Leninist totalitarianism.

A wide-ranging historian of ideas who had grown up in Riga and Petrograd, Isaiah Berlin had seen, up close and personal, the human and political effects of passionately held ideas. Berlin knew in his bones that ideas are not intellectuals' toys: ideas have consequences, for good and for ill, in what even intellectuals sometimes call the "real world." In "Two Concepts of Liberty," Berlin mounted an extended defense of what he understood to be the liberal idea of freedom against its principal modern political competitors, fascism and communism. At the same time, he raised an alarm against what he regarded as the tendency in social democratic theory and among democratic socialists to weaken individual freedom in the name of other social goods. As the title of his lecture signals, Berlin's basic intellectual move was to distinguish between "negative liberty" and "positive liberty," and then to defend the former as the only concept of liberty that could be actualized in the real world of conflicting interests, diverse concepts of the good, and competing human projects.

"Negative liberty" for Isaiah Berlin is freedom *from:* freedom from interference in personal matters, which implies the circumscription of state power within a strong legal framework.[2] As biographer Michael Ignatieff summarizes Berlin's argument, the primary purpose of a liberal political community is to create the public circumstances in which men and women are left alone "to do what they want, provided that their actions [do] not interfere with the liberty of others."[3] "Positive liberty," on the other hand, is "freedom *to*": freedom to realize some greater good in history. At the heart of the fascist and communist projects, Berlin warned, was a determination to use political power to liberate human beings, whether they liked it or not, for the realization of some higher historical end. That determination, Berlin argued, inevitably leads to repression.

Isaiah Berlin was not a libertarian. Rather, the man who had first worked at the intersection of ideas and power during his World War II service at the British Embassy in Washington was a Russo-English exponent of classic American New Deal liberalism: a liberal who believed that government had the obligation to help ensure the economic, social, and educational conditions under which people could truly exercise their liberty. Berlin broke with the social-democratic left, though, in insisting that liberty, equality, and justice were, are, and always will be in tension. To adopt an example from Ignatieff: a progressive income tax may arguably be just; according to Berlin, however, it is absurd to argue that such a tax does not constitute an infringement on someone's liberty for the benefit of someone else's.[4]

Isaiah Berlin was never willing (or perhaps able) to sort out the tensions or to define the boundaries between liberty and justice. Still, his insistence that politics is not therapy, his resolute refusal to deny the reality of conflicts among social goods, and his insistence that utopian politics inevitably become coercive politics (and, in the modern world, extraordinarily brutal coercive politics) were all important ideas to defend, in Europe and America, against the coercive utopians of the 20th century. In this specific sense, Isaiah Berlin was a champion of pluralism in an age in which too many other political theorists had cast their lot with monisms of one sort or another — monisms, otherwise known as totalitarianisms, of a most lethal sort. A robust pluralism, Berlin suggested, was both an expression of liberty rightly lived and political liberty's surest guarantee.

So high marks to Isaiah Berlin for identifying the perversion of liberty that was at the root of the totalitarian project, and for defending a concept of liberty-as-non-interference that, in setting legal limits to coercive state power, has deep resonances in those parts of the Western democratic political tradition most influenced by Edmund Burke. A half-century after "Two Concepts of Liberty," though, one has to ask whether Berlin's analysis of the problem of freedom reaches the crux of the matter today.

In a thoughtful assessment of Isaiah Berlin's achievement, Norman Podhoretz argued that, despite its important contribution in its time, Berlin's essay is at bottom intellectually unsatisfying: it does not propose a principled, but only a pragmatic, defense of pluralism, and it fails to grapple satisfactorily with a problem that Berlin notes but never seriously addresses — the problem of moral relativism. For while Berlin correctly recognized, in Podhoretz's words, "the spinelessness that can develop from the rejection of any absolutes and the correlative failure to develop rock-bottom convictions," his liberal skepticism about the possibility of philosophically defensible "rock-bottom convictions" could not provide an antidote to "spinelessness."[5] The response to the events of September 11, 2001, in at least some of the higher altitudes of the intellectual class in both the United States and Europe, illustrates with almost painful clarity the truth of Podhoretz's critique of Berlin on this point. To that diagnosis, I would add another disease to which relativism is susceptible, especially when it encounters the afterburn of New Left thought and politics in the United States, or post-"1968" sensibilities in Europe: namely, the absolutizing of moral relativism, and indeed its erection as a kind of constitutionally mandated national (or, in the case of the European Union, transnational) political creed.

In the final analysis, though, Isaiah Berlin's "two concepts" of liberty are unsatisfactory because Berlin does not drive the analysis deeply enough, historically or philosophically. His two concepts are both children of the Enlightenment, and there is virtually no reckoning in his essay with the possibility that pre-Enlightenment thinkers might have some important things to teach us about freedom. Berlin himself concedes that "conceptions of freedom directly derive from what constitutes a self, a person, a man," and goes on to argue that, given "enough manipulation of this definition of man...freedom can be made to mean whatever the manipulator wishes."[6] But this is to dodge the crucial question, which is precisely the question of the truth about man — the truth about the human person — on which any defense of human freedom with real traction must ultimately rest. Isaiah Berlin's philosophical anthropology, his concept of the human person even as *homo politicus*, is exceedingly thin. The net result is to reduce freedom to a matter of one human faculty — the will — alone.

And here, I suggest, is a clue that can lead to a deeper analysis of the problem of freedom today. For the identification of freedom with the will is not, contrary to much conventional wisdom, an Enlightenment innovation. It is the product of a great intellectual chasm that opened up in the High Middle Ages. The nature of that fissure can be depicted in what we might call a tale of two friars. So let us return to the 13th and 14th centuries, when two men of genius had two very different ideas about freedom — ideas that would prove to have immense consequences in the lives of individuals, in politics among nations, and in the character of a civilization.

A Tale of Two Friars

St. Thomas Aquinas, the Dominican friar known to the history of theology as the "Angelic Doctor," was born c. 1225 in his family's *castello* near Roccasecca in what was then the Kingdom of Naples, and died in 1274 at the abbey of Fossanuova, southeast of Rome, en route to the Council of Lyons. His monumental achievement, in such epic works as the *Summa Contra Gentiles* and the *Summa Theologiae,* was to marry the wisdom of a millennium of Christian philosophy and theology to the "new philosophy" of Aristotle that had been rediscovered in Europe in the early 13th century, largely through the mediation of Arabic philosophers. This intellectual marriage between classical Christian philosophy and theology and Aristotelian reason yielded a rich, complex, and (to use the precisely right word a few centuries before its time) deeply *humanistic* vision of the human person, human goods, and human destiny. Embedded in that Thomistic vision of the human person was a powerful concept of freedom.

According to one of his most eminent contemporary interpreters, the Belgian Dominican Servais Pinckaers, Aquinas's subtle and complex thinking about freedom is best captured in the phrase *freedom for excellence.* Freedom, for St. Thomas, is a means to human excellence, to human happiness, to the fulfillment of human destiny. Freedom is the capacity to choose wisely and to act well as a matter of habit — or, to use the old-fashioned term, freedom is an outgrowth of *virtue.* Freedom is the means by which, exercising both our reason and our will, we act on the natural longing for truth, for goodness, and for happiness that is built into us as human beings.

Freedom is something that grows in us, and the habit of living freedom wisely must be developed through education, which among many other things involves the experience of emulating others who live wisely and well. On St. Thomas's view, freedom is in fact the great organizing principle of the moral life — and since the very possibility of a moral life (the capacity to think and choose) is what distinguishes the human person from the rest of the natural world, freedom is the great organizing principle of a life lived in a truly human way. That is, freedom is the human capacity that unifies all our other capacities into an orderly whole, and directs our actions toward the pursuit of happiness and goodness, understood in the noblest sense: the union of the human person with the absolute good, who is God.

Thus virtue and the virtues are crucial elements of freedom rightly understood, and the journey of a life lived in freedom is a journey of growth in virtue — growth in the ability to choose wisely and well the things that truly make for our happiness and for the common good. It's a bit like learning to play a musical instrument. Anyone can bang away on a piano; but that is to make noise, not music, and it's a barbaric, not humanistic, expression of freedom. At first, learning to play the piano is a matter of some drudgery as we master exercises that seem like a constraint, a burden. (Well do I remember my first temptation to book-burning, which involved an instrument of torture for neophyte pianists entitled *Scales, Chords, and Arpeggios.*) But as our mastery of the instrument grows, we discover a new, richer dimension of freedom: we can play the music we like, we can even create new music on our own.

Language works the same way. Hearing and speaking a new language are the best way to learn it (as everyone knows from learning their first language). As some point, though, we have to learn the basic rules of grammar and we have to develop a working vocabulary, both of which are sets of rules. Rules make language possible, for speech without rules is just noise. Speech within rules is what's truly human: it's language, communication, a way of meeting and engaging others. Here we meet what Pinckaers calls a "new kind of freedom": living within a set of rules, we are nonetheless free to choose the words we like to make our sentences — and to make sense. This new freedom is not the freedom to make mistakes, as if mistakes meant nothing; it's the freedom to avoid mistakes without thinking about it. In a word, it's the habit, or virtue, of speaking well.

Freedom, then, is a matter of gradually acquiring the capacity to choose the good and to do what we choose with perfection. Which means that law has a lot to do with freedom. Law can educate us in freedom. Law, rightly understood, is not a work of heteronomous (external) imposition but a work of wisdom, and good law facilitates our achievement of the human goods that we instinctively seek because of who we are and what we are meant to be as human beings.[7]

Aquinas was fully aware that human beings can fail, and in fact do evil — often great evil. No exponent of Aristotelian realism like St. Thomas, indeed no one formed by biblical religion as well as ancient philosophical wisdom, could deny the undeniable. Yet, even in the face of manifest evil, Thomas insisted that we have within us, and we can develop, a freedom through which we can do things well, rightly, excellently. Evil is not the last word about the human condition, and an awareness of the pervasiveness of evil is not the place to start thinking about freedom, or indeed about political life in general. We are made for excellence. Developed through the four cardinal virtues — prudence (practical wisdom), justice, courage, and temperance (perhaps better styled today, "self-command") — freedom is the method by which we become the kind of people our noblest instincts incline us to be: the kind of people who can, among other possibilities, build free and virtuous societies in which the rights of all are acknowledged, respected, and protected in law.[8]

It was not for nothing (although it was an aside tinged with a characteristic sense of irony) that Father John Courtney Murray, S.J., the great American Catholic public philosopher of freedom, once called Thomas Aquinas "the first Whig."[9]

Our second mendicant friar, William of Ockham, was born in England about a dozen years after Aquinas's death, joined the Franciscans, was educated and later taught at Oxford, and died in 1347 in Munich after a life of considerable turbulence, both intellectual and ecclesiastical. Those who have never studied philosophy will recognize his name as the author of "Ockham's Razor" — the principle (still used in the sciences as well as in philosophy) that the simpler of two explanations should be preferred. Professional philosophers consider him the chief exponent of "nominalism," a powerful late medieval philosophical movement which denied that universal concepts and principles exist in reality — they exist only in our minds. To take an obvious and critical example: according to the nominalists, there is no such thing as "human nature" per se. "Human nature" is simply a description, a name (hence "nominalism"), we give to our experience of common features among human beings. The only things that exist, according to nominalism, are particulars.

Often presented as a crucial moment in the history of epistemology, the theory of knowledge, nominalism also had a tremendous influence on moral theology. And because politics, as Aristotle taught, is an extension of ethics, nominalism's impact on moral theology eventually had a profound influence on political theory. To return to that obvious and critical example: if there is no human nature, then there are no universal moral principles that can be read from human nature. Morality, on a nominalist view, is simply law and obligation, and that kind of law is always external to the human person. Law, in other words, is always coercion — divine law and human law, God's coercion of us and our coercion of each other.

The implications of Ockham's nominalism for the moral life and for politics are not hard to tease out of this brief sketch of his basic philosophical position. In his history of medieval philosophy, the German scholar Josef Pieper writes that, with Ockham, "extremely dangerous processes were being set in motion, and many a future trouble was preparing."[10] Servais Pinckaers, perhaps the premier Catholic analyst of the history of moral philosophy and moral theology of the late 20th century, goes so far as to describe Ockham's work as "the first atomic explosion of the modern era." "The atom he split," though, "was...not physical but psychic," for Ockham shattered our concept of the human soul and thereby created a new, atomized vision of the human person and, ultimately, of society.[11]

With Ockham, we meet what Pinckaers has called the *freedom of indifference*. Here, freedom is simply a neutral faculty of choice, and choice is everything — for choice is a matter of self-assertion, of power. Will is the defining human attribute. Indeed, will is the defining attribute of all of reality. For God, too, is supremely willful, and the moral life as read through Ockhamite lenses is a contest of wills between my will and God's imposition of his will through the moral law.

Ockham's radical emphasis on the will is an idea with very serious, real-world consequences. It not only severs the moral life from human nature (which, for a nominalist, doesn't exist). At the same time, and because of that, it severs human beings from one another in a most dramatic way. For there can be no "common good" if there are only the particular goods of particular men and women who are each acting out their own particular willfulness.

Here, in the mid-14th century, is the beginning of what we call today the "autonomy project": the claim that each of us is a radically autonomous, self-creating Self, whose primary relationship to others is one of power. From its Ockhamite beginning, as Pinckaers writes, "freedom of indifference was...impregnated with a secret passion for self-affirmation."[12] Thus, over time, freedom was eventually led into the trap of self-interest from which Immanuel Kant tried, unsuccessfully, to rescue it by appeals to a "categorical imperative" that could be known by reason and that would, it was hoped, restore a measure of objectivity to morality.[13] On a long view of the history of ideas, and freely conceding the twists and turns of intellectual fortune along the way, William of Ockham is the beginning of the line that eventually leads to Nietzsche's will-to-power and its profound effect on the civilization of our times.

Freedom, for Ockham, has little or no spiritual character. The reality is autonomous man, not virtuous man, for freedom has nothing to do with goodness, happiness, or truth. Freedom is simply willfulness. Freedom can attach itself to any object, so long as it does not run into a superior will, human or divine. Later in the history of ideas, when God dropped out of the equation, freedom came to be understood in purely instrumental or utilitarian terms. And if the road on which Ockham set out eventually led to Nietzsche, it also led, through even more twists and turns, to Princeton's Peter Singer (author of the major article on "Ethics" in the *Encyclopaedia Britannica*), and to Singer's claim that parents ought to be able to wait for a few weeks before deciding whether their newborn child should be allowed to live. Ideas, indeed, have consequences.

From the Greeks down to Aquinas, every moral philosopher of note had assumed that the pursuit of happiness is the issue that focuses serious and sustained reflection on the moral life: how should I live, in order to be happy? With William of Ockham, the profound linkages among freedom, virtue, and the pursuit of happiness are sundered. And thus morality is mere obligation, while freedom is mere willfulness. When Western thought took a decisively subjectivist and inward-looking turn in the 17th century, and when that subjectivism eventually gave birth over time to a principled skepticism about the human capacity to know anything with confidence, the result, which is much with us today, was the emergence of an intellectual culture of radical moral relativism lacking any thick notion of the common good. By positing a profound tension between freedom and reason (or, in his construction, will and reason), Ockham created a situation in which there are only two options: determinisms of a biological, racial, or ideological sort, or the radical relativism that, married to irrationalism, eventually yields nihilism. In either case, freedom self-destructs.[14]

This tale of two friars sheds light on why Isaiah Berlin's "two concepts of liberty" are finally unsatisfactory. Although Berlin concedes at the outset that "political theory is a branch of moral philosophy," he simply does not conjure with the "atomic explosion" that Ockham created in moral theory or with its results in political thought.[15] When Berlin writes that "I am normally said to be free to the degree to which no man or body of men interferes with my activity," such that "political liberty is simply the area within which a man can act unobstructed by others," he is taking an Ockhamite tack from the outset.[16] Berlin openly admits that his "positive liberty" begins in "an act of will." In fact, however, his formulation of "negative liberty" also assumes that freedom is essentially a matter of the will.[17] "Negative liberty" is simply that which allows me to avoid too many unpleasant collisions with the wills of others.[18] But this concept of "negative liberty," as Norman Podhoretz correctly noted, doesn't tell us much about how we resolve the inevitable conflicts between wills without raw coercion, or even why we should do so. "Negative liberty" accurately describes one important aspect of the political organization of freedom: the need to circumscribe and regulate coercive state power by law. But Berlin's "negative liberty" cannot provide an account of why that freedom has any moral worth beyond its being an expression of my will. Life, liberty, and the pursuit of happiness are drastically disconnected here.

Berlin goes so far as to suggest that, for a "schoolman" like Aquinas, as well as for the Jacobins and communists of the modern period, it is legitimate to force others into living their freedom rightly.[19] That kind of crude coercion was certainly true of Jacobins and communists, but it is no part of Thomas Aquinas's theory of freedom. For as the Catholic Church came to recognize over centuries of debate, culminating in the teaching of the Second Vatican Council and of Pope John Paul II, the philosophical anthropology that underwrites Aquinas's freedom for excellence — an anthropology that contains thick moral convictions about the inalienable dignity and value of every human life — demands a commitment to the method of persuasion in politics. Indeed, as the history of the past three decades has shown, it is today's devotees of "negative liberty" as reinterpreted by postmodern radical skeptics and relativists who are the primary exponents of coercion in the name of "tolerance" and "diversity" — coercion that can be mediated through the United States Supreme Court, or the European Parliament, or the regulatory agencies of the democracies on both sides of the Atlantic.

Isaiah Berlin could not escape — and perhaps did not even recognize — Ockham's trap. That is why his "two concepts of liberty" ultimately break down. And that is why we require, as individuals and as democratic societies, a deeper understanding of the nature of freedom today — an understanding that challenges the freedom of indifference with freedom for excellence.

The Idea of Freedom We Need

In addition to illuminating a crucial episode in the history of ideas, this tale of two friars also sheds light on grave public issues today. And in doing so, it reminds us that a clash of civilizations is being played out within the Western democracies, as well as between ourselves and hostile forces from outside the civilizational orbit of the West, forces bent on our destruction.

In the aftermath of the communist crack-up in 1989–91, a tremendous wave of euphoria rippled through what was then rightly called the "free world." This euphoria went far beyond the undeniable satisfaction of seeing a great evil overcome; more than one otherwise sober-minded observer was heard to propose that the democratic project — the great carrier of the modern quest for freedom — was now inevitably and irreversibly triumphant. In the first decade of the new century, we have been abruptly reminded of the fragility of freedom — of the hard fact, chiseled in stone on the Korean War Memorial on the National Mall in Washington, D.C., that "freedom is never free." Which is to say, we have been reminded of the fact that democracy is always an unfinished experiment, testing the capacity of each generation to live freedom nobly.

The first wake-up call came in the aftermath of dramatic advances in genetics, including the decryption of the human genome, and the biotechnologies this new knowledge rapidly spawned. Suddenly, Francis Fukuyama's image of the "end of history" seemed overrun by Aldous Huxley's "brave new world." Human beings, it became clear, would soon have the capacity to remanufacture the human condition — precisely by manufacturing or remanufacturing human beings. The new tyranny on the horizon was not the jackbooted totalitarian state of Orwell's *1984;* that was the tyranny that had haunted our dreams during what Jeane Kirkpatrick once aptly described as the "Fifty-Five Years' Emergency" — the civilizational crisis that ran from Hitler's military re-occupation of the Rhineland in 1936 to the collapse of the Soviet Union in 1991. Rather, the new and ominous possibility on the near-term horizon was something quite different: the mindlessly pleasurable, thoroughly dehumanized, and massively coercive dystopia of Huxley's brilliant imagination.

Do I exaggerate? I think not. Scientists and biotech industry executives now talk freely, if usually behind closed doors, of what Leon Kass has called the "immortality project." Here, they confidently tell us, is a possible future world without suffering, even without death — except perhaps death freely chosen as a remedy for terminal boredom. But as Huxley presciently discerned decades before the unraveling of the DNA double-helix, such a world would ultimately be an inhuman world: a world of souls without longing, without passion, without striving, without surprise, without desire — in a word, a world without love.

And here, too, we can find long-term radioactive traces from Ockham's "atomic explosion" in the 14th century. Ockham's was a world without purpose, a world of willful means detached from ends. So is the brave new world as Aldous Huxley described it. As one of the World Controllers muses in Huxley's novel, "Once you began admitting explanations in terms of purpose — well, you didn't know what the results would be. It was the sort of idea that might easily decondition some of the more unsettled minds among the higher castes — make them . . . take to believing . . . that the goal was somewhere beyond, somewhere outside the present human sphere; that the purpose of life was not the maintenance of well-being, but some intensification and refinement of consciousness, some enlargement of knowledge. Which was, the Controller reflected, quite possibly true. But not, in the present circumstances, admissible."[20] Tyranny thrives in a world in which means always trump ends. The freedom of indifference cannot sustain a truly free society.

The debate over cloning and embryo-destructive stem cell research in various Western democracies ought to have given us pause, and precisely on this point. With rare exceptions, the first great public debates of the biotech era were conducted in largely utilitarian terms (when they were not reduced to appeals to compassion that did not constitute anything resembling a serious moral argument). What can be done to put this urgent and unavoidable discussion onto more secure moral-philosophical ground? I suggest that that will require a rigorous reckoning with the degree to which the freedom of indifference has become the operative notion of freedom in much of Western high culture, in the media, among many political leaders, in considerable parts of the mainline Protestant religious community, among many Jewish intellectuals and religious leaders, in the academy, and in the biotech industry. Challenging the freedom of indifference with freedom for excellence is essential if we are to deploy our new genetic knowledge in ways that lead to human flourishing rather than to the soulless dystopia of the brave new world.

There will be — there already are — appeals to "pluralism" in these debates. Pluralism, however, is not mere plurality, as John Courtney Murray never tired of repeating. Plurality is sheer difference: a sociological fact, a staple of the human condition. Pluralism is a civilizational achievement: the achievement of what Murray called an "orderly conversation" — a conversation about personal goods and the common good, about the relationship between freedom and moral truth, about the virtues necessary to form the kind of citizens who can live their freedom in such a way as to make the machinery of democracy serve genuinely humanistic ends.

That kind of orderly conversation cannot begin with the radical epistemological skepticism and moral relativism that inform today's Ockhamites and their defense of freedom as willfulness. It must begin, as Jefferson began the American democratic experiment, with the assertion and defense of truths. As Father Murray once wrote, in words than can be applied to other democracies as well, "the American Proposition rests on the...conviction that there are truths; that they can be known; that they must be held; for if they are not held, assented to, worked into the texture of institutions, there can be no hope of founding a true City."[21] The orderly conversation that is the lifeblood of democracies must begin, in other words, with a reaffirmation of freedom for excellence as the freedom to which we, like the Founders, can pledge our lives, fortunes, and sacred honor. It is past time to bid farewell to Ockham's distorted idea of freedom, and to re-embrace the more humanistic vision of Aquinas.

The second challenge to what many commentators have styled America's "holiday from history" came, of course, on September 11, 2001 — a day of infamy that marked the true beginning of the 21st century as a distinctive historic epoch, as the guns of August 1914 had marked the true beginning of the 20th. The world has changed and acknowledging that, however difficult, is imperative. The holiday from history is over. Not only the American republic and the freedoms it embodies, but the entire civilizational project we call "the West," is in grave peril from a new form of irrationalism and nihilism that expresses itself, often violently, through a perverse form of monotheistic religion. The struggle against this new and present danger may well last several generations.

The roots of this new struggle run deep into history. Some argue, and I would not disagree, that they run more than thirteen hundred years into the past, and that what confronts us today is the contemporary expression of a civilizational contest that has ebbed and flowed for well over a millennium. Because its roots run so deeply into the religious and cultural subsoil of history — because we have been forcefully reminded since 9/11 that the deepest currents of world-historical change are religious and cultural — analyzing the causalities that brought us to September 11, 2001, is no simple business. Yet amidst the inevitable complexities of history understood as an arena of moral responsibility, there was also some welcome, and perhaps long overdue, simplicity.

For in the immediate aftermath of the attacks on New York and Washington, there was, in America, a remarkable resurgence of simple, indeed robust, moral clarity in a country that had long been told, by everyone from Alan Wolfe to Jerry Falwell, that it was awash in moral relativism. That moral clarity, and the resolve that accompanies it, showed significant staying power — for a while.

Among certain sectors of the American intellectual class, however, it lasted, by my count, approximately ninety-six hours after 9/11.

For the commentariat seems to have established a statute of limitations, according to which radical moral relativism and its off-spring in the worlds of political analysis and commentary must be given free rein in public debate, no matter how kinetically they have been refuted by events. Thus, less than a week after 9/11, Americans began hearing appeasement strategies, moral equivalence theories, "root cause" analyses of terrorism, nonsense about "violence begetting violence" (as if a justly conducted war were the same thing as turning a 767 into a weapon of mass destruction), and self-loathing anti-Americanism of the most vulgar sort. At the outset, these intellectual and moral aberrations were reasonably well confined to the woolier fringes of the American chattering classes. But they were already well-entrenched in Europe a month after 9/11, and they began to have a corrosive effect on the American political conversation in the run-up to the 2004 presidential election. The rifts that opened then, and that remained afterward, had everything to do with four things analyzed above: the deterioration of the idea of freedom into willfulness, the detachment of freedom from moral truth, an obsession with "choice," and the consequent inability to draw the most elementary moral conclusions about the imperative to resist evil — or to recognize and describe evil as such, rather than to deny its reality by an appeal to psychiatric or quasi-Marxist political categories.

The initial response to 9/11 demonstrated that the American people are still capable of moral common sense. In that same initial moment of crisis, the American national commitment to tolerance and the basic human decencies in a religiously diverse society, which held firm then and which has remained firm since, has demonstrated the enduring power of the Judeo-Christian tradition to ground that commitment, which is not being sustained today by

ACLU-style theories of liberty or by other, alternative religious traditions. So let us gratefully take note of the fact that, at a moment of
national emergency unprecedented in two generations, the American people acquitted themselves with the dignity, decency, and
determination that come from deeply rooted moral convictions.

What, however, will sustain us — meaning, not only Americans, but the peoples of the West — over the long haul? In the
United States of 2001 (as distinguished from the United States of
that low decade, the 1970s), there was a remarkable resurgence of
uncomplicated, unapologetic patriotism in the aftermath of foreign aggression: flags, not the yellow ribbons of the era of Jimmy
Carter and the preemptive cringe, were the icons of the day. But
this welcome recovery of patriotism — which was paralleled iñ
other democracies by the outpouring of sympathy for and solidarity with the United States — cannot be indefinitely sustained
during a multi-generational struggle against jihadism unless it becomes, once again, the expression of a nobler concept of freedom
than mere willfulness. The questions posed here are emphatically
not for Americans only. Is happy hedonism that for which we of the
West are prepared to make the sacrifices that will be required of us?
Or is it more likely that the acids of the relativism that accompany a
merely negative concept of freedom as non-interference will eventually bring us to the point where "appeasement" will once again
become a respectable word in the Western political vocabulary?

A society without convictions about moral goods tethered to
truths cannot defend itself against aggressors motivated by a distorted sense of "ought." We should have been reminded of that
when reading those chilling letters from the hijackers the week after
9/11. The answer to a distorted concept of the good cannot be a
radical relativism about the good. It must be a nobler concept of
the good.

And that brings us back, finally, to our tale of two friars.

Freedom for excellence is the freedom that will satisfy the deepest yearnings of the human heart to be free. It is more than that, though. The idea of freedom for excellence and the disciplines of self-command it implies are essential for democracy and for the defense of freedom.

Homo Voluntatis, Willful Man, cannot exploit the new genetic knowledge so that it serves the ends of freedom and avoids the slippery slope to the brave new world. Why? Because *Homo Voluntatis* cannot explain why some things that can be done should not be done.

Homo Voluntatis cannot defend himself or the institutions of democracy against the new jihadist dangers to national security and world order. Why? Because *Homo Voluntatis* cannot give an account of a freedom worth sacrificing, even dying, for.

There are, indeed, two ideas of freedom. Both ideas have consequences. One of them is worthy of the West. One of them will see us through to a future worthy of free peoples.

Chapter Eight

Thinking World Politics: A Catholic Optic

In 2002, I was invited by the Columbus School of Law at the Catholic University of America to deliver the school's annual Pope John XXIII Lecture. Having long been convinced that John XXIII's 1963 encyclical, Pacem in Terris, *marked a developmental peak from which a once-vital Catholic international relations theory had begun to decompose, and concerned that post-Johannine patterns of thought on world politics in many Catholic circles (including the Vatican) were ill-fitted to address the moral pressures being put on statesmen in the post-9/11 global environment, I decided to use the John XXIII Lecture to propose a revival of the very idea of a distinct Catholic international relations theory. The classic intellectual structure of this way of thinking about the world had important, enduring truths to teach; yet the theory itself needed, not only recovery, but development, given the realities of the new world disorder. My Pope John XXIII Lecture —"The Just War Tradition and the World after September 11"—was subsequently published by the* Catholic University of America Law Review, *and became a source for both this essay and the essay that follows, "Moral Clarity in a Time of War."*

In light of the debates over the wars in Afghanistan and Iraq, I extensively revised the Pope John XXIII Lecture as I prepared the twenty-sixth annual Thomas Merton Lecture, which I delivered at Columbia University in New York in October 2003, and revised it further still for an academic conference on the future of Catholic thought about world politics, which was held in Rome in April 2004 under the joint sponsorship of the School of Philosophy of the Pontifical Gregorian University and the Ethics and Public Policy Center. In a slightly shortened form, and without the apparatus, that form of the essay was published in First Things *in May 2004 under the title, "World Order: What Catholics Forgot."*

The idea that there is, in fact, such a thing as "Catholic international relations theory" and that it deserves both retrieval and renewal remains to be firmly re-established. That this has not been done—that so many contemporary Catholic commentators insist that there is no such thing as Catholic international relations theory, such that their commentary on world politics is indistinguishable in content from that of others—is a bad thing for both the Church and the world.

Once upon a time — and not all that long a time ago — educated Catholics knew that there was a distinctively Catholic way to think about world politics.[1] They also understood that Catholics brought more than a sensibility to the debate over world affairs; Catholics brought ideas, and those ideas were organized in a distinctive way that led to distinctive insights and a distinctive method of moral analysis. That moral analysis and the ideas that informed it are even more important today than they were in what might be called the Golden Age of Catholic international relations theory, the middle decades of the 20th century. Yet what ought to have been stretched and developed to meet the new realities of international public life has in fact been largely abandoned. That is a serious problem, for the Catholic Church and for the world.

Catholic International Relations Theory

What was this distinctive Catholic tradition of moral reflection about the politics of nations?

It was first forged by Augustine in *De Civitate Dei*, and then developed by Aquinas in his commentaries on ethics and politics, the *De Regimine Principum* and the relevant sections of the *Summa Theologiae*. It was refined by theologians like Francisco de Vitoria and Francisco Suárez in the Counter-Reformation period. It was further developed by the 20th-century papal magisterium during the pontificates of Pius XII and John XXIII. Needless to say, the world changed from the last days of the Roman Empire to the *Gotterdamerung* of Hitler's Thousand-Year Reich. Yet from Augustine to John XXIII, this distinctive Catholic way of thinking about world politics displayed certain consistent features. It was a tradition of moral realism, built around three key insights.

First, the Catholic tradition insisted that politics is an arena of rationality and moral responsibility. Unlike those theorists of international relations who insisted that world politics is an arena of amorality or immorality, classic Catholic thinking about international relations taught that every human activity, including politics, takes place within the horizon of moral judgment, precisely because politics is a human activity and moral judgment is a defining characteristic of the human person. That is true of politics-among-nations, the Catholic tradition insisted, even if there are distinctive aspects to the moral dimension of world politics.

This basic stance toward politics was itself built on more fundamental Catholic moral-theological convictions: that mankind is not "totally depraved," as some Reformation traditions taught; that society is a natural reality; that governance has a positive, not merely punitive or coercive, function; that political community is a good in its own right, an expression of the sociability that is part of the God-given texture of the human condition. Politics, the Catholic tradition of moral realism insisted, always engages questions of virtue, questions of public goods, questions of how we ought to live together.

Second, the Catholic tradition taught a classic understanding of power: power is the capacity to achieve a corporate purpose for the common good. The idea of power is not to be reduced, or traduced, such that "power" becomes a synonym for "violence." On the contrary, violence is a limit-case testing the boundaries of a rational and ethical politics. Power thus has a positive dimension; its proper exercise is a form of human creativity. Power is also related to governance. Political communities exist to achieve common purposes — that is, to exercise power. Absent power, there is anarchy. Thus the Catholic question was never, should power be exercised? Rather, the Catholic question was, how is power to be exercised? To what ends, by what authority, through what means? Power, in this understanding, is not the antinomy of peace (which is one of the goods to be sought by public authority); power, rightly understood, is a means to the achievement of the good of peace.

Third, the Catholic tradition had a distinctive understanding of peace. The peace to be sought in the politics-of-nations was not the interior peace that comes only to the individual through a right relationship with God. Nor was the peace to be sought in world politics the eschatological peace of a conflict-free world, which Catholic moral realism deemed a utopian fantasy. Catholic moral realism understood that the biblical peace of the shalom kingdom envisioned in Isaiah 2:2–4 cannot be built by human effort in this world. Something else could be built, however — the peace of political community, in which freedom, working through just structures of governance and law, advances the common good in ways that lead political communities toward that *caritas* [charity] that is their proper and most noble end.

This Catholic tradition of moral realism had a considerable, if often unremarked, effect on the evolution of world politics in the modern period. It formed part of the intellectual foundation on which the Dutch Protestant Hugo Grotius based his 17th-century reflections on what he termed the "community of nations," his early attempts to apply the category of "law" to world politics, and his development of just war thinking. If Grotius be the father of international law, and thus the father of today's international system, then the grandfather of that system is the moderate realism of what can properly be called Catholic international relations theory.

As might have been expected from a tradition that defined peace as *tranquillitas ordinis* [the tranquillity of order], Catholic international relations theory in the mid-20th century stressed international legal and political institutions as a remedy for the threat of modern war and as the natural evolution of human political development. The high point of this line of thought came in 1963, with John XXIII's encyclical *Pacem in Terris* [Peace on Earth]. There, the Pope taught that the "universal common good" required the development of a "universal public authority."

John XXIII was not a world federalist. He did not specify the structure of the universal public authority for which he called, and he did not discuss in any detail the relationship of that "universal public authority" to existing nation-states. Rather, he pointed out that, as there were obviously certain grave problems on the global agenda that could be addressed only on a global basis, there ought to be some form of legal/political entity capable of resolving global questions in a global way. Pope John was also careful to stress that the universal public authority he envisioned must operate according to the principle of subsidiarity (i.e., not drawing all political authority into itself, but respecting the legitimate prerogatives of "lower" forms of public authority and the free associations of civil society). Moreover, according to *Pacem in Terris,* the universal public authority must take as one of its primary objectives the defense of human rights.

A Fallow Period, a New Set of Questions

In the four decades after *Pacem in Terris,* the encyclical's stress on the imperative of public authority at the global level was given concrete diplomatic effect in the diplomacy of the Holy See and in commentary by officials of the Holy See on world politics and international conflict. At the theoretical level, however, Catholic international relations theory entered a rather fallow period in the years immediately following *Pacem in Terris.* Indeed, very few Catholics in the early 21st century have ever heard of a "Catholic international relations theory" — including, alas, very few scholars and bishops. That there is a distinctively Catholic way of thinking about world politics, rooted in the distinctive understandings that ground Catholic social ethics, has not been a dominant theme among Catholic political theorists and international relations specialists since the mid- to late 1960s.

This is troubling in many ways, not least because there were two interesting developments in the Catholic Church's interaction with world politics during the pontificate of Pope John Paul II that would seem to call for a development of Catholic moral-theological reflection on world politics — and precisely at the level of theory.

Taking up an insight of John XXIII, John Paul II insisted for more than a quarter-century that human rights are the moral core of the "universal common good" and that religious freedom is the first of these human rights to which the institutions of international public life must attend. This papal theme was a fruit of the Second Vatican Council, an expression of John Paul II's own experience with totalitarian regimes, and a specification of Karol Wojtyła's philosophical reflections on the dynamic structure of the human person. To insist that religious freedom is the first of human rights, and that international legal and political institutions must defend and promote it, was not, for John Paul, a matter of institutional special pleading. Rather, it was a function of the Pope's teaching that all thinking about society, even international society, must begin with a sound philosophical anthropology of the human person, which recognizes in the human quest for transcendent truth and love the defining characteristic of our humanity.

The second signal development in John Paul's pontificate was the emergence of the Office of Peter — the papacy — as an office of global moral witness with real effect within and among nation-states. The most obvious example of this, of course, was the Pope's pivotal role in the collapse of European communism — by igniting a revolution of conscience in Poland in June 1979, John Paul II had a decisive impact on shaping the nonviolent politics that eventually produced the Revolution of 1989 in east central Europe, and the collapse of the Soviet Union in 1991. But other examples could be adduced, including the Pope's tacit support for the People Power revolution that displaced the Marcos regime in the Philippines; the Pope's role in supporting democratic transitions in Latin America, with special reference to El Salvador, Nicaragua, Chile, and Argentina; and the Pope's role in arousing an effective international opposition to the Clinton administration's efforts to have abortion-on-demand declared a fundamental human right at the 1994 Cairo World Conference on Population and Development.

The emergence of the pope, the holder of the world's oldest institutional office, as a global moral witness has been an intriguing phenomenon in its own right. It becomes even more interesting when another aspect of the situation comes into focus. For while John Paul II was taking moral arguments directly to the people of individual states and to the people of the world, going around or beyond their governments or the relevant international organizations, the diplomacy of the Holy See (which enjoys full diplomatic relations with more than 170 states as well as Permanent Observer status at the U.N. and diplomatic representation at the European Union, the Organization for Security and Cooperation in Europe, and the Organization of American States) has continued to function through the normal grooves of bilateral relations and multilateral institutions. Is there a tension here? I think so.

John Paul II was a moral witness speaking truth to power in world politics; his diplomatic representatives were, by definition, players according to the established rules-of-the-game. Sometimes those roles got confused. Some would argue that that was the case during the debate prior to the Iraq War, when the prudential judgments of Vatican diplomats and agency heads were often reported (and perceived) as if they were decisive moral judgments by the man the world had come to recognize as its foremost moral authority — Pope John Paul II.

Then there was, and is, the question of how the Holy See, which is not a state, is to function in international forums in which every other actor of consequence is a state. How is it possible for the Holy See to function like a state without being a state and without damaging the Catholic Church's moral witness? To take one issue that arose under John Paul II and is sure to reoccur under his successors: Can the Holy See, without damaging the moral witness of the Catholic Church, form practical alliances for purposes of defending the family and the inalienable right to life with Muslim states whose policy and practice deny what the Catholic Church claims is the moral core of the universal common good — religious freedom?

This tension between the moral witness of the Successor of Peter and the Church, on the one hand, and the diplomacy of the Holy See, on the other, is not likely to be resolved anytime soon — nor should it be prematurely resolved in either direction (i.e., by muting the moral witness of the Office of Peter, or by the Holy See's withdrawal from bilateral and multilateral diplomacy). In the early 21st century, when the Catholic Church is the world's premier institutional challenger to utilitarianism as the default position in international politics and in the understanding of the human person implicit in international organizations, the world needs the Church, working through the Holy See, to promote the dignity of the human person as the foundation of any worthy politics, including international politics. And if that means the Church must live with ambiguity and tension, then so be it. In the face of the jihadist threat (which only intensifies the temptation to create a naked international public square), the world also needs a demonstration that publicly assertive religion is not necessarily violent or aggressive religion; the Catholic Church, acting through the Holy See, is the only available candidate for making that demonstration at the global level. And, again, if that results in a certain tension and ambiguity, so be it.

But given this inevitable tension and ambiguity, it is all the more urgent to reconvene a conversation that has lapsed for some forty years — the conversation over the development of Catholic international relations theory. Its central insights into the nature of politics and public life remain true; moreover, these insights could play a crucial leavening role in a debate often dominated by less noble (and indeed less true) conceptions of the human person, human community, human origins, and human destiny. Catholic international relations theory, developed, would also offer a dramatic alternative to what is now the other prominent religiously grounded moral reading of world politics, namely, the ideology of Islamism and its most radical expression, jihadism. And Catholic international relations theory, developed, would represent an important challenge to the amoral Realpolitik that has corrupted Western European thinking about world politics and that is always a danger in the formulation of U.S. foreign policy.

Reading the Signs of These Times

According to the instruction of the Second Vatican Council to read the "signs of the times," the development of Catholic international relations theory, while remaining faithful to the moral truths that are its foundation, must reckon with at least five new realities of international public life.

A New World Disorder

We no longer live in a world structured according to the political realities that prevailed at the end of the Second World War. With the collapse of the Soviet Union and the end of the Cold War, the world is no longer divided into two opposing ideological and military camps whose rivalry set the framework for much of international public life between 1945 and 1991. The preponderance of U.S. military, economic, and cultural power in the world is one facet of the new situation. Other relevant factors include the absolute and relative decline of western European influence in the world; the emergence of China, India, and Japan as international actors with potentially global impact; the new influence of international economic and financial institutions such as the World Bank, the International Monetary Fund, and the World

Trade Organization; the impact of international non-governmental organizations on the world political debate; the global communications revolution and the emergence of a "real-time" global politics; and the new assertiveness of religious conviction as a factor in the politics of nations. All of these must be taken into account in thinking through the development of Catholic international relations theory.

The Enduring Nation-State

A developed Catholic international relations theory must also reckon with the enduring reality of the nation-state system. Despite the emergence of a plethora of international legal, political, and economic institutions, and the increasing impact of non-state actors on world affairs, the nation-state remains the basic organizing unit of world politics. That seems unlikely to change in the 21st century. The 21st-century world is not going to be structured according to pre-1914 patterns of empire; but neither is the 21st-century world going to evolve swiftly toward a post-nation-state structure in which international legal and political institutions are the dominant actors.

New Actors on Stage

There are new actors in world politics with which a developed Catholic international relations theory must contend. I have already mentioned the impact of global financial and economic institutions and international non-governmental organizations. But one must also wrestle here with the fact that other non-state actors have become increasingly important in shaping politics-among-nations. Transnational terrorist organizations and networks are the most prominent, and lethal, examples of this phenomenon. Transnational criminal cartels — trafficking in human persons, for example — are another.

The Crisis of International Organizations

Catholic international relations theory must also contend with the unavoidable fact that existing international organizations are in a troubled state. Founded to save humanity from the scourge of war, the U.N. system has proven incapable of doing so, even as it is proven largely incapable of dealing with the new reality of aggressive non-state actors (including terrorist organizations) and with the often-lethal reality of complex humanitarian emergencies caused by failed states or collapsing states. The 20th-century Catholic commitment to the evolution of effective international legal and political organizations is not going to be reversed in the 21st century, nor should it be. But that commitment must now be tempered by a new sobriety, in the Holy See and among Catholic social ethicists, about the failures of the U.N. and its affiliated agencies to deal with such post–Cold War crises as the Rwandan genocide, the collapse of Yugoslavia, the hijacking of Afghanistan by the Taliban, widespread famine in sub-Saharan Africa, the African AIDS pandemic, and the breakout of SARS from China. Catholic international relations theory must, in other words, face squarely the moral and political failures of a U.N. system in which Libya can chair the U.N. Human Rights Commission, Saddam Hussein's Iraq can lead a major international meeting on disarmament, the Security Council becomes a dysfunctional obstacle to its own ends because its structure and procedures are incongruent with the realities it must address, and U.N. peacekeeping operations (as in Kosovo) too often serve to create new dependencies rather than functioning civil societies.

The Dictatorship of Relativism

While a developed Catholic international relations theory for the 21st century must take account of the failures of the U.N. system, precisely in order to help create conditions for the possibility of reforming that system, it must also take account of the anti-democratic (and often anti-Catholic) bias in regional associations like the European Union, and a new and dangerous form of judicial activism in international legal institutions. The latter is particularly troubling, as international courts or national courts claiming international jurisdiction have imitated activist U.S. appellate courts and become vigorous contestants in an international culture war over issues like marriage, the family, abortion, euthanasia, human sexuality, and the emerging biotechnologies. A developed Catholic international relations theory must recognize that the world will not come into greater conformity with Catholic understandings of the universal common good, or with Catholic understandings of the peace of order, if the tyranny of unelected judges supplants the tyranny of some governments, or if democratically achieved agreements within countries are summarily abrogated by activist courts in other countries. The problem here is not simply theoretical; it can damage progress toward the peace of order within and among states. Nothing did more to enhance the reputation of Slobodan Milosevic and his political party in Serbia than his trial in the Hague by the International Criminal Tribunal for the former Yugoslavia; a local war-crimes trial, run by his own people, would have been far more likely to produce a verdict that would have advanced, rather than retarded, the cause of Serbian democracy.

Catholic international relations theory must also come to grips with the ideological bias at work in both international tribunals and national courts seeking an expanded international role. When a Spanish court overrides the democratically rendered judgment of the Chilean people by issuing an international arrest warrant for former Chilean dictator Augusto Pinochet, when Pinochet was in London for medical treatment, something is clearly awry. And that "something" is made worse by the fact that Spanish courts dismissed attempts to conduct similar proceedings against Fidel Castro when he was within their alleged sphere of jurisdiction. One suspects that something other than a newly discovered commitment to judicial restraint was at work in the latter case. A parallel set of problems has emerged with attempts to subvert national laws on marriage, abortion, and euthanasia through the European Parliament.

Priority Issues

Read against the pattern of Catholic moral reflection on world politics noted at the outset, these "signs of the times" suggest certain priority issues for the intellectual development of Catholic international relations theory in these early years of the 21st century. Four of these issues are of particular urgency.

Hard Power and Soft Power

Catholic international relations theory must develop a sophisticated understanding of the relationship of what Harvard political scientist Joseph Nye has termed "hard power" and "soft power" in the pursuit of *tranquillitas ordinis,* the peace of order that is composed of freedom, justice, and security.[2]

The accomplishments of soft power in recent decades have been impressive. The nonviolent Revolution of 1989 in east central Europe, which began with John Paul II's revolution of conscience in Poland, is the preeminent example, but one could also cite the democratic transformation of Latin America, the People Power revolution in the Philippines, and the democratic transitions in Taiwan and South Korea as further examples. The question to be pressed, though, is whether those experiences can be universalized.

The answer is almost certainly "No." Take what is the cockpit of so much of world conflict today, the Middle East. Had the nascent state of Israel opted for a soft power approach to being invaded by several Arab states in 1948, the Jews would have been driven into the sea in a mass slaughter. Conversely, had the Palestinians

opted for a soft power approach in 1967, at the end of the Six-
Day War, they would have been preparing in 2007 to celebrate
the thirty-fifth anniversary of independent Palestine. In the 1948
case, a soft power approach would have led to disaster; in 1967, it
likely would have led to the dramatic amelioration of conflict. The
effective deployment of soft power requires a certain context.

That was certainly true of the Revolution of 1989, which seems
to be taken by some in the Holy See as a kind of paradigmatic
case for the efficacy of soft power. Yet the liberation of east central
Europe from communist control — which was indeed a brilliant
example of effective soft power in the form of nonviolent cultural
and, ultimately, political resistance — took place within a hard
power context set by numerous factors, among them, Western re-
armament during the 1980s. Absent that hard power context, it is
not easy to see that the Revolution of 1989 would have happened
when it did and how it did. Thus the question of how proportionate and discriminate hard power can set the context in which soft
power can be effective requires careful study.[3]

This, in turn, should prompt a more careful Catholic reflection on the relationship between the "force of law" and the "law
of force," a binary trope that got considerable attention in the debate prior to the Iraq War of 2003, but perhaps without shedding
as much light on the present and future as its proponents hoped.
To juxtapose an undefined "law of force" over-against the "force of
law" in an absolute antimony seems unsatisfactory, empirically and
morally. All law, of whatever sort, ultimately requires the sanction
of enforcement if "law" is to mean anything other than a vague
expression of good intentions. This is a perennial feature of the
human condition, it seems. Imagine, for example, a world ordered
according to the vision of John XXIII in *Pacem in Terris,* a world in
which effective, just, and democratically accountable international
legal and political institutions for resolving international conflict
are, in fact, in place. Human nature being what it is, someone

would undoubtedly breach the peace, and in some instances that breach of the peace (and that challenge to John XXIII's universal public authority) would have to be met by the use of proportionate and discriminate armed force.

Law is not self-vindicating or self-enforcing. Catholic international relations theory in the 21st century must take that into account in thinking through the relationship between hard power and soft power, and between the rule of law and the use of armed force, in international public life.

The Morally Legitimate First Use of Force

Both contemporary international law and much recent Catholic commentary seem to have come to the settled view that the first use of armed force is always bad, while the second use of armed force (in response to that always-bad first use) may be morally justifiable. This is not, however, the classic Catholic view, and 21st-century Catholic international relations theory is going to have to think about first use/second use of armed force in a more nuanced way. This, in turn, requires refining our understanding of what constitutes "aggression" and refining the criteria by which the international community and individual states can judge, with moral legitimacy, that aggression is under way.

Classic Catholic thinking about the morally legitimate deployment of armed force did not restrict legitimacy to second use. Thomas Aquinas, for example, did not begin his just war thinking with a "presumption against war" (as that phrase is currently understood in much Catholic debate). Indeed, St. Thomas believed that there were occasions when the first use of force is morally justified — for example, to punish systematic and organized wickedness, or to prevent innocents from coming to harm.[4] Pondering these examples, one readily thinks of Pope John Paul II's address to the U.N. Food and Agricultural Organization in Rome in 1992, when the Pope stressed the moral duty of "humanitarian

intervention" in situations of an impending or ongoing genocide —
but without specifying on whom that duty fell, or how it was to be
fulfilled.

In any case, is it possible to begin to refine the criteria by which
the first use of armed force would be morally justifiable because
of a responsible judgment that aggression was indeed under way?
In the early phase of the Iraq War, the president of the American
Society of International Law suggested that aggression could reasonably be said to be "under way" when three conditions had been
met: (1) when a state possessed weapons of mass destruction or exhibited clear and convincing evidence of intent to acquire weapons
of mass destruction, (2) when grave and systematic human rights
abuses in the state in question demonstrated the absence of internal
constraints on that state's behavior internationally, and (3) when
the state in question had demonstrated aggressive intent against
others in the past.[5] The author suggested that these three criteria set a high threshold for the first use of armed force in the face
of aggression, while recognizing that there are risks too great to
be countenanced by responsible statesmen. A revitalized Catholic
international relations theory would engage this proposal, help refine it, and indeed open a broader discussion that would include
filling in the criteria by which John Paul II's "duty" of humanitarian intervention is satisfied by the use of armed force when other
remedies fail.

By Whose Authority?

As noted above, the popes of the mid-20th century, Pius XII and
John XXIII, laid considerable emphasis on international legal and
political institutions. Thus it should hardly be surprising that the
Holy See has been as consistent a supporter of the United Nations
as is to be found anywhere in the world. What is perhaps surprising
is that this support has intensified in the past two decades, even as
the United Nations and its affiliated agencies have adopted policies

with respect to abortion, the family, and the proper response to the AIDS pandemic in Africa that are opposed to the moral teaching of the Catholic Church and the policy preferences of the Holy See. In the debate prior to the Iraq War, for example, at least one senior official of the Holy See insisted that only the United Nations, through the Security Council, can legally authorize and morally legitimate the use of armed force in the pursuit of peace, security, and order. And while that statement does not constitute the authoritative teaching of the Catholic Church or the settled policy of the Holy See, it certainly reflects a cast of mind that is deeply skeptical about any use of armed force in the world that is not formally authorized by the Security Council. (Indeed, as the experience of the 1990–91 Gulf War shows, the Holy See's skepticism about the use of armed force extends to actions authorized by the Security Council. But that is a matter to be discussed in a moment.)

What is striking about the early-21st-century commentary from officials of the Holy See on the Security Council's monopoly of legitimating authority in the matter of using armed force is that this monopoly has been asserted, not argued. The sheer fact of the U.N. system seems to be taken to constitute a new moral reality; states which adhere to the U.N. Charter are deemed to have forfeited attributes of their sovereignty that the Catholic Church had long recognized as morally legitimate. Perhaps that is the case. But that case has to be made, not assumed.

And in arguing the case, certain facts of international public life cannot be denied. Since 1945, 126 out of 189 U.N. member states have been involved in 291 armed conflicts in which some 22 million people have been killed.[6] Given this record, it is difficult to argue that the "international community" (a phrase of dubious utility) has agreed in practice to be bound by the U.N. Charter and its rules on the use of force. It is even more difficult to argue that the international community has ceded an effective monopoly on the use of force to those actions sanctioned by the Security Council. Perhaps it should; perhaps it someday will. But to assert as a matter of fact that this transfer of authority has taken place seems counter-factual today.

Classic Catholic international relations theory, tutored by Augustine and Aquinas, was an expression of moral realism. Thus a developed Catholic international relations theory must wrestle with several hard realities of the U.N. system today. The first and perhaps most urgent is that the present structure of the Security Council is thoroughly unrealistic. Ascribing veto power on the Security Council to five states — China, France, Great Britain, Russia, and the United States — does not reflect the realities of contemporary world politics, but rather a set of political accommodations reached for various reasons (most of them unworthy) at the end of the Second World War. The rotation of the other nine Security Council seats takes place through a process which, again, does not reflect the realities of power. These structural problems themselves should raise questions about the moral standing of the Security Council and the claim that it alone is the locus of moral authority over the use of armed force in world politics.

If we probe a little deeper, other problems emerge as well. How, for example, is moral legitimacy conferred by the Security Council when three of its permanent members — China, France, and Russia — formulate their foreign policies on explicitly Realpolitik grounds that have little or nothing to do with moral reasoning about world politics as the Catholic Church understands it? Can an amoralist calculus yield a decisive and morally binding result? If so, it remains to be shown how.

To raise these questions is not to suggest that international organizations must always be a snare and a delusion, as some critics from the starboard side of American politics argue. The Catholic Church, which existed for a millennium and a half before the modern nation-state and which is the bearer of truths about the human person that must always stand in judgment on the nation-state (as they stood in judgment on previous forms of political organization), cannot regard the nation-state as the final form of human political organization. By the same token, however, it is surely true, from the point of view of a realistic moral analysis of the situation, that not every institution, agency, or process that labels itself "international" constitutes an advance for the cause of humanity and for the struggle to build the peace of order in world politics. Some are; but some are not.

Thus a developed Catholic international relations theory for the 21st century must undertake a critical evaluation of contemporary international organizations, asking openly, frankly, and without preconceptions whether and how those organizations contribute to the pursuit of *tranquillitas ordinis,* and to the freedom, justice, and security that are the component parts of the peace of order. That kind of critical examination is crucial for the integrity of the Catholic analysis of world politics; it also seems crucial for the possible reform of international organizations. No other global institution is as likely to bring the skills of moral reasoning to bear on the task of international organizational reform as the Catholic Church. On the other hand, were the Catholic Church, expressing its convictions through the diplomacy of the Holy See, to resemble ever more closely the World Council of Churches in the latter's undifferentiated embrace of the current U.N. system, much would be lost — for the Church, but also for the world.

Beyond Functional Pacifism

During the 1990–91 Gulf War, the Holy See seemed to oppose the use of armed force to reverse Iraq's invasion and occupation of Kuwait, even though the use of force had been authorized by the Security Council. Concern for embattled minority Christian communities in the Middle East played a role here; so did the judgment, correct in my view, that it is not the task of the Holy See or the pope to "bless" a war. Yet the Holy See's opposition to a Gulf War authorized by the Security Council, on the one hand, and its opposition to the deposition of the Saddam Hussein regime by a coalition facing opposition from permanent and rotating members of the Security Council, on the other, raises an important question: Is the Catholic Church's position on the morally legitimate use of armed force (whether that position is manifest in the personal witness of the pope, in the diplomacy of the Holy See, or as the default position in the relevant Vatican agencies) a kind of functional pacifism — a way of thinking that retains the intellectual apparatus of the just war tradition of moral reasoning but that always comes down, at the bottom line, in opposition to the use of armed force?

Recent events might seem to justify a positive answer to that question. But then what is one to do with John Paul II's insistence on a duty of humanitarian intervention, which would presumably include the use of proportionate and discriminate armed force, in cases of impending or actual genocide? And what is one to make of the virtual silence of the Holy See in respect of other armed interventions in the post–Cold War period, notably including French interventions in Africa?

This complex pattern of commentary from the Holy See suggests that the time is ripe for a thorough re-examination of the just war tradition. In the classic Catholic understanding of the just war tradition, just war thinking is not simply a calculus of means — a set of hurdles that religious leaders pose for politicians. Rather, the just war way of thinking is a tradition of statecraft within the broader ambit of Catholic international relations theory. The just war tradition is that part of Catholic international relations theory that addresses the question of whether, under certain specific circumstances and by certain specific means, the use of proportionate and discriminate armed force can help build the peace of order. The just war tradition does not exist in intellectual isolation from politics;

it is an integral part of a larger, more comprehensive conception of world politics.

Several of the "priority issues" I have been discussing here bear on the re-examination of just war thinking for the post–Cold War world: the question of what constitutes "aggression under way" (which bears on the classic just war criteria of just cause and last resort), and the moral status of the U.N. system (which touches the just war criterion of competent authority). Another reality of the contemporary world with which a re-examined and refined just war tradition would have to wrestle is the fact that real-time battlefield intelligence, precision-guided munitions, and other forms of high-tech weaponry now make it more likely that a responsible country can use military force in ways that satisfy the just war criteria of no-more-force-than-necessary (i.e., proportionality of means) and non-combatant immunity (i.e., discrimination).

Refining Catholic thinking on these questions is essential to the revitalization of Catholic international relations theory.

The Path Ahead

Commenting on *Pacem in Terris* in 1963, Father John Courtney Murray, S.J., one of the last American exponents of classic Catholic international relations theory, wrote the following:

[The Pope's] acute sense of the basic need of the age is evident in the word that is so often repeated in the encyclical and that sets its basic theme. I mean the word "order." This does seem to be the contemporary issue. The process of ordering and organizing the world is at the moment going forward. The issue is not whether we shall have order in the world; the contemporary condition of chaos has become intolerable on a worldwide scale, and the insistent demand of the peoples of the world is for order. The question is, then, on what principles is the world going to be organized?[7]

Murray was prescient here. After the communist crack-up, after the Cold War, after 9/11, the question indeed is, on what principles is the world going to be organized? A developed Catholic international relations theory, mediated through the catechesis and preaching of the Catholic Church, the witness of the papacy, and the diplomacy of the Holy See could play an important role in answering that question. Indeed, it is not Catholic special pleading, but only a recognition of the realities, which suggests that the Catholic Church must play such a role in the 21st century and the third millennium, if the question of the principles on which the world is to be organized is going to be grasped in its moral depth.

The Catholic Church is a world Church, and the development of a refined Catholic international relations theory must therefore be the subject of a global conversation. Within that global conversation, however, there will be many other distinct Catholic conversations, and one of them strikes me as particularly important — the conversation between the Holy See and the Roman intellectual milieu that informs its perceptions, on the one hand, and the United States, on the other. The world's most potent moral authority and the world's leading political, economic, and military power must be in regular and intense conversation, not only at the formal diplomatic level (important as that is), but also in a mutual exchange of ideas and perceptions between U.S.-based scholars and their counterparts in the Roman Curia and the Roman universities.

That conversation, not unlike the conversation about Catholic international relations theory in general, has not been as robust as it might be. The reasons why involve all parties, and it is not my purpose to parcel out relative responsibilities here. But now, surely, is the time to get the conversation going again. The United

States, for all its faults, is not a Realpolitik power — and, I would suggest, it cannot be, given the nature of the American Founding and the enduring moral commitments of the American people. The Catholic Church, because it is the bearer of a great tradition of moral realism applied to world politics, is distinctively positioned to broker a new and wiser conversation throughout the world about the way in which moral truths impinge on the politics-of-nations. The Church's effort to do so will be respected by the United States, its government, and its people; it will not be respected by other powers.

And that, too, suggests that a new conversation is in order — a conversation about order, the principles that will guide the ordering of the world, and the principles that will guide public authorities' response to the multiple disorders of the world. That conversation should result in the revitalization of Catholic international relations theory, which is good for the Church and good for the world.

Chapter Nine

Moral Clarity
in a Time of War

*The second William E. Simon Lecture, which I delivered in
Washington in December 2002, was an effort to think through
in greater detail some of the urgent questions posed by a post-9/11
world marked by jihadist terrorism, the proliferation of weapons of
mass destruction, the incapacities of existing international organizations, and rogue or outlaw states. The lecture also continued
my two-decade-long critique of the way most contemporary just
war theorists understood the just war way of thinking, even as it
offered a sharp challenge to those analysts who, in the post-9/11
environment, deemed "moral analysis" a luxury the West could ill
afford. In a sense, then, this essay continued the work I had begun
in the 1987 book,* Tranquillitas Ordinis: The Present Failure
and Future Promise of American Catholic Thought on War
and Peace, *applying some of what I had discussed there to a post–
Cold War context. The essay was used as teaching material in
several service academies and armed forces graduate schools, and
was circulated throughout the U.S. government and the Vatican.*

It was published in a slightly shorter form in the January 2003 issue of First Things.

In the spring of 2003, I was lecturing in England and had the opportunity to meet the newly appointed archbishop of Canterbury, Dr. Rowan Williams. Knowing Dr. Williams's longstanding interest in these questions, I gave him a copy of the Simon Lecture at the end of our discussion in Lambeth Palace. Some months later, Dr. Williams made a critique of my position the basis of a lecture he delivered at the Royal Institute of International Affairs, familiarly known as Chatham House. Dr. Williams subsequently agreed to the publication of his Chatham House remarks, to which I was permitted a response, in the March 2004 issue of First Things, *under the title "War and Statecraft: An Exchange." I owe a debt of gratitude to Dr. Williams for his commentary, which prompted me to reshape parts of the original essay into the form that follows.*

I N BOOK THREE of Tolstoy's epic *War and Peace,* the hero, Pierre Bezukhov, arrives at the battlefield of Borodino to find that the fog of war has descended, obscuring everything he had expected to be clear. There is no order; there are no familiar patterns of action; all is contingency. He could not, Count Bezukhov admits, "even distinguish our troops from the enemy's."[1] And the worst is yet to come, for once the fighting begins, chaos is master of all.

From the *Iliad* to Tolstoy to Evelyn Waugh and beyond, that familiar trope, "the fog of war," has been used to evoke the millennia-old experience of the radical uncertainty and contingency of combat. The gut-wrenching opening scenes of *Saving Private Ryan,* and the HBO miniseries *Band of Brothers,* brought this ancient truth home to a new generation of Americans: in even the most brilliantly planned military campaign, such as the Allied invasion of Europe, contingency is soon king, and prevailing amidst the radical contingency of combat draws on a man's deepest reserves of courage and wit.

Some analysts, however, take the trope of "the fog of war" a philosophical step further and suggest that warfare takes place beyond the reach of moral reason, in a realm of interest and necessity where moral argument is a pious diversion at best and, at worst, a lethal distraction from the deadly serious business at hand.

To which men and women formed by biblical religion, by the great tradition of Western moral philosophy, or by the encounter between biblical religion and moral philosophy that we call moral theology must say: "No, that is a serious mistake." Nothing human takes place outside the realm of moral reason or beyond its reach. Every human action is susceptible to moral analysis and moral judgment.

Thus moral muteness in a time of war is, in fact, a moral stance. It can be a stance born of fear; it can be a stance born of indifference; it

can be a stance born of cynicism about the human capacity to promote freedom, justice, and order, all of which are moral goods. But
whatever its psychological, spiritual, or intellectual origins, moral
muteness in wartime is a form of moral judgment — a deficient
and dangerous form of moral judgment.

That is why the venerable just war tradition — a form of moral
reasoning that traces its origins to St. Augustine in 5th-century
North Africa — is such an important public resource. For fifteen
hundred years, as it has been developed amidst the historical whitewater of political, technological, and military change, the just war
tradition and the just war way of thinking have allowed men and
women to avoid the trap of moral muteness, to think through the
tangle of problems involved in the decision to go to war and in
the conduct of war itself — and to do all that in a way that recognizes the distinctive realities of warfare. Indeed, in the 21st-century
American debate precipitated by jihadist terrorism and the threat
of outlaw states armed with weapons of mass destruction, we can
hear echoes of the moral reasoning of Augustine and his successors:

+ What is the just cause that would justify putting our armed
  forces, and the American homeland, in harm's way?

+ Who has the authority to wage war? The president? The president and Congress? The United States acting alone? The United
  States with a sufficient number of allies? The United Nations or
  its Security Council?

+ Is it ever right to use armed force first? Can going first ever be,
  not just morally permissible, but morally imperative?

+ How can the use of armed force contribute to the pursuit of
  freedom and justice, order and security in world affairs? Which
  is to say, can war help make peace?

That these are the questions that instinctively emerge in the American national debate suggests that the just war tradition remains

alive in our national cultural memory. And that, for the reasons suggested just a moment ago, is a very good thing. But it is also a somewhat surprising thing. For the past forty years have witnessed a great forgetting of the classic just war tradition among those who had long been assumed to be its primary intellectual custodians: the nation's moral philosophers, moral theologians, and religious leaders. That forgetting has been painfully evident in much of the post-9/11 commentary from religious leaders on world politics, commentary that is often far more dependent on political and strategic intuitions of dubious merit than on solid moral reasoning. The fact of the matter today is that the just war tradition, as a historically informed method of rigorous moral reasoning, is far more alive in America's service academies and armed forces graduate schools than in our divinity schools and on our faculties of theology; the just war tradition "lives" more vigorously in the American officer corps, in the Uniform Code of Military Justice, and at the higher levels of the Pentagon than it does at the National Council of Churches, in certain offices at the United States Conference of Catholic Bishops, or on the faculties of Berkeley's Graduate Theological Union and the Duke Divinity School.

This forgetting in the places where the just war tradition has been nurtured for centuries has led to confusions about the tradition itself. Those confusions have, in turn, led to distorted and, in some cases, irresponsible analyses from the quarters to which Americans usually look for moral guidance. That is why it is imperative that the just war tradition be retrieved and developed in these first perilous decades of the 21st century. At issue is the public moral hygiene of the Republic, our national capacity to think with moral rigor about some very threatening realities of today's world, and our ability to give an account of our actions before the bar of contemporary world public opinion and before the bar of history.

That process of retrieval and development must begin at the beginning. We must begin by remembering and reclaiming precisely what the just war tradition is, what the just war tradition does — and for whom.

A Theory of Statecraft

In one of 2001's notable books, *Warrior Politics,* veteran foreign correspondent Robert Kaplan suggested that only a "pagan ethos" can provide us with the kind of leadership capable of safely traversing the global disorder of the 21st century.[2] Kaplan's pagan ethos has several interlocking parts. It is shaped by a tragic sense of life, which recognizes the ubiquity, indeed inevitability, of conflict. It teaches a heroic concept of history: fate is not all, and wise statecraft can lead to better futures. It promotes a realistic appreciation of the boundaries of the possible. It celebrates patriotism as a virtue. And it is shaped by a grim determination to avoid "moralism," which Kaplan (following Machiavelli, the Chinese sage Sun-Tzu, and Max Weber) identifies with a morality of intentions, oblivious to the peril of unintended or unanticipated consequences.[3] For Robert Kaplan, exemplars of this pagan ethos in the past century include the two Roosevelts, Theodore and Franklin, and Winston Churchill.

Reading *Warrior Politics,* and reflecting on the concept of morality that informs it, reminded me of a story that I hadn't thought of for years. During the Korean War, the proudly Protestant Henry Luce, son of China missionaries, found himself confused by the debate over "morality and foreign policy" that Harry Truman's police action had stirred up. What, Luce asked his friend, Father John Courtney Murray, S.J., did foreign policy have to do with the Sermon on the Mount? "What," Father Murray replied, "makes you think that morality is identical with the Sermon on the Mount?"[4]

Robert Kaplan, a contemporary exponent of foreign policy realism, seems to share Henry Luce's mis-impression that the moral life is reducible to the ethics of personal probity and interpersonal relationships. The implication is that issues of statecraft exist somewhere "outside" the moral universe. The classic just war tradition takes a very different view.

The classic tradition insists that no aspect of the human condition falls outside the purview of moral reasoning and judgment—including politics. Politics is a human enterprise. Because human beings are creatures of intelligence and free will—because human beings are inescapably moral actors — every human activity, including politics, is subject to moral scrutiny.[5] There is no Archimedean point outside the moral universe from which even the wisest pagan statesman can leverage world politics.

Indeed, what Robert Kaplan proposes as a pagan ethos is a form of moral reasoning that would be enriched by a serious encounter with the classic just war tradition. One need not be a pagan, as Kaplan proposes, to understand the enduring impact of original sin on the world and its affairs; Genesis 1–3 and a good dose of Augustine's *City of God* will do the job just as well, and arguably better. One need not be a pagan to be persuaded that moral conviction, human ingenuity, and wise statecraft can bend history's course in a more humane direction; one need only reflect on the achievement of Pope John Paul II and the Church-based human rights resistance in central and eastern Europe in helping rid the world of the plague of communism. A realistic sense of the boundaries of the humanly possible in given situations is not foreign to the classic moral tradition of the West; prudence, after all, is one of the cardinal virtues. Nor is patriotism necessarily pagan; indeed, in a country culturally configured like the United States, patriotism is far more likely to be sustained by biblical rather than pagan moral warrants. As for "moralism" and its emphasis on good intentions, I hope I shall not be thought unecumenical if I observe that that is primarily a Protestant problem; moreover, Catholic moral theology in the authentic Thomistic stream is very dubious about voluntaristic theories of the moral life and their reduction of morality to a contest of wills between the divine will and my will.

Robert Kaplan notwithstanding, we can get to an ethic appropriate for leadership in world politics without declaring ourselves pagans. And, as Brian Anderson argued in a thoughtful review of Kaplan's book, we can get there while retaining "a crucial place for a transcendent *ought* that limits the evil governments can do."[6] An ethic for world politics can be built against an ampler moral horizon than Robert Kaplan suggests.

As a tradition of statecraft, the just war tradition recognizes that there are circumstances in which the first and most urgent obligation in the face of evil is to stop it. Which means that there are times when waging war is morally necessary, to defend the innocent and to promote the minimum conditions of international order. The post-9/11 world is one of those times. Grasping that does not require us to be pagans. It only requires us to be morally serious and politically responsible. Moral seriousness and political responsibility require us to make the effort to connect the dots between means and ends.

Thus the just war tradition is best understood as a sustained and disciplined intellectual attempt to relate the morally legitimate use of proportionate and discriminate military force to morally worthy political ends. In this sense, the just war tradition shares Clausewitz's view of the relationship between war and politics: unless war is an extension of politics, war is simply wickedness. For Robert Kaplan, Clausewitz may be an archetypal pagan. But on this crucial point, at least, Clausewitz was articulating a thoroughly classic just war view of the matter, one that would have been agreeable to St. Thomas Aquinas. Good ends do not justify any means. But as Father Murray liked to say in his provocative way, "If the end doesn't justify the means, what does?" In the classic just war tradition of statecraft, what justifies the resort to the means of proportionate and discriminate armed force — what makes war make moral sense — is precisely the morally worthy political ends being defended and/or advanced.

That is why the just war tradition is a theory of statecraft, not simply a method of casuistry. And that intellectual fact is the first thing about the just war tradition that must be retrieved today, if we seek a public moral culture capable of informing the national and international debate about war, peace, and international order.

Identifying the Starting Point

The second crucial idea to be retrieved in the contemporary renewal of the just war tradition is the distinction between *bellum* and *duellum,* between warring and "duelling," so to speak. As intellectual historian and just war theorist James Turner Johnson has demonstrated in a number of seminal works, this distinction is the crux of the matter in moral analysis.[7] *Bellum* is the use of armed force for public ends by public authorities who have an obligation to defend the security of those for whom they have assumed responsibility. *Duellum,* on the other hand, is the use of armed force for private ends by private individuals. To grasp this essential distinction is to understand that, in the just war tradition, "war" *is* a moral category. Moreover, in the classic just war tradition, armed force is not inherently suspect morally. Rather, as Johnson insists, the classic tradition views armed force as something that can be used for good or evil, depending on who is using it, why, to what ends, and how.[8] Thus those scholars, activists, and religious leaders who claim that the just war tradition begins with a "presumption against war" (sometimes confusingly re-named a "presumption against violence") are quite simply mistaken. It does not begin there, and it never did begin there (except in the most generic sense: for any morally serious person, non-military means of resolving conflict are preferable to war, when those means are available). To suggest otherwise is not merely a matter of misreading intellectual history, although it is surely that; to suggest that the just war tradition begins with a "presumption against war" inverts the structure of moral analysis in ways that inevitably lead to dubious moral judgments and distorted perceptions of political reality.

The classic tradition, to repeat, begins with the presumption — better, the moral judgment — that rightly constituted public authority is under a strict moral obligation to defend the security of those for whom it has assumed responsibility, even if this puts the magistrate's own life in jeopardy. That moral truth helps clarify one reason why Thomas Aquinas locates his discussion of *bellum ius-tum* within the treatise on charity in the *Summa Theologiae*.[9] That moral truth is why the late Paul Ramsey, who revivified Protestant just war thinking in America after World War II, described the just war tradition as an explication of the public implications of the Great Commandment of love-of-neighbor (even as he argued that the commandment sets limits to the use of armed force).[10]

If the just war tradition is a theory of statecraft, to reduce it to a casuistry of means-tests that begins with a "presumption against war" is to begin at the wrong place. The just war tradition begins somewhere else. It begins by defining the moral responsibilities of governments, continues with the definition of morally appropriate political ends, and only then takes up the question of means. By reversing the analysis of means and ends, the "presumption against war" starting point collapses *bellum* into *duellum* and ends up conflating the ideas of "violence" and "war." The net result is that warfare is stripped of its distinctive moral texture. Indeed, among many American religious leaders today, the very notion of warfare as having a moral texture seems to have been forgotten.

The "presumption against war" starting point is not only fraught with historical and methodological difficulties. It is also theologically dubious. Its effect in moral analysis is to turn the tradition inside-out, such that war-conduct [*in bello*] questions of proportionality and discrimination take theological precedence over what were traditionally assumed to be the prior war-decision [*ad bellum*] questions: competent authority, just cause, and right intention; reasonable chance of success, proportionality of ends, and last resort. This inversion explains why, in much of the religious commentary after the terrorist attacks of 9/11, considerable attention was paid to the necessity of avoiding indiscriminate non-combatant casualties in the war against terrorism, while little attention was paid to the prior question of the moral obligation of government to pursue national security and world order, both of which were directly threatened by the terrorist networks.

This inversion is also theologically problematic because it places the heaviest burden of moral analysis on what are inevitably contingent judgments. There is nothing wrong, per se, with contingent judgments; but they are, well, contingent. In the nature of the case, we can have less surety about *in bello* proportion and discrimination (and about *ad bellum* proportionality, chance of success, and last resort) than we can on the *ad bellum* questions of competent authority, just cause, and right intention, which specify certain moral duties that can be known by reason.[11] The tradition logically starts with *ad bellum* questions because the just war tradition is a tradition of statecraft: a tradition that attempts to define morally worthy political ends. But there is also a theo-logic — a theological logic — that gives priority to the *ad bellum* questions of competent authority, just cause, and right intention, for these are the questions on which we can have some measure of moral clarity.

The "presumption against war" and its distortion of the just war way of thinking can also lead to serious misreadings of world politics. One such misreading, precisely from this intellectual source, may be found in the 1983 U.S. bishops' pastoral letter "The Challenge of Peace" [TCOP]. TCOP was deeply influenced by the emphasis laid on questions of *in bello* proportionality and discrimination because of the threat of nuclear war. No doubt these were important issues. But when that emphasis drove the moral analysis, as it did in TCOP, the result was a distorted picture of reality and a set of moral judgments that contributed little to wise statecraft. Rather than recognizing that nuclear weapons were one (extremely dangerous) manifestation of a prior conflict with profound moral roots, the bishops' letter seemed to suggest that nuclear weapons could, somehow, be factored out of the conflict between the West and the Soviet Union by arms control. And in order to achieve arms control agreements with a nervous, even paranoid, foe like the Soviet Union, it might be necessary to downplay the moral and ideological (i.e., human rights) dimensions of the Cold War. That, at least, was the policy implication of the claim that the greatest threat to peace (identified as such because *in bello* considerations and the "presumption against war" trumped everything else) was the mere possession of nuclear weapons.

The opposite, of course, turned out to be true. Nuclear weapons were not the primary threat to peace during the Cold War; communism was. When communism went, the threat posed by the weapons was dramatically reduced. As the human rights resistance in central and eastern Europe brought massive regime change inside the Warsaw Pact, creating dynamics that eventually led to the demise of the USSR itself, the risks of nuclear war were greatly diminished and real disarmament (not arms control) began. The "presumption against war" starting point, as manifest in TCOP, produced a serious misreading of the political realities and possibilities.

The claim that a "presumption against war" is at the root of the just war tradition cannot be sustained historically, methodologically, or theologically. If the just war tradition is a tradition of statecraft, and if the crucial distinction that undergirds it is the distinction between *bellum* and *duellum*, then the just war tradition cannot be reduced, as too many religious leaders reduce it today, to a series of means tests that begins with a "presumption against war." To begin here — to imagine that the role of moral reason is to set a series of hurdles (primarily having to do with *in bello* questions of proportionality and discrimination) that statesmen must overcome before the resort to armed force is given moral sanction — is to begin at the wrong place. And beginning at the wrong place almost always means arriving at the wrong destination. The retrieval and development of classic just war thinking must include a recovery of the classic structure of the just war argument. That means getting the starting point right.

Just War and Achievable Peace

Fifteen years ago, before I had learned something about literary marketing, I published a book entitled *Tranquillitas Ordinis: The Present Failure and Future Promise of American Catholic Thought on War and Peace.*[12] There I argued that, as a theory of statecraft, the just war tradition contained within itself a *ius ad pacem,* in addition to the classic *ius ad bellum* (the moral rules governing the decision to go to war) and *ius in bello* (the rules governing the use of armed force in combat). By coining the phrase *ius ad pacem,* I was trying to prize out of the just war way of thinking a concept of the peace that could and should be sought through the instruments of politics — including, if necessary, the use of armed force. Like the just war tradition itself, this concept of peace finds its roots in Augustine: in *The City of God,* peace is *tranquillitas ordinis,* the "tranquillity of order," or as I preferred to render it in more contemporary terms, the peace of "dynamic and rightly-ordered political community."[13]

In Augustine's discussion of peace as a public or political issue, peace is not a matter of the individual's right relationship with God, nor is it a matter of seeking a world without conflict. The former is a question of interior conversion (which by definition has nothing to do with politics), and the latter is impossible in a world forever marked, even after its redemption, by the *mysterium iniquitatis,* the mystery of evil. In the appropriate political sense of the term, peace is, rather, *tranquillitas ordinis:* the order created by just political community and mediated through law.

This is, admittedly, a humbler sort of peace. It coexists with broken hearts and wounded souls. It is to be built in a world in which swords have not been beaten into plowshares, but remain: sheathed, but ready to be drawn in the defense of justice and freedom. Its advantage, as Augustine understood, is that it is the form of peace that can be built through the instruments of politics.

This peace of *tranquillitas ordinis,* this peace of order, is composed of freedom, justice, and security. The peace of order is not the eerily quiet and sullen "peace" of a well-run authoritarian regime; it is a peace built on foundations of a just constitutional order and a civil society's commitment to the several forms of justice. It is a peace in which freedom, especially religious freedom, flourishes. The defense of basic human rights is thus an integral component of work for peace.[14]

This is the peace that has been achieved in and among the developed democracies. It is the peace that has been built in recent decades between such ancient antagonists as France and Germany. It is the peace that we defend within the richly diverse political community of the United States, and between ourselves and our neighbors and allies. It is the peace that must be defended in the war against jihadist terrorism and against aggressor states seeking weapons of mass destruction.

Terrorism of the jihadist sort — of which Americans had a direct national experience on September 11, 2001 — is a deliberate assault, through the murder of innocents, on the very possibility of order in world affairs. That is why the terror networks must be dismantled and destroyed. The peace of order is also under grave threat when vicious, aggressive regimes acquire weapons of mass destruction—weapons that we must assume, on the basis of their treatment of their own citizens, these regimes will not hesitate to use against others. That is why there is a moral obligation to ensure that this lethal combination of irrational and aggressive regimes + weapons of mass destruction + credible delivery systems does not go unchallenged. That is why there is a moral obligation to rid the world of this threat to the peace and security of all. Peace, rightly understood, demands it.

This concept of peace-as-order can also enrich our understanding of that much-bruited term, the "national interest."

The irreducible core of the national interest is composed of those basic security concerns to which any responsible democratic statesman must attend. But those security concerns are related to a larger sense of national purpose and international responsibility: we defend America because America is worth defending, in itself and because of what it means for the world. Thus the security concerns that make up the core of the national interest should be understood as the necessary inner dynamic of the exercise of America's international responsibilities. And those responsibilities include the obligation to contribute, as best we can, to the long, hard, never-to-be-finally-accomplished domestication of international public life: to the quest for ordered liberty in an evolving structure of international public life capable of advancing the classic goals of politics—justice, freedom, order, the general welfare, and peace. Empirically and morally, the United States cannot adequately defend its national interest without concurrently seeking to advance those goals in the world. Empirically and morally, those goals will not be advanced if they are pursued in ways that gravely threaten the basic security of the United States.

In eradicating global terrorism and denying aggressive regimes weapons of mass destruction, the United States and those who walk this road with us are addressing the most threatening problems of global disorder that must be resolved if the peace of order, the peace of *tranquillitas ordinis*, is to be secured in as wide a part of the world as possible in the 21st century. Here, national interest and international responsibility coincide.

Issues for Intellectual Development

Moral clarity in any time of war requires that we grasp the idea of the just war tradition as a tradition of statecraft, the classic structure of just war analysis, and the concept of peace as *tranquillitas ordinis*. Moral clarity in this particular time of war also requires us to develop and extend the just war tradition to meet the political exigencies of a new century, and to address the international security issues posed by new weapons technologies. There are three areas in which the *ad bellum* ("war-decision") criteria of the just war tradition require retrieval and development; the sketch that follows suggests certain possible policy implications of these developments.

Just Cause

In the classic just war tradition, "just cause" was understood as defense against aggression, the recovery of something wrongfully taken, or the punishment of evil. As the tradition has developed since World War II, the latter two notions have been largely displaced, and defense against aggression has become the primary, even sole, meaning of just cause.[15] This theological evolution has parallels in international law: the defense-against-aggression concept of just cause shapes Articles 2 and 51 of the Charter of the United Nations. In light of 21st-century international security realities, it is imperative to re-open this discussion and to develop the concept of just cause.[16]

As recently as the Korean War (and, some would argue, the Vietnam War), defense against aggression could reasonably be taken to mean a defensive military response to a cross-border military aggression already under way. New weapons capabilities and outlaw or rogue states require a development of the concept of defense-against-aggression. To take the obvious example: it makes little moral sense to suggest that the United States must wait until an enemy actually launches a ballistic missile tipped with a nuclear, biological, or chemical weapon of mass destruction before the U.S. can, with moral legitimacy, do something about it. This instinctive moral intuition raises an important and delicate question: In the hands of certain kinds of states, does the possession of weapons of mass destruction constitute an aggression or, at the very least, an aggression-waiting-to-happen?

This regime factor is crucial in the moral analysis, for weapons of mass destruction are clearly not aggressions-waiting-to-happen when they are possessed by stable, law-abiding states. No Frenchman goes to bed nervous about Great Britain's nuclear weapons, and no sane Mexican or Canadian worries about a preemptive nuclear attack from the United States. Every sane Israeli, Turk, or Bahraini, on the other hand, is deeply concerned about the possibility of an Iran with nuclear weapons and ballistic missiles. If the regime factor is crucial in the moral analysis, then the first use of armed force to deny the rogue state that kind of destructive capacity would not, in my judgment, contravene the defense-against-aggression concept of just cause. Indeed, it would do precisely the opposite, by giving the concept of defense-against-aggression real traction in the world we must live in, and transform.

Some will argue that this violates the principle of sovereignty and risks a global descent into chaos. Yet the post-Westphalian notions of state equality and sovereign immunity assume at least a minimum of acquiescence to minimal international norms of order. Today's rogue states cannot, on the basis of their behavior, be granted that assumption. Therefore, they have forfeited that immunity. The regime factor ought to be a determinative element in the moral analysis in these extreme instances, even if the determination that just cause exists does not, in and of itself, determine the precise response required to the aggression in question (a determination that engages other just war criteria). To deny rogue states the capacity to create lethal dis-order, precisely because their possession of weapons of mass destruction threatens the minimum conditions of order in international public life, strengthens the cause of world order; it does not undermine it. Surely the lessons of the 1930s are pertinent here.

On the matter of just cause, the tradition also needs development in terms of its concept of the relevant actors in world politics. Since 9/11, some analysts have objected to describing the West's response to the international terrorist networks as "war" because, they argue, al-Qaeda and similar networks are not states, and only states can, or should, wage war, properly understood. There is an important point at stake here, but the critics misapply it.

Limiting the legitimate use of armed force to those international actors who are recognized in international law and custom as exercising sovereignty has been one of the principal accomplishments of just war thinking as it has shaped world political culture and law; over a period of centuries, the classic distinction between *bellum* and *duellum* has been concretized in international law. At the same time, however, it does not fudge or blur this crucial distinction to recognize that al-Qaeda and similar networks function like states, even if they lack certain of the attributes and trappings of sovereignty traditionally understood. Indeed, terrorist organizations provide a less ambiguous example of a legitimate military target, because, unlike conventional states (which are always admixtures of good and evil, against whom military action sometimes threatens the good as well as the evil), the parasite entities that are international terrorist organizations are unmitigated evils whose only purpose is wickedness — the slaughter of innocents for ignoble political ends.[17] Thus the exigencies of the current situation require us to think outside the Westphalian box, so to speak, but to do so in

such a way as to avoid dismantling de facto the distinction between
bellum and *duellum*.

Competent Authority

Two questions involving the *ad bellum* criterion of competent authority have been raised since 9/11: the question of the relationship
between a government's domestic and foreign policy and its legitimacy as a belligerent, and the question of whether competent
authority now resides exclusively in the United Nations (which
means, for all practical purposes, the Security Council).

One of the more distasteful forms of post-9/11 commentary
can be found in suggestions that there were "root causes" to terrorism — root causes that not only explained the resort to mass
violence against innocents, but made the use of such violence humanly plausible, if not morally justifiable. The corollary to this
was the suggestion that the United States had somehow brought
9/11 on itself, by reasons of its dominant economic and cultural
position in the world, its Middle East policy, or some combination
thereof. The moral-political implication was that such a misguided
government lacked the moral authority to respond to terrorism
through the use of armed force.

The root causes school blithely ignores the extant literature on
the phenomenon of contemporary terrorism, which is emphatically not a case of the wretched of the earth rising up to throw off
their chains.[18] It is, however, the moral-political implication the
root causes school draws that must be addressed here. And on this
issue, Lutheran scholar David Yeago has been a wise guide. Writing
in the ecumenical journal *Pro Ecclesia*, Yeago clarified an essential
point:

> The authority of the government to protect the law-abiding
> and impose penalties on evil-doers is not a *reward* for the
> government's virtue or good conduct.... The protection of

citizens and the execution of penalty on peace-breakers is the commission which *constitutes* government, not a contingent right which it must somehow earn. In the mystery of God's providence, many or indeed most of the institutional bearers of governmental authority are unworthy of it, often flagrantly so, themselves stained with crime. But this does not make it any less the vocation of government to protect the innocent and punish evil-doers. A government which refused to safeguard citizens and exercise judgment on wrong out of a sense of the guilt of past crime would only add the further crime of dereliction of duty to its catalog of offenses.[19]

The question of alliances and international organizations must also be addressed in the development of just war thinking about competent authority. Must any morally legitimate military action be sanctioned by the U.N. Security Council? Or, if not that, then is the United States obliged, not simply as a matter of political prudence but as a matter of moral principle, to gain the agreement of allies (or, more broadly, coalition partners) to any use of armed force in response to terrorism, or any military action against aggressive regimes with weapons of mass destruction?

That the U.N. Charter itself recognizes an inalienable national right to self-defense suggests that the Charter does not claim for the Security Council sole authority to legitimate the use of armed force. According to the Charter, if you are under attack you don't have to wait for the permission of China, France, Russia, or others of the veto-wielding powers to defend yourself. Moreover, the manifest inability of the U.N. to handle large-scale international security issues suggests that assigning a moral veto over U.S. military action on these fronts to the Security Council would be a mistake. Then there is the question of what we might call the Security Council "neighborhood": what kind of moral logic is it to claim that the U.S. government must assuage the Realpolitik interests of the

French foreign ministry and the strategic aims of the repressive Chinese government — both of which are in full play in the Security Council — in order to gain international moral authority for the war against terrorism and the defense of world order against outlaw states with weapons of mass destruction? A very peculiar moral logic, indeed, I should think.

Building coalitions of support for dismantling the international terror networks and denying rogue states lethal weapons capacities is politically desirable (and in some instances militarily essential). But I doubt that it is morally imperative from a classic just war point of view. The United States has a unique responsibility for leadership in the war against terrorism and the struggle for world order; that is not a statement of hubris but of empirical fact. That responsibility may have to be exercised unilaterally on occasion. Defining the boundaries of unilateral action while defending its moral legitimacy under certain circumstances is one crucial task for a developing just war tradition.

Last Resort

Among those who have "forgotten" the just war tradition while retaining its language, the classic *ad bellum* criterion of last resort is often understood in quasi-mathematical terms: the use of proportionate and discriminate armed force is the last point in a series of options, and prior, non-military options (legal, diplomatic, economic, etc.) must be serially exhausted before the criterion of last resort is satisfied. This is both an excessively mechanistic understanding of last resort and a prescription for danger.

The case of international terrorism again compels a development of this *ad bellum* criterion. For what does it mean to say that all non-military options have been tried and found wanting when we are confronted with a new and lethal type of international actor, one which recognizes no other form of power except the use of violence and which is largely immune (unlike a conventional state) to international legal, diplomatic, and/or economic pressures? The charge that U.S. military action after 9/11 was morally dubious because all other possible means of redress had not been tried and found wanting misreads the nature of terrorist organizations and networks. The "last" in "last resort" can mean "only," in circumstances where there is plausible reason to believe that non-military actions are unavailable or unavailing.

As for rogue states developing or deploying weapons of mass destruction, a developed just war tradition would recognize that here, too, last resort cannot be understood as the terminal point of a lengthy series of non-military alternatives. Can we not say that last resort has been satisfied in those cases when a rogue state has made plain, by its conduct, that it holds international law in contempt and that no diplomatic solution to the threat it poses is likely, and when it can be demonstrated that the threat the rogue state poses is intensifying? I think we can. Indeed, I think we must.

Some states, because of the regime's aggressive intent and the lack of effective internal political controls on giving lethal effect to that intent, cannot be permitted to acquire weapons of mass destruction. Denying them those weapons through proportionate and discriminate armed force — even displacing those regimes — can be an exercise in the defense of the peace of order, within the boundaries of a developed just war tradition. Until such point as the international political community has evolved to the degree that international organizations can effectively disarm such regimes, the responsibility for the defense of order in these extreme circumstances will lie elsewhere.

The Virtue of Responsibility

Finally, moral clarity in this time of war requires a developed understanding of the location of the just war tradition in our public discourse and its role in responsible governance.

If the just war tradition is indeed a tradition of statecraft, then the proper role of religious leaders and public intellectuals is to do everything possible to clarify the moral issues at stake in a time of war, while recognizing that what we might call the virtue or moral habit of political responsibility lies elsewhere — with duly constituted public authorities, who are more fully informed about the relevant facts and who must bear the weight of responsible decision-making and governance. It is simply clericalism to suggest that religious leaders and public intellectuals own the just war tradition in a way that constitutes them as a parallel competent authority in determining when the use of proportionate and discriminate armed force is necessary in defense of peace.

Many of today's religious leaders and public intellectuals have suffered severe amnesia about core components of the tradition, and can hardly be said to own it in any serious intellectual sense of ownership. But even if today's religious leaders and public intellectuals were fully in possession of the tradition, the burden of decision-making would still lie elsewhere. Religious leaders and public intellectuals are called to nurture and develop the moral-philosophical riches of the just war tradition, and to do so in conversation with public authorities (who, conversely, must be open to that conversation). The tradition itself, however, does not exist to serve religious leaders and public intellectuals. It exists to serve statesmen, as the *Catechism of the Catholic Church* acknowledges, when it states, in concluding its review of some of the traditional just war criteria, "The evaluation of these conditions for moral legitimacy belongs to the prudential judgment of those who have responsibility for the common good."[20]

The vocation of public service ought to be understood to include growth in the virtue of political discernment. Duly constituted public authority can, and does, get it wrong, of course. But that fact of life does not suggest that bishops, stated clerks, rabbis, imams, or ecumenical and interreligious agencies have developed the virtue of political discernment by reason of their ordination, consecration, investiture, or highest earned degree. Moral clarity in a time of war demands moral seriousness from public officials. It also demands a measure of political modesty from religious leaders and public intellectuals in the give-and-take of democratic deliberation, in which they, of course, play an important role.

Amidst the new world disorder of the post-9/11 world, some have suggested that the just war tradition is obsolete. To which I would reply: to suggest that the just war tradition is obsolete is to suggest that politics — the organization of human life into purposeful political communities — is obsolete. By the same token, the traditional custodians of the just war tradition in the religious community and the academy must recognize that to reduce the just war tradition to an algebraic casuistry is to deny the tradition its capacity to shed light on the irreducible moral component of all political action. What we must do, in this generation, is to retrieve and develop the just war tradition to take account of the new political and technological realities of the 21st century. The events of 9/11, what has followed, and what lies ahead have all demonstrated just how urgent that task is.

Chapter Ten

Just War and
the Iraq Wars–I

In January 2006, I delivered the fifth William E. Simon Lecture in Washington under the title, "Just War and the Iraq War, Three Years Later." The lecture was subsequently published in a revised form by First Things *in April 2006 and entitled, "Iraq: Then and Now."*

The goal of the fifth Simon Lecture was to analyze the first three years of the war in Iraq, in light of the developed just war tradition for which James Turner Johnson and I had been calling for over a decade and a half. As Johnson and I had suggested, questions of the ius ad bellum *— the war-decision criteria of the tradition — had returned to a prominent place in the debate, yet without, Johnson and I believed, being properly understood in themselves or in their relationship to each other. These difficulties were compounded by the continuing influence of the 1983 pastoral letter by the Catholic bishops of the United States, "The Challenge of Peace," which Johnson and I judged to have misstated the traditional just war criteria and how they functioned in classic just war analysis. Both Johnson and I were fully agreed* *that the just war way of thinking needed development; but that development would be a genuine development, rather than a de facto abandonment of the tradition, only were it to proceed from a clearer understanding of the "theo-logic" of the just war way of thinking than was being offered by many religious leaders, moral philosophers, and moral theologians. Their commentary, before, during, and after the invasion of Iraq in March 2003, reinforced the suspicion that the just war tradition was being traduced into a form of what I had once termed "functional pacifism," in which the outward forms of the tradition remained while its philosophical and theological substance was lost.*

The fifth Simon Lecture was dedicated to the memory of Thomas K. Doerflinger, killed in action in Iraq on November 11, 2004.

EVEN AS HISTORY continued to unfold — and explode — in ancient Mesopotamia and throughout the Middle East, one thing about the Iraq War that began in March 2003 quickly became clear: this was the most consequential international political event of the post–Cold War period.

It changed, and continues to change, the political, psychological, and perhaps even theological landscape of the Middle East.

It drove great wedges between America and many of its oldest European allies for a time; it brought the Anglo-American "special relationship" to a high point of cooperation not seen for decades; it strengthened the U.S. strategic partnership with Australia; and it suggested the possibility of important alliances with the new democracies of central and eastern Europe, even as it likely precipitated new thinking in emerging powers like India and China.

It exposed in painful detail the incapacities and corruptions of the United Nations, which turned out to be an accomplice, witting or not, in Saddam Hussein's efforts to escape international sanctions and recommence his quest for regional hegemony.

It roiled the domestic politics of the United States and western Europe as they had not been shaken since the nuclear freeze demonstrations of the early 1980s. Yet even as it sent political shock waves throughout the West, the Iraq War was also creating conditions for the possibility of something actually resembling "politics" in Iraq itself, as well as in Lebanon, Jordan, Egypt, the Gulf emirates, Pakistan, and perhaps even Saudi Arabia, Libya, and Syria.

Moreover, the often-bloody drama of the post-war transition to responsive and responsible government in Iraq — a society that suffered for thirty years under the lash of a regime that rivaled those of Pol Pot and Kim Il Sung for viciousness — has guaranteed that the seismic shocks generated by the Iraq War will affect world politics for years, and likely decades, to come.[1]

The Iraq War also had a dramatic impact in the world of ideas. In policy documents like the 2002 *National Security Strategy of the United States* [NSS-2002], the administration of President George W. Bush, convinced that 9/11 defined a pivotal moment in world politics, laid down a challenge to certain well-entrenched ideas about the nature of realism in international affairs, even as its policy on-the-ground challenged numerous conventions of post–World War II international public life. Perhaps most dramatically, the Bush administration, in its effort to define a more truly realistic approach to world politics, was willing to challenge the seemingly settled consensus that the Middle East is a region so politically volatile, economically important, and culturally retrograde that it can only be managed, never transformed. These three challenges have, in turn, led to a remarkable reversal, even an inversion, in the geography of ideas in American public life. Who would have imagined, fifty years ago, that a commitment to the democratic transformation of the world would find its primary American political home in (at least some) conservative circles? Who would have imagined, fifty years ago, that much of American liberalism, rather than making the moral and political case for deposing a genocidal brute, would find itself in de facto alliance with the status quo forces in world politics? It is impossible to know with any confidence where this dramatic alteration in the political location of great ideas will take the United States, or the world. But if ideas really do have consequences, the impact is likely to be significant.

The Guilds' Dissent

In a related realm of ideas, the war to depose Saddam Hussein crystallized the tensions that had been apparent in just war thinking for the past several decades. The debates before and after the brief major combat phase of the war demonstrated that contemporary distortions of classic just war thinking—in particular, confusions over the nature of the classic *ad bellum* or war-decision criteria and their relationship to each other — continue to affect the judgment of many of the philosophers, theologians, and religious leaders who are presumed to be the among the chief custodians of this venerable method of moral reasoning. No comprehensive survey of opinion in these quarters has been made, to my knowledge. But if it were, it's a safe bet that such a survey would find that an overwhelming majority of Western religious leaders thought the Iraq War imprudent at best and unjust at worst, a judgment for which they would have found ample support among most contemporary just war philosophers and theologians.[2]

In my view, that judgment — that the decision to invade Iraq to enforce the will of the United Nations, depose a tyrant, and accelerate the pace of desirable political change in the Middle East did not satisfy the war-decision criteria of the just war tradition — is mistaken. Demonstrating that does not require the moral theorist to become an apologist for every facet of Bush administration policy in Iraq, for as the administration itself has conceded, it made mistakes, some of them serious, in its appraisal of likely post-Saddam politics in Iraq, in its approach(es) to the pacification of the country, and in aspects of its counter-insurgency strategy. What demonstrating the fallacy of the consensus among many just war theorists and religious leaders against the probity of the decision to depose Saddam Hussein by force of arms does require is a willingness to think through the classic just war criteria in a classic way: that is, by understanding those criteria as a demanding yet supple framework for morally informed prudential political reasoning about the achievement of morally worthy political ends through the means of proportionate and discriminate armed force.

The just war tradition is a tradition in the service of *tranquillitas ordinis,* which was St. Augustine's definition of peace: that is, the just war tradition is a way of moral reasoning about the use of certain kinds of means toward the end of the peace that is composed of freedom, justice, and security.[3] This linkage between moral reasoning and the noblest ends of politics is what gives just war thinking its *gravitas* — and its tether to the world in which statesmen must make real decisions with life-and-death consequences. Yet even as most religious leaders, moral philosophers, and theologians who opposed the Iraq War continued to insist that theirs was the "peace" position, it was precisely this linkage between moral reasoning and the politics of peace in a conflict-ridden world that the putative custodians of the just war tradition seem to have largely forgotten.[4]

Some of the critique here bordered on the risible: thus a lengthy report by a working group of the Church of England's House of Bishops spent several pages bemoaning the alleged impact of Hal Lindsey's *Late Great Planet Earth* and Tim LaHaye's *Left Behind* novels on what the bishops deplore as aggressive American nationalism and Bush administration unilateralism.[5] Then there were the ninety-five United Methodist bishops who publicly repented their "complicity" in the "unjust and immoral" invasion and occupation of Iraq — even though these allegedly complicit clergymen had loudly opposed the war for years before March 2003.[6] Dr. Konrad Raiser, General Secretary of the World Council of Churches, simply pronounced the war "immoral, illegal, and ill-advised," and, oddly for a German whose country might still be living under the totalitarian jackboot, concluded that "wars cannot be won, only peace can."[7] Other critiques exposed the large ambitions of some intellectuals: thus the editor of *America* magazine, Father Drew Christiansen, S.J., proposed that the *Catechism of the Catholic Church* be revised in light of the Iraq War, so that it would be clear that a new shadow government of theologians, religious leaders, and activists shared public officials' responsibility for determining when the conditions for a just use of armed force had been met.[8] Where that might lead was illustrated by the Catholic bishops of the United States, who, in a letter to President Bush in September 2002, framed the just war criteria "so restrictively and prejudicially as to make [it] virtually impossible" for the criteria to be met, as one prominent just war scholar put it.[9]

The critics were not, alas, beyond misrepresentation: thus ethicist Mark Allman, among many others, wrote that "Pope John Paul II...condemned the U.S. invasion of Iraq as unjust." Yet for all his opposition to a military solution to the problem of disarming Iraq, and notwithstanding the somewhat overheated rhetoric of various Vatican officials in early 2003, the late Pope never used the word "unjust" to describe the war—perhaps in part because he knew, as Professor Allman evidently did not, that Catholic Church leaders in Iraq had thanked U.S. diplomatic representatives for liberating their country.[10] And beyond the rhetoric of opposition there was the anti-war street theater, which harped endlessly on this being a "war for oil"—a claim that ignored the fact that the only parties for whom this really was "about oil" (in the sense of a corrupt interest in a crucial commodity) were, as we shall see in a moment, Russia, France, China, various grafting U.N. bureaucrats, and Saddam Hussein.

There was, in fact, very little sustained analytical critique of the Bush administration's policy from a just war point of view. There were assertions; but there was little sustained argument.[11] Even such normally sober just war philosophers as Michael Walzer and Father John Langan, S.J., failed to make detailed critical arguments in support of their claim that the Iraq War failed the test of just war analysis. Professor Walzer, writing in a Web special edition of *Dissent* in March 2003, had this to say: "America's war is unjust. Though disarming Iraq is a legitimate goal, morally and politically, it is a goal that we could almost certainly have achieved with measures short of full-scale war....At this time, the threat that Iraq posed could have been met with something less than the war we are now fighting. And a war fought before its time is not a just war."[12] Addressing the Pacific Section of the Society of Christian Ethics, Father Langan simply averred that "both the general policy of preventive war advocated in the 2002 National Security Strategy and the exercises in deception and self-deception which led up to the invasion of Iraq constitute an unacceptable aberration from the concern for maintaining international order and for building a peaceful world of free and equal states which has been at the heart of U.S. foreign policy over the last century" — and then proposed that the assembled ethicists and their colleagues issue a "repudiation of those politicians and their advisors who brought the war about."[13]

Insofar as one can tease an argument out of what amounted to an array of sometimes confused and often confusing assertions, the just war case against the Iraq War, as implied by the more serious critics, went something like this. Granted that Saddam Hussein ran an odious regime that had brutalized the Iraqi people and that, rearmed, posed a grave security threat to the Middle East (and perhaps beyond), it was unnecessary tactically and unjust morally to depose him and effect regime change by means of an Anglo-American invasion and occupation. The U.N. sanctions regime had Saddam "in the box"; maintaining sanctions (or perhaps intensifying them, which was Michael Walzer's proposal, echoed by the U.S. Catholic bishops) would either keep Saddam in "the box" or would lead to his eventual overthrow. Moreover, to invade Iraq without an explicit mandate from the United Nations violated international law and further weakened the already delicate fabric of international public life. These claims were often set in the context of a more comprehensive rejection of the Bush Doctrine of preemption as articulated in NSS-2002, which most moral theorists and religious leaders judged to be in conflict with both the just war tradition and international law.

New circumstances inevitably give rise at times to confused analyses; that is as true of moral reasoning as it is of the foreign policy process. So, in the absence of a detailed, sustained just war critique of the Iraq War to which to respond, let me offer a just war defense of the moral probity of the decision to remove Saddam by armed force, with specific focus on the classic *ius ad bellum* (or war-decision) criteria that are the intellectual and moral core of the just war tradition. Such a defense will, I hope, demonstrate the unpersuasiveness of the assertions and judgments implicit in the unarticulated just war critique of the war that so dominated the moral rhetoric in both America and Europe in the years surrounding the March 2003 invasion of Iraq.

The Just War Case for the War

Three just war criteria were prominent in the pre-invasion debate, if not in precisely the way that a classic understanding of just war reasoning would conceive their use. Each of these criteria belonged to the *ius ad bellum,* or war-decision law: competent authority, just cause, and last resort. An examination of each is essential in making a comprehensive just war case for the war against Saddam Hussein.

Competent Authority

As James Turner Johnson, the world's premier historian of the just war tradition, has argued endlessly (and, it seems, rather fruitlessly), the just war method of moral reasoning begins with the legitimate sovereign's responsibility to defend and promote the peace of *tranquillitas ordinis,* the peace of order. In other words, the just war tradition is, first and foremost, a tradition of prudential political reasoning about good political ends, informed by the natural moral law; the natural law dimension of just war reasoning also creates the possibility of a public moral grammar for the public deliberation of public goods. The just war tradition begins, not with casuistry about this or that particular military or non-military option, and not with a set of hurdles that moral theorists set before statesmen, but with the legitimate sovereign's moral obligation to defend and promote right order. Thus, in the just war tradition, war is not

an abandonment of the moral realm; war *is* a moral category —
"war" is the use of proportionate and discriminate armed force by
legitimate public authority in order to secure certain worthy public
goods. Anything else is brigandage, in one form or another.

Although this moral-political starting point for just war thinking — the defense and pursuit of peace by legitimate sovereign
authority — has been largely forgotten by many of those who speak
to and from the just war tradition, the question of the location of
competent authority for legitimate war-making was, in fact, one of
the questions at issue in the claim that the United Nations alone
could authorize the resort to armed force to compel Saddam Hussein to comply with the obligation of disarmament laid on him
by the 1991 truce agreement that followed the first Gulf War and
by a host of subsequent U.N. resolutions. All authority to make
war in the world had been remanded over to the U.N. — or so the
assertion went.

That assertion raises any number of questions. If we are reasoning in classic just war terms, the first question to be asked is
whether the United Nations in fact constitutes a competent sovereign authority. Some would undoubtedly answer "yes," but a far
more persuasive case can be made that the U.N., as it is presently
structured and as it currently functions, lacks many of the crucial
attributes of sovereignty as the just war tradition has understood
the term. Its Charter describes the U.N. as an organization of sovereign states, not a superstate to which core attributes of national
sovereignty have been deputed. Thus it is not at all clear that the
state-members of the United Nations consider the organization a
"sovereign" entity — a suggestion grimly confirmed by the fact that,
since 1945, more than twenty million people have been killed in the
more than 150 armed conflicts *not* authorized by the U.N. Then
there is the question of accountability: the present U.N. system is
only weakly accountable to the people of the world, for member-
states alone can hold the organization accountable for its policies

and practices (and frequently fail to do so). Further, when the question turns to the legitimate use of armed force, the U.N.'s lack of sovereignty is suggested by the fact that the organization has no military capability of its own and exercises an extremely limited form of command-and-control over the forces that act in its name; that, in turn, suggests that the U.N. cannot responsibly direct those forces, which is another core characteristic of sovereignty. To assert, without further ado, that the U.N. exercises genuinely sovereign authority — the core *ad bellum* question with which just war reasoning begins — is to abandon moral reasoning and enter a realm of highly contingent legal argument, about which lawyers will likely wrangle *per omnia saecula saeculorum.*[14]

Why? Because there is a serious question as to whether the U.N. Charter claims for itself the monopoly on the legitimate use of force that some claim for it. Article 51 of the Charter recognizes that U.N. member-states possess an inherent right of self-defense: if your country is being invaded or attacked — if, in other words, you are the victim of aggression — you do not have to secure the permission of the Security Council or the General Assembly to do something about it. American, British, and continental European scholars have widely different readings of the meaning of Article 51.[15] But that itself suggests that, from a just war point of view, the question on which the argument turns is not the highly controverted one of whether the U.N. has been ceded a legal monopoly on the moral authority to authorize armed force in defense of the peace of order; rather, the far more decisive moral question raised by Article 51 is a just cause question: how does one make the judgment that aggression is, indeed, under way?

This is one of the crucial questions that a developed, classic just war analysis must address: how is "aggression" defined in a world where the minimum requisites of order are threatened by bellicose regimes with weapons of mass destruction, ballistic missile capability, and no domestic political checks on their leaders' actions?

That question and its implications for the question of sovereign authority had to be faced in 2002–3, when competent national authorities reached the judgment, but could not persuade the Security Council to accept the judgment, that aggression was indeed under way (if not yet in the classic cross-border sense of the term), and that a proportionate and discriminate military response was not only legitimate, but was necessary as an exercise of the national sovereign's moral responsibility.

Then there were the realities of contemporary U.N. practice, which were, to be plain, ugly in the years between the first Gulf War and March 2003. For assertions about the U.N.'s singular moral authority to wage war today must contend with the hard facts of the U.N.'s deep corruption, which is now beyond reasonable doubt. It is bad enough when U.N. "peacekeepers" in Africa become complicit in the sex-trafficking of young girls; still, any large organization has its share of reprehensible characters, whose odious behavior does not call into question the moral legitimacy of the organization as a political actor of consequence. What does raise that question with respect to the U.N. and Iraq are the Congressional inquiries, and the investigations of the Volcker Commission appointed by Secretary General Kofi Annan, into the U.N.-run Oil-for-Food program in Iraq. These inquiries and investigations strongly suggest — some would say, decisively prove — that the Security Council process in the debate over Iraq was thoroughly corrupted, with French and Russian diplomats admitting to having been paid off with illegal oil vouchers by the Iraqi regime.[16] It is not unreasonable to believe that others were similarly bribed. Indeed, the U.N. Oil-for-Food program was the crucial component in a colossal swindle in which Saddam Hussein embezzled some $21 billion in oil money over a dozen years.

But there was more, and it was worse. For, according to the September 2004 Duelfer Report, the embezzled billions (of which the bulk were from Oil-for-Food) were used by Saddam Hussein both to maintain his regime's economic viability and to sustain his pursuit of weapons of mass destruction. As the Duelfer Report puts it, "The introduction of the Oil-for-Food Program (OFF) in late 1996 was a key turning point for the regime. OFF rescued Baghdad's economy from a terminal decline created by sanctions. The regime quickly came to see that OFF could be corrupted to acquire foreign exchange both to further undermine sanctions and to provide the means to enhance dual-use infrastructure and potential WMD-related development."[17] The U.N. itself, in other words, was materially complicit in Saddam Hussein's success in running what the *Wall Street Journal* succinctly called "the largest bribery scheme in the history of the world."[18] And that scheme was not simply aimed at lining the pockets of Saddam, his family, and his Baathist party. It had a strategic purpose: to enable Iraq to break the sanctions regime, escape the so-called "box," and revive the very weapons programs which it was the stated goal of more than a dozen U.N. resolutions to end. Thus, as I suggested above, the only people for whom this really was "all about oil" were French, Russian, and Chinese diplomats and their governments; grafting U.N. bureaucrats; and the Saddam Hussein regime, which used oil to corrupt the U.N. political process in an unprecedented way.

All of which reinforces the grave questions about the U.N. as a locus of sovereign authority that classic just war thinking would want to pose, even prior to a sober analysis of the U.N.'s current dysfunctionality. In light of these questions and in the wake of the U.N.'s performance in the seven years before the Iraq War, the burden of proof lies squarely on those moral theorists who would claim a monopoly on the legitimate use of armed force for an organization that arguably lacks sovereignty, rightly understood; that concedes a legitimate right of self-defense to states in its Charter; and that, through the Oil-for-Food program, was the de facto financial partner of a tyrant and the agent of its own political corruption.

Just Cause

From a classic just war perspective, there were multiple and mutually reinforcing rationales for making the moral judgment that the removal of Saddam Hussein and his regime, and the creation of a new political order in Iraq, satisfied a developed version of the war-decision criterion of just cause. The Iraqi regime was in clear violation of more than a dozen U.N. resolutions demanding its disarmament, and, according to those resolutions, the burden of proof was on Saddam Hussein to prove that he had in fact disarmed; absent such proof, the assumption had to be that he had not, with severe consequences to follow. The regime had been a massive violator of human rights for decades, its signature activities having included rape as an instrument of state policy, various grotesque forms of torture, and the use of chemical weapons against its own citizens. The mass graves dug up all over Iraq in the aftermath of the major combat phase of the war bore powerful testimony to the fact that Saddam's Iraq was a killing field of systematized brutality and lethality — a model case, some might argue, for "humanitarian intervention" to depose a despotic, murderous regime.[19] Saddam's Iraq had long since proven itself a threat to regional stability, having conducted a long and bloody war against Iran (with, alas, misguided U.S. support), during which it had used ballistic missiles and weapons of mass destruction.[20] Moreover, Saddam's ambitions to be a new Saladin were well-known in the neighborhood; the fear that Saddam aroused in his neighbors was only intensified after the 1991 decision to leave him in power, and was evident in efforts by key Persian Gulf leaders to get rock-solid assurances from the United States in 2002 and 2003 that America really would see through regime change in Baghdad this time.[21] That Saddam, who had once harbored such scoundrels as Abu Nidal and Abu Abbas, was still involved with terrorists, including al-Qaeda terrorists, no serious person doubted; those convictions have been amply confirmed by documents captured during and after the war, which demonstrate that the Saddam Hussein regime trained hundreds, even thousands, of jihadist terrorists in camps around Iraq in the years immediately preceding the war.[22] The Iraqi regime thus posed a severe threat to regional security, to international order, and to the national security of the United States.

Then there was the Iraqi regime's lust for weapons of mass destruction [WMD]. Everyone — the Clinton administration, the United Nations, the Russians, the French, the Chinese, the British, and a host of U.S. intelligence agencies — was convinced that Saddam Hussein had retained stockpiles of chemical and biological weapons after the 1991 Gulf War and was actively seeking a nuclear weapons capability. No small part of the reason why the world was convinced that Saddam Hussein retained a WMD capacity and sought to enhance it was because of the Iraqi regime's recalcitrant behavior in dealing with international weapons inspectors. U.S. war plans for Iraq assumed that the Iraqi army would use chemical weapons, at least, as witness the deployment of expensive protective equipment for U.S. forces.

The Bush administration's stress on WMD as a crucial component of the case for war against the Iraqi regime was due to at least three factors: the administration's sincere conviction that Saddam had a WMD capacity and sought to grow it; the belief that Iraq's defiance of U.N. disarmament resolutions made the strongest case for military action at the Security Council; and the political needs of British prime minister Tony Blair, who had told the American administration that the WMD rationale for deposing Saddam had to be emphasized in order for him to hold his Labor Party back-benchers in the House of Commons. In the event, as the McKay and Duelfer Reports disclosed, Iraq's WMD capability had been essentially destroyed after 1991, even as Saddam retained the human and technical infrastructure necessary to reconstitute his WMD programs (if with a different mix of capabilities) once he had broken out of the "box" of U.N. sanctions — and even as he refused to comply with U.N. disarmament requirements, in order to maintain the fear-driven mystique (and power) that his previous possession and use of WMD had afforded him. The fact that coalition troops did not find caches of WMD in Iraq points to a serious intelligence failure on the part of virtually every actor of consequence on the world stage, as it underscores both Saddam's duplicity and his megalomania.[23] But does the absence of WMD in Iraq in March 2003 fundamentally change the just war calculus?

It does not. Prudent statecraft rightly assumed that Saddam had WMD; the debate was over what to do about that. And, as James Q. Wilson pointed out, whatever else can be said about pre-war intelligence failures, we now know for certain than an aggressive Iraqi regime does not have WMD with which to threaten the region and the world.[24] Ensuring the disarmament of Iraq was one facet of the just cause argument in favor of deposing Saddam by military force; that desirable and morally defensible end has been achieved.

The just cause and competent authority criteria intersect at the WMD issue. Regime change in Iraq had been U.S. policy since the Clinton administration in 1998 — because regime change was understood to be the only way to guarantee Iraq's WMD disarmament, end the suffering of its people, and achieve a measure of stability in the Persian Gulf area. That judgment was shared by the Bush administration, if now in the radically changed post-9/11 strategic environment. For 9/11 had intensified legitimate concerns that neither the Middle East nor the United States could be safe in a world in which the Saddam Hussein regime remained in power. Further, by invading Iraq and deposing the Baathist regime, the United States, Great Britain, and their allies were enforcing, de facto if not de iure (although that, too, remains a contested legal point), Iraq disarmament resolutions that the U.N. was unwilling or unable to enforce for a variety of reasons — including, as we now know, massive financial corruption. The fecklessness displayed by both the League of Nations and the great powers when National Socialist Germany militarily reoccupied the Rhineland in 1936 is widely thought to have eroded the foundations of world order in the 1930s — with lethal results. Would a similar fecklessness in the face of U.N. disarmament demands have strengthened world order? It seems very unlikely. And cannot a case be made that, over the long haul, the work of a coalition of the willing to enforce the international consensus embodied in those U.N. resolutions will strengthen the foundations of the peace of order?

By its international and domestic behavior, its weapons capabilities and ambitions, and its stated intentions, the Iraq regime of Saddam Hussein had shown that it constituted, de facto, an "aggression under way." Responding to that aggression through a proportionate and discriminate use of armed force was not only morally legitimate, according to classic just war understandings of just cause; it was, reasonable analysts could argue, morally necessary.

Last Resort

But had everything possible been done, short of full-scale war, to achieve the morally worthy ends of peace, security, and freedom in Iraq — and a changed political equation in the Middle East? Michael Walzer, for example, suggested in late 2002 and early 2003 that Saddam's regime could be contained by expanding the no-fly zones in Iraq to cover the entire country, by robustly supporting U.N. weapons inspectors, and by tightening sanctions. Walzer was under no illusions about the wickedness of Saddam's regime, and, like everyone else, he was convinced that Saddam had WMD and sought more WMD. But Walzer's moral and political realism seems to have failed him, in this instance.[25]

In 1999, three years before Walzer proposed drastically strengthening it, the sanctions regime against Iraq was crumbling, with only the U.S. and Great Britain, among the permanent members of the Security Council, supporting its extension; China, France, and Russia were all seeking ways to ease the sanctions regime into virtual or legal non-existence. As the Duelfer Report indicated, the combination of tens of billions of Oil-for-Food dollars and the collapsing political support at the U.N. for sanctions led the Iraqi regime to the not-unreasonable conclusion that it was, in fact, about to get out of "the box," at which point it could resume its WMD programs. There is no reason to think that the Walzer proposal for "sanctions plus" or an intensified "little war" would have commanded support within the Security Council or, if imposed by the U.S. and Great Britain alone, would have had the desired effect within Iraq. Moreover, the effects of a draconian sanctions regime on Iraq's long-suffering civilian population would have been so severe as to call the moral probity of the strategy into serious question. In other words, by March 2003 every morally reasonable option for enforcing Iraqi disarmament short of war had been exhausted.

Preemption, or Justified First Use of Force?

The debate over last resort was also a debate over the Bush administration's doctrine of preemption, as articulated in its September 2002 *National Security Strategy of the United States* [NSS-2002]. That debate can be located at the intersection of the competent authority, just cause, and last resort criteria of a developed, classic just war analysis of the pre-invasion Iraq situation.

The tone of NSS-2002, with its blunt affirmation of "unprecedented" and "unequaled" American strength and influence in the world, was undoubtedly grating at points, perhaps especially on allies. The document's determination to advance a "distinctly American internationalism that reflects the union of our values and our national interests" raised immediate cautions in the mind of anyone schooled by Augustinian realism to recognize that, in politics, even the best intentions will come into conflict with unavoidably imperfect policy options from time to time.[26] Read as a whole, however, NSS-2002 was neither a sermon nor an exercise in triumphalism, but rather a sober-minded attempt to define a morally sound security strategy by which the United States and its allies could advance the cause of the peace of order in the 21st century.

According to NSS-2002, the strategy of deterrence that saw the free world through to safety in the Cold War is unavailing against terrorist organizations and networks and against the most extreme rogue states; to rely solely on a "reactive posture" is too dangerous. Thus the first use of military force must be considered an available option under the doctrine of "imminent danger" that international law has recognized "for centuries." While the United States "will not use force in all cases to preempt emerging threats," the United States "will, if necessary, act preemptively."[27] Such first use of military force will be one of the means by which the United States seeks to defend the order that exists in international public life and to expand the zone of freedom (and hence of order) in the world; other available means include public diplomacy, foreign aid, and coalitional activity with allies whose purposes in the world are the same.[28]

Ever since it was issued, criticism of NSS-2002 has focused primarily on its call for preemptive military action — although NSS-2002 spends far more time discussing cooperative international diplomatic, economic, and political activity in support of the peace of order than it does discussing preemptive military action. Preemption, however, was the strategic new thing being proposed by the U.S. government in response to the dramatically altered circumstances of post-9/11 international public life. That, plus the fact that the word "preemption" seemed to imply a settled skepticism about the role of international legal and political institutions in managing conflict, made it inevitable that preemption would be perceived as the centerpiece of NSS-2002.

Suppose, however, that NSS-2002, rather than using the language of preemption, had adopted language derived more explicitly from the just war tradition — which can indeed imagine the morally legitimate first use of armed force? Substituting just war–derived language for the words "preemption" and "preemptively" (and their synonyms) in NSS-2002 yields the following, interesting results:

While the United States will constantly strive to enlist the support of the international community, we will not hesitate to act alone, if necessary, to exercise our right of self-defense by *the first use of armed force* against such terrorists, to prevent them from doing harm against our people and our country....[29]

The United States has long maintained the option of *the first use of armed force* to counter a sufficient threat to our national security. The greater the threat, the greater is the risk of inaction — and the more compelling the case for *the first use of armed force,* even if uncertainty remains as to the time and place of the enemy's attack. To forestall or prevent such hostile acts by our adversaries, the United States will, if necessary, *engage in the first use of armed force.* The United States will not use force in all cases to *forestall* emerging threats, nor should nations use *[our] first use of armed force* as a pretext for aggression.[30]

We will always proceed deliberately, weighing the consequences of our actions. To support options *involving the first use of armed force,* we will...build better, more integrated intelligence capabilities...coordinate closely with allies...[and] continue to transform our military forces. The purpose of our *first use of armed force will* always be to eliminate a specific threat to the United States or our allies and friends. The reasons for our actions will be clear, the force measured, and the cause just.[31]

If classic just war language had been substituted for the language of preemption in the relevant sections of the document, NSS-2002 might have been received as what I expect its authors intended it to be: an effort to describe a morally serious and politically feasible national security strategy in which the use of armed force, as one necessary instrument of statecraft, is understood according to the canons of a developed just war tradition. Given the political and media contexts into which NSS-2002 was launched, however, the sound-bite language of preemption readily fed the perception that NSS-2002 marked a breach with the just war tradition and with the tenets of international law. Using the classic language of the morally responsible first use of armed force would have been truer to the logic of NSS-2002, and might have helped accelerate needed fresh thinking among just war analysts and churchmen.

James Turner Johnson offered a historical perspective on this facet of the Iraq War debate in these terms:

> Classic statements of the just war idea did not stigmatize first resort to force because their concern was with responding to injustice, however it might be manifest. They did not prioritize defense against armed attack, and certainly did not define just cause in terms of such self-defense, reflecting Augustine's conception of just war [as one in which] a Christian might justifiably use force to protect an innocent neighbor against harm. Augustine's aim was not, as [Paul] Ramsey later saw clearly, to justify use of force to respond to prior use of force — one did not have to wait until the neighbor had been harmed to act — but to show how force might be morally justified to prevent harm from being delivered.... From the perspective of classic statements of the just war idea, there was no question that one might justifiably use force to prevent an attack by a wrongdoer as well as to repair the injustice caused by such an attack or to punish the attacker.[32]

Extending the Just War Tradition

Strikingly, there were few just war criticisms of the *in bello* (war-conduct) practices of U.S.-led coalition forces during the brief major combat phase of the war — which reflects the fact that advances in military technology, including real-time intelligence, global positioning systems, and precision-guided munitions, have made it more possible than ever before for responsible political authorities to use what the classic just war tradition would consider truly proportionate and discriminate armed force in the service of worthy political ends.[33] Insofar as there were grave violations of just war–fighting during the ground combat phase of the Iraq War, they were committed by Iraqi forces — a fact that remained largely unremarked by either the just war critics of the war or by the media. Still, the predominance of *ad bellum* or war-decision issues in the Iraq debate suggests that the focus of just war debate for the future has decisively shifted to this cluster of questions.

But perhaps another set of questions, which dominated the debate since late 2003, will continue to hold center stage in the years ahead. For some time now, certain just war thinkers have suggested that there is a third cluster of questions to be pursued in a thorough just war analysis: that, in addition to the war-decision questions of the *ius ad bellum* and the war-conduct questions of the *ius in bello,* there are questions of what Michael Walzer has called the *jus post bellum.* As Walzer writes, "It seems clear that you can fight a just war, and fight it justly, and still make a moral mess of the aftermath."[34] James Turner Johnson has expressed the same concerns in a different way, arguing that satisfying the classic *ad bellum* or war-decision criterion of right intention includes the commitment to securing a just peace after the conclusion of combat.[35] Whether one deems this cluster of questions the third part of an expanded just war tradition or an extension of one of the classic *ad bellum* criteria, this is obviously an area in which considerable criticism of the Iraq war has been focused — whether the issue at hand involves the scandals at Abu Ghraib prison, interrogation methods, de-Baathification policies, counter-insurgency strategies and tactics, or the provisions of the new Iraqi constitution with respect to religious freedom and the role of Islamic law in post-Saddam Iraq.

These issues are, obviously, important in themselves; similar issues are likely to become important in the future, because the Bush doctrine and its application in Iraq have launched the United States and indeed the world into uncharted waters, where new military, political, and moral challenges abound. As NSS-2002 made clear, the United States will actively seek to shape events and thereby reshape the contours of world politics. Given the new realities of the post-9/11 world disorder, I believe there was no responsible alternative to setting sail on those uncharted waters. That conviction, however, reinforces a prudent concern that our navigation be as intelligent and precise as possible as we head out into inevitably rough seas.

The administration's 2005 *National Strategy for Victory in Iraq* was an effort to get the navigation right. But the fact that it was issued two and a half years after major combat had ended illustrates the truth of British historian Niall Ferguson's suggestion that the United States, lacking a classic imperial instinct, has lacked what we might call an imperial playbook on the British model, and that something resembling such a playbook is a moral and political necessity, if the goals of NSS-2002 are to be achieved.[36]

It is beyond my competence even to outline, much less comment in detail on, the myriad questions involved in thinking through this dense thicket of issues. But perhaps I can conclude with a brief comment on one crucial facet of the problem, which involves what has come to be known as "public diplomacy." And by "public diplomacy," I mean the U.S. government's responsibility to identify the goals of U.S. policy, to explain the strategies and tactics (military and non-military) being deployed to achieve those goals, to make the case for the moral probity of American goals, strategies, and tactics — and to do all of this both at home and abroad.

The war against terrorism is a long-haul business; the maintenance of national focus and morale is no easy thing in such a war, not least because one cannot plot the war's progress as my parents' generation plotted the progress of the war against Germany and Japan, six decades ago. Regular, prime-time presidential reports to the nation, even if only fifteen minutes in length, would have been a useful tool in maintaining that national focus and in challenging, if only indirectly, the largely negative reporting on the war in Afghanistan, the Iraq War, and the war against al-Qaeda. Such exercises in presidential leadership would be a useful tool in the future, as the struggle for Iraq continues, the battle against al-Qaeda and similar terrorist networks unfolds, and the threats to world order posed by Iran and North Korea continue — and perhaps intensify.

Still, if the administration did not always do a very good job of determining the public narrative in America about the war against terrorism or the Iraq War, it never even got started in Europe. U.S. embassies in both old and new Europe have largely been bunkers rather than beachheads from which to carry moral and political arguments into Europe's centers of public opinion. American commentators with European credibility should have been deployed throughout the continent, in person and through the electronic media, to challenge the virtually unchallenged cartoon of American evangelical cowboys running riot in the world — a cartoon that helps explain, at least in part, the vapors of Anglican bishops in the U.K. who imagine that Tim LaHaye's fictional speculations on the Book of Revelation play a formative role in U.S. foreign policy. No doubt the crisis of civilizational morale that besets western Europe in the first years of the 21st century would have made things difficult in any event; but they didn't have to be as difficult as they have been. And in any event, it is a simple matter of self-respect to get into the argument and fight.

Moreover, a commitment to making public arguments on behalf of the probity and prudence of what the United States and its allies were attempting in Iraq would have helped shape a more rational international public discourse than we have seen since 9/11. Truth is often thought to be the first victim of war. Yet if all just wars aim at the establishment or recovery of the peace of order, then vigorous truth-telling about the American decision to go to war, about America's conduct of the war, and about America's postwar efforts at reconstruction and pacification in Iraq are important components of the pursuit of a just peace. In his first address to the diplomatic corps accredited to the Holy See, Pope Benedict XVI spoke forcefully of the relationship of truth to the peace of order; as he put it, "commitment to truth is the soul of justice"; "commitment to truth establishes and strengthens the right to freedom"; and "commitment to truth opens the way to forgiveness and reconciliation."[37] Those three points are worth pondering far beyond the Apostolic Palace in Rome. The truth liberates, in many ways.

The world knows — and the American people know — just about everything that went wrong in Iraq. Serious mistakes were made after major combat ended, and while that was perhaps inevitable in fighting this new kind of war — in which major combat defined the battlefield for the military, social, economic, and political struggle in which we are currently engaged — it does not excuse the mistakes. Still, that story has been told, over and over again. But there were other stories that could have and should have been told, far more effectively: the story of a murderous regime deposed; the story of successful reconstruction efforts in a long-suffering country; the story of three elections conducted by brave citizens in the face of homicidal threats, elections that eventually produced a government that, for all its deficiencies, enjoyed the greatest democratic legitimacy in the modern history of the Middle East; the story of Libya defanged and politics briefly reshaped in Lebanon's "Cedar Revolution"; the story of changing perceptions of the politically possible and the morally desirable throughout the Arab Islamic world. Those stories strongly suggest that those who made the ultimate sacrifice in what they rightly believed was a morally justified war in Iraq, and those who will carry the wounds of that war for the rest of their lives, served in a morally worthy cause.

The world needs to know that, and so do the American people.

Chapter Eleven

Just War and
the Iraq Wars—II

*In January 2007, I delivered the sixth William E. Simon Lecture
in Washington under the title, "The Learning Curve: What We
Must Know, Five Years after 9/11." A considerably expanded form
of this lecture formed the basis of my book* Faith, Reason, and the
War Against Jihadism: A Call to Action.

The editors of First Things, *having paid considerable attention to the moral debate over Iraq for several years, invited me to
take that part of the sixth Simon Lecture that had been devoted
to what we ought to have learned during the first four years of the
war in Iraq, and to develop that into an article that would up-
date my previous writing on Iraq for the journal. I was happy to
do so, not least because it gave me the opportunity to develop the
idea that the United States, often without understanding it, had
in fact been involved in four wars in Iraq, each of which posed
distinct and urgent questions for the just war tradition. The sixth
Simon Lecture was delivered at a time when the American consensus on Iraq was beginning to unravel. Thus it seemed to me
that those who had offered a just war justification for the decision*

to depose the Saddam Hussein regime by force of arms were under an obligation — not to recant, as so many of our critics insisted — but to propose a just war analysis of precisely what had gone wrong since the defeat of the Saddam regime, and what the obligation of peacemaking implied by the theo-logic of the just war way of thinking could teach us about situations like Iraq.

In that sense, the sixth Simon Lecture was a continuation of the effort to develop a 21st-century just war tradition out of classic materials and a classic way of reasoning, both of which the traditional custodians of the tradition seemed, by and large, to have forgotten.

THE FIRST PHASE of the Iraq Wars came to a dramatic — and, as things turned out, ominously prophetic — denouement on that heady day in April 2003 when U.S. Marines, having stormed into central Baghdad, pulled down a statue of Saddam Hussein that the local citizenry couldn't quite manage to topple. Several months later, James Turner Johnson, our foremost historian of the just war tradition, wisely observed that neither the Iraq War (in its largest sense) nor the just war debate about the war was going to end any time soon. Just war thinking, as Johnson reminded us, is not only about the justification of the resort to armed force or the way in which that force is deployed. Just war thinking also includes a serious moral analysis of the goal of peace, to which the use of armed force must be ordered. Just war in the age of global jihadist terrorism, he wrote, "is not simply about the right, even the obligation, to use armed force to protect ourselves, our societies, and the values we cherish; it is not only about how we should fight in this cause; it is ultimately about the peace we seek to establish in contrast to the war the terrorists have set in motion. We are, as Augustine put it, to 'be peaceful... in warring,' that is, to keep the aim of peace first and foremost, and not only to 'vanquish those whom you war against' but also to 'bring them to the prosperity of peace....' The ideal expressed in the just war tradition... is an ideal in which the use of force serves... to create peace. This is a purpose that must not be forgotten."[1]

Just war thinking is usually taken to include the moral analysis of the *ius ad bellum* and the *ius in bello:* "war-decision law" and "war-conduct law," to use William V. O'Brien's modern nomenclature for two clusters of distinct but related moral criteria.[2] The secular-philosophical just war theorist Michael Walzer has been proposing for some years that there is another leg, so to speak, on the just war stool: a *jus post bellum* (as Walzer styles it), a set of moral criteria for defining the peace to be sought as the moral goal of the use of armed force. "It seems clear," Walzer wrote in November 2003, "that you can fight a just war, and fight it justly, and still make a moral mess of the aftermath — by establishing a satellite regime, for example, or by seeking revenge against the citizens of the defeated (aggressor) state, or by failing, after a humanitarian intervention, to help the people you have rescued to rebuild their lives."[3]

The opposite, Walzer suggested — an unjust war (*ad bellum* and/or *in bello*) that nonetheless produces a just peace — is "harder to imagine." Yet, he conceded, it's not completely beyond the realm of moral and political possibility that "a misguided military intervention or a preventive war fought before its time might nonetheless end with the displacement of a brutal regime and the construction of a decent one."[4] It is not hard to imagine the situation that Walzer — who argued in early 2003 for an intense "little war" strategy of increased sanctions and extended no-fly zones as a means of toppling Saddam Hussein — had in mind here.

James Turner Johnson has noted that Walzer, whom he credits with significant contributions to the revival of just war thinking, is nevertheless strikingly uninterested in the tradition's intellectual history. Thus it is perhaps not surprising that Johnson, a true intellectual historian as well as a man trained in theology, is inclined to think that what Walzer calls the *jus post bellum* is, in fact, already embedded in the *ius ad bellum* criterion of right intention, rightly understood. Right intention is one of the three "hard" criteria of the *ius ad bellum:* it denotes a moral duty, not merely a prudential judgment (like, for example, the *ad bellum* criterion of last resort). In this respect the criterion of right intention is like the *ad bellum* criterion of just cause: right intention is a specification of legitimate public authority's duty to do justice, which (in the case of war) does not end with repelling evil but includes the duty to build the peace of *tranquillitas ordinis,* the peace of a just public order. I am inclined to Johnson's position here, arguing as I did twenty years ago that the theo-logic of the just war way of thinking contained within itself what I then called a *ius ad pacem:* the proportionate and discriminate use of armed force must aim at the construction of the peace of order, which is composed of freedom, justice, and security.

Yet whether post-war peacemaking is conceived as a separate cluster of just war criteria, as Walzer proposes, or as an implication of right intention, *pace* Johnson, the duty to build a secure peace in the aftermath of war is intuitively grasped by morally serious people. The shoulder patch worn by the Anglo-American staff of General Dwight D. Eisenhower's Supreme Headquarters Allied Expeditionary Force [SHAEF] during World War II captured this intuition heraldically: against a black background symbolizing the darkness of Nazi aggression, a sword whose rising flames bespoke liberation and justice pointed toward a rainbow (hope) surmounted by sky blue, the colors of peace and tranquillity. Indeed, one might argue that the democratization of Germany, Italy, and Japan after World War II (motored economically by the Marshall Plan, and defended militarily by NATO and U.S. security guarantees to a disarmed Japan) was a belated recognition by the American people and their political leaders that the United States had failed the test of the *jus post bellum/ius ad pacem* in the aftermath of World War I, with globe-shaking and lethal consequences. A similar argument followed hard on the heels of the rapid victory of American-led coalition arms in the spring of 2003: How, if at all, is America to help secure the peace in Iraq after the conclusion of what was then called, somewhat innocently, the "major combat" phase of the war?

The Four Iraq Wars

Framing that debate correctly in just war terms means recognizing that there have been, in fact, four Iraq Wars since a U.S.-led coalition invaded Iraq in March 2003.

The first was the war to depose the Saddam Hussein regime and to create the political and military conditions for the possibility of responsible and responsive government in Iraq; it was quickly concluded at a very low cost in coalition military and Iraqi civilian casualties. The second—the war against Baathist recalcitrants and other Saddamist die-hards—erupted shortly after a decisive military victory had been achieved in the first war; both coalition and civilian casualties increased significantly. As jihadists like the late, unlamented Abu Mussab al-Zarqawi of "al-Qaeda in Iraq" flooded into the country, they deliberately created a third Iraq war, whose aims included not only driving the infidels from Mesopotamia but destabilizing the fragile Iraqi democracy they regarded as an offense against Islam. The fourth war—between Sunni "insurgents" (terrorists, in fact) and Shia death squads and militias—broke out in earnest after the bombing of a major Shia shrine, the Golden Mosque of Samarra, in February 2006: a decisive event in which al-Qaeda operatives seem to have played a part. The second, third, and fourth wars obviously overlapped at several points, making the situation on the ground more complex, more lethal, and more difficult to understand.

While there has been relatively little criticism of the *in bello* conduct of the first of these four wars (the war to depose the Saddam Hussein regime), the relevant academic guilds, such as the Society of Christian Ethics and the Catholic Theological Society of America, seem, in the main, to have concluded that the invasion of March 2003 did not satisfy the *ad bellum* criteria of a just war. Yet that conclusion was more often asserted than argued. Advocates of intensified "little war" like Michael Walzer failed to show how "sanctions-plus" would have resulted in the regime change in Baghdad they agreed was imperative; nor did proponents of this view meet the criticism that sanctions-plus would have placed morally unsustainable burdens on the civilian population of Iraq, given the totalitarian character of Saddam's Baathist regime. Proponents of more diplomacy — even those who would, in the final analysis, have reluctantly approved the use of armed force if more diplomacy failed — seemed unwilling or unable to reckon with the recalcitrance exhibited by several permanent members of the U.N. Security Council in late 2002 and early 2003. When Dominique de Villepin, then the French Foreign Minister, told U.S. Secretary of State Colin Powell that France would never, under any circumstances, approve the use of armed force to enforce the U.N.'s Iraq resolutions (much less to depose Saddam Hussein), he meant it. And there was nothing in the international record of Vladimir Putin since his accession to power to suggest that he would eventually have come around on the question of Iraq. Had the coalition not invaded Iraq and deposed the Baathist regime, Saddam Hussein would have slipped out of the so-called box (a favorite trope of Madeleine Albright) and, as the authoritative Duelfer Report makes clear, would have been back in the weapons-of-mass-destruction business in relatively short order — this time, politically strengthened throughout the region by his successful defiance of the Great Satan and its allies. That, in turn, would have encouraged jihadists everywhere to think, as they did in the 1990s, that the Great Satan was feckless: Osama bin-Laden's infamous "weak horse."

One of the less-than-helpful media games that confused debate on Iraq for years involved asking politicians whether Iraq was a "war of necessity" or a "war of choice." The fact is that it was both. That a revitalized Saddam Hussein regime which had successfully defied more than a decade of U.N. sanctions would have been a mortal peril to its neighbors and to world order cannot be seriously doubted. Regime change in Iraq was a necessity: it was necessary for the people of Iraq; it was necessary for peace in the Middle East; it was necessary to vindicate the fragile steps toward world order than had been taken since Eisenhower'sstaff wore those flaming-sword shoulder patches; and it was necessary in order to challenge Arab self-delusion, out of which had emerged, among other things, contemporary jihadism. The only "choice" in the matter involved who and when: Who would depose Saddam Hussein and his regime (and would they act under yet another U.N. resolution)? And when would this be done?

Saddam is gone, literally. But while significant parts of Iraq had been pacified (and the Kurdish north was doing well) by early 2007, there was precious little of the peace of order in Baghdad and in Anbar province at that time. Thus those who would continue to argue for the moral rectitude of the decision to use armed force to depose the Saddamist regime must also wrestle with the questions posed by Walzer's *jus post bellum* and Johnson's right intention, rightly understood. That wrestling must include a recognition of the many mistakes made by analysts and U.S. policymakers before, during, and after the so-called "major combat" phase of the war. The primary failure of American policy-planning was summarized neatly by the *New York Times*'s Michael Gordon and General Bernard Traynor in a fine book, *Cobra II: The Inside Story of the Invasion and Occupation of Iraq*: "What was missing was a comprehensive blueprint to administer and restore Iraq after Saddam was deposed, and identification of the U.S. organizations that would be installed in Baghdad to carry it out."[5] That lack of a strategic blueprint for post-Saddam Iraq reflected, even as it led to, other errors.

Iraq and Jihadism

American analysts and U.S. policymakers miscalculated the degree to which post-Saddam Iraq would quickly become a battlefield in the wider war against jihadism — which, in Iraq, unleashed a series of bloody events that have made the political stabilization of the country far more difficult. In *The Foreigner's Gift*, Fouad Ajami wrote that the quick collapse of a Saddamist regime that had cowed much of the Middle East exposed the "false world" in which Arabs had been living: a world characterized by that distinctive and self-delusory "Arab mix of victimology and wrath" which had defined the Middle East's politics for decades.[6] Such exposure was intolerable — to the remaining Baathists in Iraq and Syria, to the forces of the status quo among the Arab leadership, to the apocalyptics in Tehran, and to jihadists everywhere. And so each of them, in their several ways, worked to impede the success of the "foreigner's gift" to Iraq of political freedom and the forms of democratic self-government.

Had we recognized that the "links" between Iraq and jihadist terrorism were of a different sort than the conspiracies for which Western intelligence agencies were searching — had we understood that, in the jihadists' worldview, a democratic Iraq, midwifed by American military and economic power linked to Iraqi people power, was quite simply intolerable — then we might have understood that the jihadists would bend every effort to turn Iraq into what Ajami calls a "devil's playground," the porous borders of which "were a magnet for jihadists looking for a field of battle" — Jordanians, Syrians, Lebanese, Saudis, Palestinians, Iranians, all of whom grasped the fact that, if America were to succeed in Iraq, and Iraq to succeed as a modern Islamic society, their various dreams would be dealt a major, perhaps lethal, blow. On this field of battle, of course, the jihadists *stricte dictu* were de facto allies of other miscreants: the Syrian government, the Iranian government, and the Hamas government of the Palestinian Authority, none of whose behavior toward Iraq was seriously challenged by the forces of so-called Arab "moderation" (Egypt, Jordan, Saudi Arabia) or by the United States and its allies.[7]

In sum, American analysts and policymakers did not anticipate and, in the event, did not grasp quickly enough, that major combat in Iraq had only defined the battle that was coming next — a counter-insurgency war against Baathist and Iraqi military die-hards and jihadists (in which America's information-technology military advantage would be gravely weakened), followed by, and in some respects coterminous with, a sectarian conflict between Iraqi Sunni and Iraqi Shia dominated by terrorist tactics. Even though executing the war plan had required a lot of improvisation along the road to Baghdad and in the capture of Baghdad itself, the United States was well prepared for the first Iraq war: the war to depose Saddam Hussein and create the possibility of responsible and responsive Iraqi government. America was neither prepared militarily nor politically for the three wars that followed — the war against the remaining Iraqi Baathists and their allies; the war against al-Zarqawi and other jihadists; and the post-Samarra war between Shia and Sunni. In sum, American policy-planners were unprepared for Iraq's immediate post-major-combat ungovernability; and American policymakers remained somewhat tone-deaf to the deep religious dimensions of the fourth war in Iraq, which too many Sunnis and Shia in fact welcomed.

Damaged Goods

American analysts and policymakers badly miscalculated the degree of damage done to the fabric of Iraqi civil society by more than a quarter-century of Baathist totalitarianism. This, in turn, led to seriously underestimating the difficulties in accelerating a return to a functioning economy in the aftermath of the overthrow of the Saddam Hussein regime. As Robert Kaplan wrote, describing the situation as he experienced it in the spring of 2004:

> The social and cultural refuse created by the [Baathist] regime was everywhere, overwhelming the American authorities. While clichés abounded about the talent of the Iraqi people and their ability to quickly build a vibrant capitalist society, officers of the 82nd Airborne who had been [in Iraq] for months told another, more familiar story: of how Iraqis, like their Syrian neighbors, had in recent decades not experienced

Western capitalism so much as a diseased variant of it, in which you couldn't even open a restaurant or a shop without having connections to the regime. Above the level of the street vendor, in other words, capitalism [in Iraq] would have to be learned from scratch.[8]

The social incapacities induced by Saddam Hussein's totalitarianism intersected with the depredations to civil society caused by the wider Arab Islamic culture of "false redeemers and pretenders" (as Fouad Ajami described it) to make the formation of a rudimentary democratic political culture in Iraq extremely difficult. That problem has been compounded, in turn, by the capacity of al-Jazeera and other new-technology Arab-language media to spread lies; as Ajami noted in *The Foreigner's Gift*, "the new technology was put at the service of an old and stubborn refusal to face and name things as they are."[9]

Reconstruction on the Cheap

Inadequate resources were allocated for post-Saddam reconstruction in Iraq. As Max Boot put it *War Made New:*

> ... a dangerous [post-Saddam] security vacuum [was exacerbated by a] ... lack of reconstruction assistance. Only $2.5 billion had been budgeted initially to rebuild Iraq, an amount that would prove grossly inadequate, given the dilapidated condition in which Saddam Hussein's misrule and a decade of sanctions had left the country and especially its oil industry. (Administration officials would later claim that they had no idea in advance of how run-down everything was, but private experts had foreseen the need for at least $25 billion to $100 billion in reconstruction aid.) In November 2003 Congress voted $18.4 billion in further aid for Afghanistan and Iraq, but the money had to flow through so many bureaucratic

brooks and eddies that only a trickle reached its ultimate destination. As of December 2004, just $2 billion had been spent in Iraq — and much of that went for security and overhead costs incurred by American contractors.[10]

Here, as in the days before 9/11, the American intelligence community did not provide policymakers and planners what they needed, for American intelligence failed to grasp just how much damage had been done to Iraq's infrastructure by the Gulf War, Saddam Hussein's perverse priorities in the 1990s, and sanctions-driven economic stagnation. To make matters worse, there was a serious lack of bureaucratic coordination among American agencies responsible for reconstruction efforts in Iraq from the beginning. The lack of coordination was exacerbated by struggles between the Department of Defense and the Department of State over which of the two would be the lead agency in post-war Iraq — struggles which the White House could have resolved, but did not. According to Gordon and Traynor in *Cobra II,* then–Secretary of Defense Donald Rumsfeld distrusted the State Department's capacity to lead and coordinate, and feared that the bureaucratic sluggishness at Foggy Bottom would end up balkanizing Iraq; Rumsfeld may also have believed that Defense could restore order in Iraq as efficiently as the U.S. military and its allies had defeated Saddam's army. This bureaucratic leadership vacuum made it even more difficult to recognize that the original levels of reconstruction aid anticipated were gravely deficient. The administration did not grasp quickly enough the truth of one of General David Petraeus's observations on fighting a post-liberation counter-insurgency war like those in which the United States found itself in Iraq (or Afghanistan): "Money is ammunition."[11]

Why, though? Bush administration officials may, as Gordon and Traynor suggest, have brought a settled skepticism about "nation-building" to their thinking about post-Saddam Iraq. But state-building was in fact the responsibility we had taken on by determining that regime change in Iraq was a necessity. Strengthening the severely attenuated sinews of Iraq civil society, and building the rudiments of democratic self-governance amidst massive economic dislocations (and bad economic habits), proved far more difficult than anticipated. All of this should have been thought through more carefully before March 2003 — not to mention when it became unmistakably clear a year after the post–"major combat" phase of the Iraq Wars.

Losing the Information War

American policy-makers failed to devise an effective "hearts-and-minds" strategy for post-Saddam Iraq. After dominating the information dimensions of the first of the four Iraq Wars (the war against the Saddam Hussein regime), the U.S. too often left the information field to sources of misinformation and disinformation like al-Jazeera, with serious strategic consequences. Max Boot described the deleterious effects of this default on the first battle for Fallujah in April 2004, a crucial moment in the second of the four Iraq Wars:

> On April 4, 2004, two Marine battalions launched an assault on Fallujah. Five days later, while Marines were still battling their way into the city, the offensive was suspended because of inflammatory media coverage, primarily on the Arabic satellite news channel al-Jazeera, which claimed that Marines were deliberately targeting mosques and civilians. [Coalition Provisional Authority head Paul] Bremer, [General John] Abizaid, and other senior officials feared that, if the operation continued, support for the U.S. would crumble throughout the country....
>
> In Fallujah, negative news coverage succeeded in doing what Saddam Hussein's military had failed to do: it stopped

the mighty U.S. military in its tracks. As Lieutenant General James Conway, commander of the 1st Marine Expeditionary Force, put it, "Al-Jazeera kicked our butts." The Marines had to leave Fallujah, handing the insurgents their most notable victory.[12]

That disinformation-driven failure in Fallujah was itself a blow to building responsible government in Iraq, and it would only be reversed months later at the cost of numerous American and Iraqi casualties.

Taking Stock

This broad inventory does not exhaust the catalogue of American military and political failures in Iraq, which are described in painful detail in *Cobra II*. The looting and the general breakdown of public order that followed the collapse of the Saddam Hussein regime, and the virtual disappearance of Iraq's borders (the openness of which permitted, indeed encouraged, large numbers of jihadists to enter the country), should have been met with a far firmer response; but, unwilling to appear as anything other than liberators, and lacking the troops to maintain public order and patrol the borders, the U.S. and its allies let the window of opportunity they had opened by the swiftness of their military victory close. That others will, in retrospect, share the blame here — where were America's allies when large numbers of troops were required for border security? — should not diminish the sense of responsibility to be borne by the U.S. and its coalition partners: we were in charge, and it seems that we had failed to think through, prior to the invasion, the worst-case scenarios, several of which were to unfold with savage rapidity. Secretary of Defense Donald Rumsfeld became, in some circles, a useful scapegoat for all this; and, indeed, his seeming refusal to understand the difference between the force-levels needed for a lightning-swift military campaign and the force-levels required for the counter-insurgency struggle that followed played no small role in the failures of post–major combat U.S. policy. Yet it should also be recognized that Rumsfeld got some things right: it was Rumsfeld who correctly insisted that the information-technology revolution meant that Saddam could be toppled with fewer troops than had been required to eject him from Kuwait in 1991, and it was Rumsfeld who, with General Tommy Franks, insisted that the field commanders get moving again when the first phase of the invasion had stalled. Moreover, the failure of imagination that resulted in both a U.S. military and a Coalition Provisional Authority unprepared for the post-war ungovernability of Iraq rests with the entire national security apparatus of the government, not just with the Defense Department. When British historian Niall Ferguson argued some years ago that the United States both lacked an imperial playbook and badly needed one, he was, it is now clear, on to something important.

Is Iraq, then, and to cite Nancy Pelosi, Speaker of the House of Representatives, "not a war to be won but a situation to be managed"? How should Americans, disheartened by the nightly scenes of mayhem in Iraq broadcast on the evening news, and seemingly in a post-post-9/11 mood, have reacted to President Bush's description of our circumstances in the 2007 State of the Union message: "This is not the fight we entered in Iraq, but it is the fight we're in. Every one of us wishes this war were over and won. Yet it would not be like us to leave our promises unkept, our friends abandoned and our own security at risk. . . . It is still within our power to shape the outcome of this battle. Let us find our resolve, and turn events toward victory." Where do second and third thoughts on Iraq, filtered through the prism of Michael Walzer's *jus post bellum* or James Turner Johnson's amplification of the just war criterion of "right intention," lead us?

Lessons for the Future

The first place they ought to lead us is to the conclusion that the worst answer to the dilemma of Iraq — the worse answer from a moral point of view and the worst answer from a strategic point of view — is to quit: to follow Congressman Jack Murtha and many others in saying, "We're out."

What would "out" mean? It would almost certainly mean a genocidal war of Balkan ferocity (and worse) within Iraq. That war would almost just as certainly draw in Iran, and then the Sunni powers of the region; if Iraq imploded, Iraqi Kurdistan would be severely tempted to declare its independence, perhaps in league with fellow-Kurds in the adjacent areas of Turkey and Iran; and then it seems almost certain that the entire region would explode, with incalculable political, economic, and human costs. In the midst of that chaos, al-Qaeda and similar networks would find themselves new Iraqi havens, as they did in the chaos of the Soviet debacle in Afghanistan — which would, in turn, likely mean that the United States would have to go back into Iraq in the future, under far, far worse circumstances than we faced in the years following major combat (and those circumstances are bad enough). The much-vaunted Iraq Study Group, not otherwise notable for its strategic insight (indeed, most notable for its reiteration of the old shibboleths of "stability"), recognized this much, at least. And yet there are those who, for a variety of reasons — a misguided pacifism, Bush Derangement Syndrome, political calculation — insist that "we're out" is the only answer. In truth, "we're out" is the only answer that utterly fails to satisfy the *jus post bellum,* however one construes it. "We're out" is contemptible, and it is dangerous.

How, then, did the administration's new surge strategy of 2007 comport with a rightly understood *jus post bellum?* As some of its friends have noted from time to time, this has not been an easy administration to help, although in my limited personal experience it has been an administration open to arguments that cut across the grain of current policy. In any event, and not minimizing the failures noted above, the Bush administration seems to have learned from its mistakes rather more than its most vociferous critics, many of whom, throughout 2007, seemed locked in 2006 campaign mode (or preemptive 2008 campaign mode). Defense Secretary Rumsfeld was replaced. A firmer line was laid down to the Iraqi government. The U.S. military did one of the things it does far better than academic, corporate, ecclesiastical, or congressional America: it learned from its mistakes. A strategic review led to a new counter-insurgency military strategy for the pacification of Baghdad and Anbar province. Leadership of that effort was given to the commander with the most impressive in-country record in Iraq, General Petraeus — a man who had thought long and hard about the failures to date of U.S. efforts in Iraq, and who had written the U.S. Army's counter-insurgency Field Manual.

No serious analyst could reasonably expect a quick turnaround in Iraq, given the amount of ground that had already been lost in the second, third, and fourth Iraq wars. But if Petraeus's clear-hold-and-build strategy blunts both Sunni and Shia terrorism and begins to show genuine results in a Baghdad in which the Iraqi government is no longer barricaded inside the Green Zone, then perhaps the next U.S. administration — which will have Iraq on its plate, whether it likes it or not — will be able to address the problem of post–major combat economic and political reconstruction in Iraq in a thoughtful way, and with a measure of bipartisan support.

And if the Petraeus strategy fails because of an intractable local situation, inadequate force levels, and/or complete breakdown of congressional support? What would the *jus post bellum* suggest then?

It would not suggest that "we're out" had automatically become the strategy of moral choice. It would be morally wrong to abandon the Kurds to their fate yet again; indeed, Charles Krauthammer has proposed that, in the event of a collapse of governance in Baghdad, the U.S. should "move much of its personnel to Kurdistan, where we are welcome and safe." Such a move would not only fulfill a moral obligation to a people we betrayed in 1991, when the George H. W. Bush administration allowed Saddam Hussein to reimpose control on Kurdish (and Shia) areas we had encouraged to rise in revolt against the Baathist regime; it would also, arguably, give us a strategic position from which to try to direct events in the region in a better direction, once the post–U.S. withdrawal intra-Iraqi civil war had been resolved. Whether any president or Congress would be capable of proposing, much less doing, that is, of course, another question entirely: should the Petraeus strategy fail, or be forced to fail because of a collapse of congressional will, the domestic political pressure for virtually complete U.S. withdrawal could become irresistible.

There has been much talk of "realism" in the wake of America's post–major combat difficulties in Iraq, much of it involving the misguided appeasement of tyrants (read: Syria) or apocalyptics (read: Iran). An older realism, a Niebuhrian realism, would not be out of place, however, in the intellectual armamentarium of those willing to think through the strategic and moral thicket that is Iraq, 2007: Iraq *in se,* and Iraq in its relationship to the larger, interconnected war against global jihadism. As the Iraq Wars should have reminded us, elements of the Christian realist sensibility — an understanding of the inevitable irony, pathos, and tragedy of history; alertness to unintended consequences; a robust skepticism about schemes of human perfection (especially when politics is the instrument of salvation); cherishing democracy without worshiping it — remain essential intellectual furnishing for anyone thinking in a morally serious way about U.S. foreign policy in the 21st century. Yet as Reinhold Niebuhr himself understood, realism, which is less a comprehensive framework for reflection than a set of intellectual and moral cautions, must always be complemented by a sense of the possibilities of human creativity in history.

Dean Acheson once recalled that, at another moment when history's tectonic plates were shifting, the world he and Harry Truman faced "only slowly revealed itself. As it did so, it began to appear as just a little bit less formidable than that described in the first chapter of Genesis. That was to create a world out of chaos...."[13] The Bush administration, notwithstanding what it got wrong, got that precisely right in its post-9/11 analysis: the challenge today is quite similar to that faced by Truman and Acheson, Marshall and Vandenberg, faced by an ideological enemy with global pretensions in the late 1940s. In building a 21st-century world out of the chaos caused by the intersection of feckless late-20th-century Western policies and global jihadism, Americans should certainly be realistic. But in being realistic, we would do well to remember the counsel of the late public philosopher Charles Frankel: "The heart of the policy-making process... is not the finding of a national interest already perfectly known and understood. It is the determining of that interest: the reassessment of the nation's resources, needs, commitments, traditions, and political and cultural horizons — in short, its calendar of values."[14]

The Bush administration's efforts to accelerate change in the Arab Islamic world were determined by a realistic assessment of the situation after 9/11: the "custodians of American power," Fouad Ajami wisely noted, "were under great pressure to force history's pace."[15] To attempt to accelerate the transition to responsible and responsive government in the Middle East was a realistic objective, given an unacceptable status quo that was inherently unstable; that was unstable because it was corrupt; and that was producing terrorists and jihadists determined to challenge those corruptions and then expand their power globally. Accelerating the transition to responsible and responsive government in the Arab Islamic world was the grand strategic idea that impelled the United States to bring the "foreigner's gift" to Iraq. The implementation of that grand strategic idea was clumsy, to the point where success was put in jeopardy; but the idea itself was a noble one. Moreover, the prescription it embodied was correct, for as Bernard Lewis has argued, "The war against terror and the quest for freedom are inextricably linked, and neither can succeed without the other."[16]

If the Iraqi phase of the quest for freedom and a new politics in the Arab Islamic world ends in defeat for the United States and bloody chaos for the people of Iraq, we may be sure that the war against jihadism will suffer commensurately, as al-Qaeda and its allies take to describing the American defeat in Iraq as the equivalent of the Soviet defeat in Afghanistan — a telling moment in which the infidels conceded to the power of jihad. No one — in the Congress, in the churches, in the academy, or on the street — can wish for that and still claim the mantle of moral seriousness.

Chapter Twelve

Is Europe Dying?
Secularist Shibboleths and
the Future of the West

*In the wake of 9/11, policy differences sharpened between the
United States and some of its European allies. These differences
were variously analyzed in terms of different readings of modern history or divergent national interests, both of which were
surely in play. Yet it seemed to me that the differences cut deeper,
and reflected a European crisis of civilizational morale, the deepest roots of which were religious, even theological. I proposed a
reading of "Europe's problem," based on Henri de Lubac's analysis
of the drama of atheistic humanism, in the 2003 Simon Lecture, stressing that the secularist bias in European high culture —
which the Jewish legal scholar Joseph Weiler had aptly described
as "Christophobia" — had its analogues in the United States.
"Europe's problem," in other words, was also America's, if in a
different form. That analysis formed the basis of my 2005 book,*
The Cube and the Cathedral: Europe, America, and Politics
without God, *which caused a satisfying fuss on both sides of the
Atlantic.*

The editors of Commentary *asked me to revisit these questions in 2006, and to explore how the intra-European culture war over the meaning of "tolerance" and the place of religiously informed moral conviction in public life intersected with Europe's struggles to assimilate its rapidly expanding Muslim populations. The result was the essay "Europe's Two Culture Wars," which appeared in the May 2006 issue of* Commentary. *Subsequently, I was able to test the article's arguments against the sharp young minds gathered by the Catholic campus ministry at Princeton University and by the Institute for Political Studies at the Catholic University of Portugal in Lisbon.*

During this same period, I came into contact with Senator Marcello Pera, a distinguished Italian philosopher of science who had co-authored with then-Cardinal Joseph Ratzinger a provocative book, Without Roots, *which explored Europe's present distress and future prospects. Senator Pera and I then shared a platform at the United Nations in November 2006, during the presentation of another Ratzinger book on Europe,* Christianity and the Crisis of Cultures, *to which Pera had contributed an introduction. My remarks on that occasion further extended the analysis in "Europe's Two Culture Wars" and have been incorporated into the text here, thus giving the essay below its final form.*

T HE CENTENARY of the "guns of August" and the beginning of the First World War loom close on the horizon. As living memories of World War I have faded, the designation of that conflict as the "Great War" has nonetheless become more secure. For as the 20th century gave way to the 21st, it became ever more clear that the Great War was the decisive event that set the 20th century on its distinctive course.

Indeed, if we define "the 20th century," not by the conventions of chronology, but by its political history, we can see that the 20th century began with the guns of August 1914 and ended when the last great political effects of the Great War were swept from the board in August 1991, with the death of the Soviet Union. Everything that happened in between — the false peace of the interwar period, the Great Depression and the rise of the totalitarian systems, World War II, the Cold War — all of these were, either directly or indirectly, the by-products of the Great War.

Much of this seems to have been understood, on both sides of the Atlantic: that the "19th century" really ran from the Congress of Vienna until August 1914; that the "20th century" began in August 1914 and ended in August 1991; and that the Great War was the axial moment that set the 20th century in motion.

Yet as the West marks the centenary of those cataclysmic events, a hard question has forced itself upon us: Can the West anticipate, with any degree of confidence, that it will have maintained its essential cultural and political form at the bicentenary, the two hundredth anniversary, of the Great War? The answer to that question is almost certainly "No."

Why can we not be sure that the West of 2114 will be in clear and unmistakable continuity with the West of 2014 and the West of 1914 — much less the West of 1514 or 714 or 314? Not because global warming (whatever that may or may not be) will result in Lisbon, New York, and Sydney sinking beneath the waves caused by melting polar ice, but because the West is a proposition culture, built on the foundation of certain ideas and truth claims. If our civilization's grasp on those truths weakens, then our civilization cannot give an account of itself, to itself or to other civilizations. And if cannot give an account, it is in mortal peril.

The West is losing its ability to give an account of its deepest political commitments, and that form of intellectual and moral disarmament is leading to grave danger. The problem is most acute in Europe, which in recent decades has been suffering from a crisis of civilizational morale. That crisis of cultural confidence began to manifest its effects in earnest in the Great War; but the contemporary European crisis of civilization morale could only have come to the surface and be seen for what it is when the political effects of the Great War were finally behind us, as they have been since August 1991.

In American coal mines, in the days before proper ventilation, miners used to take a caged canary with them into the depths of the earth. When the canary began to wobble, and eventually keeled over and fell to the floor of the cage, it was the signal that the air had become too toxic and that the miners had to leave that particular shaft. In recent decades, Europe, in its crisis of civilizational morale, has been functioning as a kind of canary-in-the-mineshaft for the entire West. Europe's present distress is a warning that the cultural air is becoming too toxic to sustain democratic life. Conversely, Europe's cultural and moral renewal could point the way to a brighter 21st century for the entire Western world, and indeed for the world as a whole. But make no mistake about it: unless Europe finds within itself the resources to emerge from its present malaise with spiritual, cultural, and political vigor — and does so in the next twenty years — then the Europe of 2114 will almost certainly not be in any recognizable continuity with the Europe of 2014, or 1914, or 314.

And that brings us to Europe's two culture wars, which came into focus in an acute way in Spain in 2004.

Bombs at Sunrise

At the height of the morning commute on March 11, 2004, ten bombs exploded in and around four Madrid train stations. Almost two hundred Spaniards were killed, and some two thousand wounded. The next day, Spain seemed to be standing firm, with demonstrators around the country wielding signs denouncing the "Murderers" and "Assassins." Yet things didn't hold, and seventy-two hours after the bombs had strewn arms, legs, heads, and other body parts over three train stations and a marshaling yard, the Spanish government of José María Aznar, a staunch ally of the United States and Great Britain in the Iraq War, was soundly defeated in an election the socialist opposition had long sought to turn into a referendum on Spain's role in the war on jihadist terrorism.

As, evidently, did the al-Qaeda operatives who set the bombs. A fifty-four-page al-Qaeda document that came to light three months after the bombings speculated that the Aznar government "cannot suffer more than two or three strikes before pulling out under pressure from its own people." For the pro-Western government of José María Aznar, it was, in the event, one strike and out — as it was for Spanish troops in Iraq, who were withdrawn, as the new prime minister, José Luis Rodríguez Zapatero, had promised the day after Spanish voters chose appeasement.

Five days short of the second anniversary of the Madrid bombings, the Zapatero government, which had already legalized marriage between same-sex couples and had sought to restrict religious education in Spanish schools, announced that the words "father" and "mother" would no longer appear on Spanish birth certificates. Rather, according to the Official Bulletin of the State, "the expression 'father' will be replaced by 'Progenitor A,' and 'mother' will be replaced by 'Progenitor B.'" The chief of the National Civil Registry, Pilar Blanco-Morales, explained to the Madrid daily *ABC* that the change simply brought birth certificates into line with Spain's same-sex marriage legislation. Irish commentator David Quinn, more acute, saw in the new regulations "the withdrawal of the state's recognition of the role of mothers and fathers and the extinction of biology and nature, all in the name of equality." A storm of protest eventually led to the rescinding of this order (which was, in fact, ironically sexist), but not before the larger point about the worldview of the Zapatero government and the European cultural forces it embodied had been made.

At first blush, the Madrid bombings and the Newspeak of "Progenitor A" and "Progenitor B" might seem tenuously connected, and only by the vagaries of electoral politics: the bombings, aggravating public opinion against a conservative government, led to the installation of a leftist prime minister, who then proceeded to do many of the things that aggressively secularizing governments have tried to do in Spain in the past. In fact, the nexus is more complex than that. For these events in Spain were a microcosm of the two interrelated culture wars that beset western Europe today.

The first of these — call it "Culture War A," following the example of Spain's birth certificates — is a sharper form of the red state/blue state divide in America: a culture war between the postmodern forces of moral relativism and the defenders of traditional moral conviction. The second — "Culture War B" — is the struggle to define the nature of civil society, the meaning of tolerance and pluralism, and the limits of multiculturalism in an aging Europe whose below-replacement-level birth rates have opened the door to rapidly growing and increasingly assertive Muslim populations. The aggressors in Culture War A are radical secularists, motivated by what Jewish legal scholar Joseph Weiler has dubbed "Christophobia."[1] They aim to eliminate the vestiges of Europe's Judeo-Christian culture from a post-Christian European Union by demanding same-sex marriage in the name of equality, by restricting free speech in the name of civility, and by abrogating core aspects of religious freedom in the name of tolerance. The aggressors in Culture War B are radical and jihadist Muslims who detest the West, who are determined to impose Islamic taboos on Western societies by violent protest and other forms of coercion if necessary, and who see such operations as the first stage toward the Islamification of Europe — or, in the case of what they often refer to as *al-Andalus,* the restoration of the right order of things, temporarily reversed in 1492 by the *Reconquista* of Ferdinand and Isabella.

The question Europe must face, but which much of Europe seems reluctant to face, is whether the aggressors in Culture War A have not made it exceptionally difficult for the forces of genuine civility, true tolerance, and authentic civil society to prevail in Culture War B.

From P.C. to the Dictatorship of Relativism

Western Europe's descent into the languors of "depoliticization," as the French political theorist Pierre Manent has called it, once seemed a matter of welfare-state politics, socialist economics, and protectionist trade policy, flavored by irritating E.U. regulations on everything from the proper circumference of tomatoes to the proper care and feeding of Sardinian hogs.[2] And, to be sure, there has been no let-up, but in fact an expansion, of Europe's seeming determination to bind itself ever more tightly in the cords of bureaucratic regulation. Visitors to Poland after its 2004 accession to the E.U. noticed that most eggs sold in Polish grocery stores carried an official, multi-digit E.U. numeric code (which, as one acerbic Polish intellectual put it, "probably includes the farmer's birthday and the chicken's, too"); hikers in the Polish Tatras noted that every sheep in sight had an official E.U. tag stapled into one of its ears. Then there is Big Brussels Brother's regulation of the workplace. In 2005, a British church had to pay almost $2,500 to change five light bulbs in its ceiling, thanks to the E.U.'s "Schedule Six of the Working-at-Heights Directive" — another glorious piece of Newspeak but, as it happens, an expensive one. Because Schedule Six's mandatory "risk assessment" precluded the village electricians from using ladders, an enormous scaffolding had to be erected inside St. Benet's in Eccles, Suffolk, and the two-day job worked out at about $500 per bulb.[3]

Yet even as Europe's regulatory passions continue to have deleterious economic consequences, they have also been sharpened to a harder ideological edge, redolent of Weiler's "Christophobia," in recent years. In October 2005, for example, the official custodians of Dutch orthographic probity decreed that, beginning in August 2006, "Christ" must be written with a lower-case "c," while "Jews" (*joden*) would be spelled with a capital "J" when denominating nationality and a lower-case "j" when indicating members of a religion.[4] In early 2006, an atheist math teacher won a discrimination case in Scotland after claiming that his application for a "pastoral care post" at a Catholic school had been declined on the grounds that the school intolerantly reserved such positions for Catholics.[5] Thus Culture War A is, in part, a determined effort on the part of secularist aggressors to marginalize the public presence and impact of Europe's dwindling numbers of practicing Christians.

Culture War A also involves crucial questions about the beginning and end of life, and nowhere are these issues more sharply posed than in the no-longer-tradition-bound Low Countries. The Netherlands has long enjoyed a reputation for legalized libertinism involving drugs and prostitution, while leading Europe along the path to euthanasia and same-sex marriage. Now, formerly stolid Belgium, land of gray skies and monastic beer, seems determined to catch up in the charge toward the brave new world of technologized begetting and technologized dying — two practices that concretize the idea of freedom as unencumbered personal license. In addition to matching their Dutch neighbors' embrace of same-sex marriage and euthanasia (half the infant deaths in Flanders in

1999–2000 were from euthanasia), the Belgians found themselves embroiled in a 2005 case in which a rent-a-uterus mother had sold the child she gestated to a Dutch couple rather than to the Belgian couple who had, so to speak, "ordered" the youngster; the Dutch couple finally won.[6] As the Italian philosopher and government minister Rocco Buttiglione put it, "Once we used to quote Karl Marx when protesting against the 'alienation,' 'objectification,' and 'commercialization' of human life. Can it be possible that, today, the left is inscribing on its banners precisely the right to commercialize human beings" — all, of course, in the name of tolerance and equality?

Culture War A also finds expression in efforts to coerce and impose behaviors deemed progressive, non-judgmental, compassionate, or politically correct in the most extreme feminist or multiculturalist terms. In recent years, this has typically taken the form of E.U. member-states legally regulating, and thus restricting, public commentary, with morally critical comments about homosexual behavior being deemed "hate speech." Thus a French parliamentarian was fined in 2005 for saying that heterosexuality was morally superior to homosexuality. But the stakes here have been raised considerably, and at the transnational level. For in February 2006, pressure from the E.U. brought down the governing coalition in one of the E.U.'s new members, Slovakia, in what may have been the world's first coup d'etat instigated by transnational quango (a quasi-autonomous non-governmental organization).

The Slovaks had negotiated a concordat (a treaty regulating the legal position of the Catholic Church in Slovakia) with the Vatican; the concordat stipulated that Slovak law would provide a conscience clause respecting the decision of doctors who, for reasons of moral conviction, chose not to perform abortions. This provision of the concordat was bitterly attacked by the E.U.'s Network of Independent Experts on Fundamental Human Rights, which is composed of one member from each of the E.U. member states and advises the European Commission and the European Parliament. According to the Network's forty-page report, medical professionals cannot be permitted *not* to participate in abortions. Why? Because, the report claims, the right to abort a child is an international human right while the right to religiously informed conscientious objection (or, indeed, any other form of conscientious objection) is "not unlimited." The ensuing parliamentary debate in Bratislava over the risks of offending the human rights mandarins of Brussels and Strasbourg — who not-so-subtly threatened economic retaliation and even suspension of Slovakia's E.U. membership if the Slovaks didn't disabuse themselves of conscience-clauses in their abortion law — destabilized the center-right coalition government to the point where the prime minister dissolved parliament and called new elections.[7]

All of which, in terms of Culture War A, was of a piece with a January 2006 resolution of the European Parliament condemning states that do not recognize same-sex marriage as "homophobic"; the resolution also referred to religious freedom as a "source of discrimination."[8] During the debate on the resolution, the threat of suspension of E.U. membership was again raised against countries like Poland and Lithuania by British Euro-MP Michael Cashman, who equated traditional marriage laws with "[a] breach [of] the human rights of gay and lesbian people."[9] Poland was similarly threatened with a suspension of voting rights in the E.U.'s ministerial meetings if it reinstituted capital punishment, as Polish president Lech Kaczynski had suggested he would do during his 2005 electoral campaign.

Demographic Suicide

Whatever else might be said about these developments, that Europe finds itself embroiled at this particular moment in its history in a bitterly contested culture war over the legal imposition of political correctness strikes even the friendliest observer as a bizarre distraction from the most dramatic fact about the continent in the early 21st century: Europe is committing demographic suicide, and has been doing so for some time. Environmental extremists like the Club of Rome and anti-natalist demagogues like Paul Ehrlich once predicted that, as the world ran out of various things by the end of the 20th century—gold, zinc, tin, mercury, petroleum, copper, lead, natural gas, and so forth—humanity would also be crushed beneath rampant "overpopulation." At the beginning of the 21st century, the world is still chock-full of natural resources. Europe, however, is running out of the most crucial resource—people.

The overall picture is sobering enough. As of 2007, not a single E.U. member state had a replacement-level total fertility rate (the 2.1 children/woman needed to maintain a stable population). Moreover, eleven E.U. countries — including Germany, Austria, Italy, Hungary, and all three Baltic states—displayed "negative natural increase" (i.e., more annual deaths than births), a clear step down into the demographic death-spiral. These figures are striking enough in the aggregate. Yet the devil is in the demographic details, which graphically illustrate what happens when a continent healthier, wealthier, and more secure than ever before refuses to produce the human future in the most elemental sense, by creating successor generations.

Thanks to generation after generation of below-replacement-level reproduction, the same Belgians who are rushing into ever more advanced forms of political correctness may well see their population drop to 4.5 million by mid-century. The Spaniards, whose government is busily dismantling traditional social and cultural life, will likely see their population cut by almost 25 percent by 2050.

German politics seems incapable of facing, much less addressing, the fiscal consequences of Germany's deliberate infertility, which has led to a dire situation in which a shrinking number of taxpaying workers attempt to support an increasing number of retirees in the state pension system, as well as the entire state-run health care system. Indeed, things have gone so far that Germany will likely lose the equivalent of the entire population of the former East Germany by mid-century. None of this is unknown, and German president Horst Köhler has made something of a public cause out of raising Germany's birth rate; but a 2006 poll indicated that 25 percent of German men and 30 percent of German women in their twenties intended to have no children — and saw no problems with a lifestyle choice that will exacerbate the problems caused by the present 1.39 birth rate.[10]

Then there is Italy. The large, extended Italian family is a staple of the world's imagination about Italian life. The truth of the matter is far different: by 2050, on present trends, almost 60 percent of Italians will not know, from personal experience, what a brother, sister, aunt, uncle, or cousin is. But this is perhaps not surprising in a country in which the average age of a man when his first child is born is thirty-three and in which the ratio of over-sixty-five-year-olds to under-fifteen-year-olds has reached 137.7:100. (Germany, Spain, Portugal, and Greece also have more over-sixty-fives than under-fifteens, in somewhat less severe ratios; the average age for first-time fatherhood in Spain is thirty or thirty-one, as it is in France.) Nor is this demographic meltdown limited to "Old Europe"; Bulgaria is projected to lose 36 percent of its population by 2050, and Estonia 52 percent.

By 2030, as an average across the E.U., numbers of workers will decline by 7 percent while over-sixty-five-year-olds will increase by 50 percent. This will create intolerable fiscal pressures on the welfare state across the continent; the resulting intergenerational strains will put great pressures on national politics; and those pressures may, in a variety of ways, put paid to the project of "Europe" as it has been envisioned since the European Coal and Steel Community, the institutional forerunner of today's European Union, was established in 1952. Demography is a very large part of destiny, and Europe's demographics of decline — which are unparalleled in human history, absent wars, plagues, and natural catastrophes — are creating enormous and unavoidable political, economic, and social problems. Even more ominously, though, Europe's demographic free-fall is the link between Culture War A and Culture War B.

The Coming of Eurabia?

History abhors certain demographic vacuums, and the vacuum created by Europe's self-destructive fertility and birth rates has, for several generations now, been filled by a large-scale immigration from throughout the Islamic world. For those who took the trouble to look, the most obvious effects of that immigration could be seen in recent decades in Europe's increasingly segregated urban landscape, in which an impoverished Muslim suburban periphery typically surrounds an affluent European urban core. Extensive Islamic immigration and high fertility rates among immigrant Muslims have changed far more than the look of European metropolitan areas, however.

The U.S. government estimates that there are more than one hundred "ungovernable" areas in France: Muslim-dominated suburbs, mainly, where the writ of French law does not run and into which the French police do not go. Similar extraterritorial enclaves, in which *shari'a* law is enforced by local Muslim clerics, can be found in other European countries, including Great Britain. Moreover, as Bruce Bawer detailed in *While Europe Slept,* European authorities pay little or no attention to practices among their Muslim populations that range from the physically cruel (female circumcision) through the morally cruel (arranged and forced marriages) to the socially disruptive (remanding Muslim children back to radical madrassas in the Middle East, North Africa, and Pakistan for their primary and secondary education) and the illegal ("honor" killings in cases of adultery and rape — the rape victim being the one killed).[11] Indeed, as Bawer showed, it is not simply a case of European governments choosing not to pay attention; Europe's welfare systems generously support immigrants who despise their host countries — and in more than a few instances turn violently against them (most notably, in the London Underground and bus bombings of July 7, 2005). Yet, thanks to the politically correct liberality of European criminal law, seditious Muslim criminals are treated in ways that seem reminiscent of the Red Queen's world of "impossible things before breakfast": thus Muhammad Bouyeri, the Dutch-Moroccan who murdered film-maker Theo van Gogh in 2004 in the middle of an Amsterdam street and then affixed a personal fatwa to his victim's chest with a kitchen knife, retains the right to vote — and could, if he wished, run for the Dutch parliament. (Meanwhile, at least two Dutch parliamentarians critical of Islamist extremism were forced by Islamist threats to live in prisons or army compounds under police or military guard; one subsequently emigrated.)

Those who imagined that the European instinct for appeasement died on September 1, 1939, have been forced to reconsider in recent years. French public swimming pools have been gender-segregated because of Muslim protests. "Piglet" mugs have disappeared from certain British retailers, after Muslim complaints that the A. A. Milne character was offensive to Islamic sensibilities; so did Burger King chocolate ice-cream swirls that reminded some Muslims of Arabic script from the Qur'an. Bawer reported that the British Red Cross banished Christmas trees and nativity scenes from its charity stores for fear of offending Muslims, while, for similar reasons, the Dutch police destroyed a piece of Rotterdam street art that proclaimed "Thou shalt not kill" in the wake of the van Gogh murder. Meanwhile, Dutch schoolchildren are forbidden to display Dutch flags on their backpacks because immigrants might think them "provocative."

The European media frequently censors itself in matters relating to domestic Islamic radicalism and crimes committed by Muslims, and, with rare exceptions, its coverage of the war against jihadist terrorism makes the American mainstream media look remarkably balanced. When certain domestic problems related to Muslim immigrants do come to light, the typical European reaction, according to Bawer, is usually one of self-critique. Thus when rapes, robberies, school-burnings, honor killings, and anti-Semitic agitations got so out of hand in Malmö that the Swedish press had to report that large numbers of native Swedes were abandoning the country's third-largest city, the Swedish government's report on the situation blamed Malmö's problems on Swedish racism, and chastised Swedes who mistakenly thought about integrating immigrants in "two hierarchically ordered categories, a 'we' who shall integrate and a 'they' who shall be integrated." Belgium, for its part, has established a governmental Centre for Equal Opportunities and Opposition to Racism [CEEOR], which once sued a manufacturer, Feryn, for "racism" because Feryn's Moroccan employees work in the company's factory and are not sent out to install the company's security garage gates in Belgian homes. Conversely, CEEOR declined to prosecute a Muslim who created a Jew-baiting cartoon series in order not to "inflame" the situation.

Perhaps predictably, European Jews have frequently played the role of the canary in the mine-shaft amidst the trials of Islamic integration in Europe. Two years ago, a Parisian disc jockey was brutally murdered, his assailant crying, "I have killed my Jew. I will go to heaven"; that same night, another Muslim murdered a Jewish woman while her daughter watched, horrified. Yet, as columnist Mark Steyn wrote, "No major French newspaper carried the story" of these homicides, despite the ominous trend they suggested. In February, the French media did report on the gruesome murder of a

twenty-three-year-old Jewish man, Ilan Halimi, who had been tor-
tured for three weeks by an Islamist gang; his screams under torture
were heard by his family during phone calls demanding ransom
"while the torturers read out verses from the Qur'an," according
to Steyn. Halimi's murder was reported in the French press — but
with disclaimers from the public authorities about anti-Semitism.
Steyn, one of the few Western op-ed regulars to pay sustained attention to all this, reported one police detective shrugging off the
jihadist dimension of this horror by saying that it was all rather
simple: "Jews equal money."[12]

There is little to be said for the sagacity of the politicians who attempted to appease totalitarian aggression in the 1930s; for all their
blindness, though, they were at least men who thought that, by
preserving peace through appeasement, they were preserving their
way of life. Bruce Bawer (following Bat Ye'or) argued, correctly,
that 21st-century Europe's appeasement of Islamists amounts to
self-inflicted "dhimmitude": in an attempt to slow the advance of
a rising Islamist tide, many of Europe's national and transnational
political leaders are surrendering core aspects of sovereignty and
turning Europe's native populations into second- and third-class
citizens, *dhimmis,* in their own countries.

These patterns of sedition and appeasement finally came to international attention in early 2006 in the Danish cartoons jihad.
Despite the fact that the Danish government was beginning to address some of the problems of Islamic non-integration into Danish
society, the original publication in the Copenhagen daily *Jyllands-
Posten* of a set of cartoons depicting the Prophet Muhammad
caused little comment, in Denmark or anywhere else. But after several Islamist Danish imams began agitating throughout the Middle
East (aided by three additional, and far more offensive, cartoons of
their own devising), an international furor erupted, with dozens
of people killed by rioting Muslims in Europe, Africa, and Asia.
As Henrik Bering wrote at the time, "The Danes were suddenly

the most hated people on earth, with their embassies under attack, their flag being burned, and their consciousness being raised by lectures on religious tolerance from Iran, Saudi Arabia, and other beacons of enlightenment."[13]

And the response from Europe, in the main, was to intensify appeasement. Thus the Italian "reforms minister," Roberto Calderoli, resigned under pressure from Prime Minister Silvio Berlusconi, because Calderoli had worn a T-shirt featuring one of the offending cartoons — which "thoughtless action," Berlusconi deduced, had caused a riot outside the Italian consulate in Benghazi in which eleven people were killed. Newspapers which ran the cartoons were put under intense political pressure; some journalists faced criminal charges; Web sites were forced to close. The pan-European Carrefour supermarket chain, bowing to Islamist demands for a boycott of Danish goods, placed signs in its stores, in both Arabic and English, expressing "solidarity" with the "Islamic community" and noting, inelegantly if revealingly, "Carrefour don't carry Danish products." The Norwegian government forced the editor of a Christian publication to apologize publicly for printing the Danish cartoons, at a press conference at which the hapless editor was surrounded (appropriately enough) by Norwegian cabinet ministers and imams. E.U. foreign minister Javier Solana groveled his way from one Arab nation to another, pleading that Europeans shared the "anguish" of Muslims "offended" by the Danish cartoons. And, not to be outdone by those appeasement-obsessed national governments which were in headlong flight from traditional concepts of freedom of the press and free speech, the E.U.'s justice minister, Franco Frattini, announced in early February that the E.U. would establish a "media code" to encourage "prudence." Which in this instance is a synonym for "surrender" — irrespective of one's view of artistic merits of, or the cultural sensitivity displayed by, the world's most notorious cartoons.

Dying from Debonair Nihilism

Bruce Bawer blames Europe's appeasement mentality and the self-imposed dhimmitude it creates on multiculturalist political correctness run amok. And there is surely something to that indictment. For, in a nice piece of intellectual irony, European multiculturalism, which is bottomed on postmodern theories of the incoherence of knowledge (and thus the relativity of all truth claims), has itself become utterly incoherent. A French Islamic organization in Champagne-Ardennes, composed of immigrants from countries where "human rights" are not, to be gentle, entirely secure, brought suit in the European Court of Human Rights in 2006, charging that the Danish cartoons were acts of "discrimination" against Muslims, who, presumably, deserve legal protection from anything they deem offensive. Or take a brace of examples from the U.K.: Prime Minister Tony Blair appoints Iqbal Sacranie, General Secretary of the Muslim Council of Britain, as one of his advisors on Muslim affairs and procures him a knighthood; Sir Iqbal tells the BBC that homosexuality "damages the very foundation of society" and, following the protests of a British gay lobby, is investigated by the "community safety unit" of Scotland Yard, whose mandate includes "hate crimes and homophobia"; then, when a Muslim lobby demands that Blair scrap the "Holocaust Memorial Day" he created several years ago, Sir Iqbal backs their demands, telling the *Daily Telegraph* that "Muslims feel hurt and excluded that their lives are not equally valuable to those lives lost in the Holocaust time." It all does seem remarkably like something from beyond Lewis Carroll's looking glass.

Yet to blame "multi-culti" p.c. for Europe's paralysis in the face of its advancing dhimmitude is to remain on the surface of things. Culture War A — the attempt to impose multiculturalism and lifestyle libertinism in Europe by limiting free speech, defining religious and moral conviction as bigotry, and using state power to enforce "inclusivity" and "sensitivity" — is a war over the very meaning of tolerance itself. What Bruce Bawer rightly deplores as out-of-control political correctness in Europe is rooted in a deeper malady: a rejection of the belief that human beings, however inadequately or incompletely, can grasp the truth of things — a belief that has, for almost two millennia, underwritten European civilization. Postmodern European high culture rejects that conviction. And because it can only conceive of "your truth" and "my truth" while determinedly rejecting any idea of "the truth," it can only conceive of tolerance as indifference to differences — an indifference to be maintained by coercive state power, if necessary. The idea of tolerance as engaging differences within the bond of civility (as Richard John Neuhaus once put it) is itself, well, intolerant. Thus those who would defend the true tolerance of orderly public argument about contending truth claims (which include religious and moral convictions) risk being driven, and in many cases are driven, from the European public square by being branded as "bigots."

Europe's soul-withering skepticism has also led to a form of what the late Alan Bloom once styled "debonair nihilism." And while Europe's depopulation has been caused by many factors (economic, social, even ideological), that nihilism is a critical factor in Europe's unwillingness to create the future by creating successor generations. Europe's infidelity to the future (which is shaped in part by a p.c. rejection of Europe's past) has, in turn, created the demographic vacuum now being filled by peoples who, even in their second and third generations, reject integration and pose a profound threat to Europe's cultural identity.

Europe's skepticism about the truth of anything has also led to a culturally corrosive moral relativism that eventually yields political paralysis. Bruce Bawer, who left America for Europe because of the influence of the Religious Right on American politics and because Europe was far more open than the United States to same-sex marriage, cannot seem to grasp that what made Europe attractive to those like himself — its moral "openness" — is what has made Europe so vulnerable to radical Islam. For it is precisely the same radical skepticism that grounds Europe's lifestyle libertinism that could lead Jacques Derrida, then one of the high priests of European postmodernism, to famously say, after September 11, 2001, "We do not in fact know what we are saying or naming in this way: September 11, *le 11 septembre,* 9/11."

Bawer proposed that Europe regain its nerve and defend its free societies by rejecting multicultural political correctness while retaining the political expression of skepticism and relativism: freedom concretized in law as radical personal autonomy. But it is the imperialism of the autonomous Self that helps maintain Europe's steep demographic decline; it is the imperialism of the autonomous Self that has led Europe to deprecate its own civilizational achievements, seeing in its history only repression and intolerance; and it is the imperialism of the autonomous Self that underwrites political correctness and its corrosive effects on Europe's capacity to defend itself against internal Islamist aggression, be that aggression violent or not.

Beyond the Dictatorship of Relativism

An alternative — and far more persuasive — analysis of early-21st-century Europe's culture wars has emerged from a remarkable dialogue that began in 2004. The partners in the conversation were, to some, a bit of a surprise: Marcello Pera, an agnostic academic turned politician (and president of the Italian Senate), and Cardinal Joseph Ratzinger, then the prefect of the Congregation for the Doctrine of the Faith, the principal theological agency of the Catholic Church. Pera gave a lecture on "Relativism, Christianity, and the West" at Rome's Pontifical Lateran University; Ratzinger, at Pera's invitation, gave a lecture in the Italian Senate on "The Spiritual Roots of Europe"; the two men then agreed to exchange letters exploring the striking convergence of analysis that had characterized their lectures. The lectures and letters were published in a small book in Italy in early 2005 and created something of a stir; the stir intensified after April 19, 2005, when Joseph Ratzinger became Pope Benedict XVI. The Ratzinger/Pera volume was subsequently published in the United States under the title *Without Roots: The West, Relativism, Christianity, Islam.*[14]

Long before becoming the 265th Bishop of Rome, Joseph Ratzinger, a widely respected intellectual who had succeeded the late Andrei Sakharov in the latter's chair at the prestigious French *Académie des Sciences Morales et Politiques,* had been warning his fellow-Europeans that their dalliance in the intellectual sandbox of postmodernism was going to cause the most severe problems for their societies and their polities. Thus Ratzinger was returning to familiar territory when he sharply criticized a Europe that "seems hollow, as if it were internally paralyzed by a failure of its circulatory system." And that circulatory failure, he argued, is at one and the same time intellectual, spiritual, and moral: the "crumbling of [European] man's original certainties about God, himself, and the universe" has led, in turn, to "the decline of a moral conscience grounded in absolute values [that] is still our problem today." All of which has led, Ratzinger concluded, to the "real danger" of "the self-destruction of the European conscience," which is being prefigured now in a "peculiar Western self-hatred that is nothing short of pathological." Why is it, Ratzinger asked, that Europe "has lost all capacity for self-love?" Why is it that Europe can see in its own history only "the despicable and the destructive; [that] it is no longer able to perceive what is great and pure?"

Marcello Pera's answer to that question, and others, about Europe's current condition was the welcome news in *Without Roots.* Europe's secularist cultural mandarins had heard critiques like Ratzinger's before, and had typically dismissed them as the special pleading of committed Christians. Now came a parallel critique from a self-described *non credente* and philosopher of science. Europe, Pera wrote, is "infected by an epidemic of relativism. It believes that all cultures are equivalent. It refuses to judge them, thinking that to accept and defend one's culture would be an act of hegemony, of intolerance, that betrayed an anti-democratic, anti-liberal, disrespectful attitude." And it is precisely the toxin of relativism, Pera argued, that has led Europe into "the prison-house of insincerity and hypocrisy known as political correctness. Europe has locked itself in this cage for fear of saying things that are not at all incorrect but rather ordinary truths, and to avoid facing its own responsibilities and the consequences of what might be said." Including the things that must be said about the difficulties of integrating Europe's Muslims, who too often come to Europe absent many of the habits of heart and mind necessary to be contributing citizens of a pluralist democracy; for as Pera insisted, "Integration does not mean having equal departure points. It means sharing an equal willingness to accept the common arrival point."

Pera was also blunt about the effects of European moral relativism on Europe's willingness to defend itself. Do Europeans understand, he wrote, "that their very existence is at stake, their civilization has been targeted, their culture is under attack? Do they understand that what they are being called on to defend is their own identity? Through culture, education, diplomatic negotiations, political relations, economic exchange, dialogue, preaching, but also, if necessary, through force? I fear that Europe has not realized this. And thus I fear that European pacifism, however noble and generous it may be, is not so much a realistic, meditated, conscious choice as a heedless, passive consequence of its angelic relativism." (Or, as another philosopher-critic of Europe's current cast of mind, France's Chantal Delsol, has aptly put it, "Our contemporary [European] cannot imagine for what cause he would sacrifice his life because he does not know what this life means."[15])

In his essay in *Without Roots,* Ratzinger adopted an idea from Toynbee and proposed that any renewal of Europe's civilizational morale can be effected only by "creative minorities" who will challenge secularism as the de facto ideology of the European Union by proposing a European re-encounter with Europe's Judeo-Christian religious and moral heritage. Pera, for his part, proposed that the needed "work of renewal...be done by Christians and secularists together," and in February 2006 gave a first demonstration of what such a new political-cultural configuration might mean when he launched a movement called "For the West, the Bearer of Civilization." The movement's manifesto began by briskly describing Europe's two culture wars: "The West is in crisis. Attacked externally by fundamentalism and Islamic terrorism, it is not able to rise to the challenge. Undermined internally by a moral and spiritual crisis, it can't seem to find the courage to react." The two culture wars have, in turn, led to paralysis: "Our affluence makes us feel guilty and we are ashamed of our traditions. Terrorism is seen as a reaction to our errors, whereas it is nothing less than an act of aggression against our civilization and against all humankind." The manifesto went on to affirm Western civilization as "a source of universal and inalienable principles," and commits its signatories (who included a center-right spread of Italian intellectual and political figures) to a broad agenda of renewal: to "deprive [terrorism] of every justification and support"; to integrate immigrants "in the name of shared values...without, in any way, accepting that the rights of any one group should prevail [over] those of its individuals"; to support "the right to life from conception until natural death"; to dismantle unnecessary bureaucracy according to "the principle of 'as much liberty as possible, as much State as necessary' "; to "affirm the value of the family as a natural partnership based on marriage"; to spread "liberty and democracy as universal values"; to maintain the institutional separation of Church and state "without giving in to the secular temptation of

relegating the religious dimension solely to the individual sphere";
and to promote a healthy pluralism in education, including "full
equality...for both state and private schools." The manifesto concluded with a call to ideological arms and a warning: "We are
committed...to highlighting the values of conservative liberalism
so that the growth of public and individual freedom may develop at
the same rate as the preservation of our common heritage. People
who forget their roots can be neither free nor respected."[16]

Pascal's Wager, Revisited

Joseph Ratzinger and Marcello Pera deepened their conversation
in another book, published a year after *Without Roots* appeared in
the United States. A close reading of Ratzinger's *Christianity and
the Crisis of Cultures,* to which Pera provided a thoughtful and
lengthy introduction, also suggested that, several years before his
now-famous September 2006 lecture at the University of Regensburg, the man who would become Pope Benedict XVI had distilled
a lifetime of reflection on the relationship between faith and reason, and on the cultural consequences of a collapse of both faith
and reason, into a challenge of prime importance for anyone who
cares about the future of the West.[17]

   In the controversy immediately following the Regensburg Lecture, it will be remembered, attention focused exclusively on Pope
Benedict's analysis of certain theological tendencies in Islam and
their unhappy consequences in the world of politics. Yet the
Regensburg Lecture was in fact addressed at least as much to the
West as to Islam. Yes, the Pope warned that an unreasonable faith
is a real and present danger to the world — a faith, for example,
in which God can be imagined capable of commanding the irrational, like the murder of innocents. But so, the Pope argued
at Regensburg, is a loss of faith in reason: that, too, is a real and
present danger. If, for example, the West limits the concept of

"reason" to a purely instrumental rationality, or, in a fit of post-modern self-indulgence, denies the human capacity to grasp the truth of anything with certainty, then the West will be unable to defend itself. Why? Because it will be unable to give an account of its political commitments and their moral foundations — to itself, or to those who would replace the free societies of the West with a very different pattern of human community, based on a very different idea of God and, consequently, of the just society.

These, of course, were points that Joseph Ratzinger had been making for years, indeed decades. In *Christianity and the Crisis of Cultures,* he synthesized his arguments into a series of finely tuned propositions. According to the first, we live in a moment of dangerous imbalance in the relationship between the West's technological capabilities and the West's moral understanding. Thus Ratzinger wrote, "Moral strength has not grown in tandem with the development of science; on the contrary, it has diminished, because the technological mentality confines morality to the subjective sphere. Our need, however, is for a public morality, a morality capable of responding to the threats that impose such a burden on the existence of us all. The true and gravest danger of the present moment is precisely this imbalance between technological possibilities and moral energy."[18]

According to Ratzinger's second proposition, the moral and political lethargy that many sense in much of Europe today is one by-product of Europe's disdain for the Christian roots of its unique civilization, a disdain which has contributed in various ways to the decline of what was once the center of world culture and world-historical initiative: "...Europe has developed a culture that, in a manner hitherto unknown to mankind, excludes God from public awareness.... God is irrelevant to public life.... [This contemporary European culture] is the most radical contradiction not only of Christianity, but of all the religious and moral traditions of humanity...."[19]

The third proposition Ratzinger advanced states that the abandonment of Europe's Christian roots implies the abandonment of the idea of "Europe" as a civilizational enterprise constructed from the fruitful interaction of Jerusalem, Athens, and Rome — biblical religion, Greek rationality, Roman law. This infidelity to the past has led, in turn, to a truncated idea of reason, and of the human capacity to know, however imperfectly, the truth of things, including the moral truth of things. There is a positivism shaping (and misshaping) much of Western thought today, a positivism that excludes all transcendent moral reference points from public life. Ratzinger asked whether such a positivism is an exercise of what the Canadian philosopher Charles Taylor describes as "exclusive humanism," and then asks whether such an exclusivist humanism, is, itself, rational. His answer was a resounding "No." As he wrote, "This philosophy expresses, not the complete reason of man, but only one part of it. And this mutilation of reason means that we cannot consider it to be rational at all. Hence it is incomplete and can recover its health only through reestablishing contact with its roots. A tree without roots dries up. . . ."[20]

And so, we may rightly suspect, do civilizations.

Finally, Ratzinger suggested that the recovery of reason in the West would be facilitated by a reflection on the fact that the Christian concept of God as *Logos* helped shape the distinct civilization of the West as a synthesis of Jerusalem, Athens, and Rome. If men and women have forgotten that they can, in fact, think their way through to the truth of things, that may have something to do with the European forgetfulness of God which Aleksandr Solzhenitsyn identified as the source of Europe's 20th-century civilizational distress. And that, in turn, has led, contrary to the expectations of the Enlightenment, to the demise of reason, not its advance. Thus Ratzinger wrote, "From the very beginning, Christianity has understood itself to be the religion of the *Logos,* to be a religion in keeping with reason. . . . [But] a reason that has its origin in the irrational and is itself ultimately irrational does not offer a solution to our problems. Only that creative reason which has manifested itself as love in the crucified God can truly show us what life is."[21]

Then, in light of these four propositions, Joseph Ratzinger laid down a challenge, frankly borrowed from Pascal:

> In the age of the Enlightenment, the attempt was made to understand and define the essential norms of morality by saying that they would be valid *etsi Deus non daretur,* even if God did not exist.... [Today] we must... reverse the axiom of the Enlightenment and say: Even the one who does not succeed in finding the path to accepting the existence of God ought nevertheless to try to live and to direct his life *veluti si Deus daretur,* as if God did indeed exist. This is the advice Pascal gave to his nonbelieving friends, and it is the advice I should like to give to our friends today who do not believe. This does not impose limitations on anyone's freedom; it gives support to all our human affairs and supplies a criterion of which human life stands sorely in need.[22]

In his introduction to *Christianity and the Crisis of Cultures,* Marcello Pera took up Pope Benedict's challenge and issued a clarion call for moral and cultural renewal throughout the West:

> This proposal should be accepted, this challenge welcomed, for one basic reason: because the one outside the Church who acts [as if God did indeed exist] becomes more responsible in moral terms. He will no longer say that an embryo is a "thing" or a "lump of cells" or "genetic material." He will no longer say that the elimination of an embryo or a fetus does not infringe any rights. He will no longer say that a desire that can be satisfied by some technical means is automatically a right that should be claimed and granted. He will no longer say that

all scientific and technological progress is per se a liberation or a moral advance. He will no longer say that the only rationality and the only form of life outside the Church are scientific rationality and an existence bereft of values. He will no longer act as only half a man, one lacerated and divided. He will no longer think that a democracy consisting of the mere counting of numbers is an adequate substitute for wisdom.[23]

With the dust settled after the Regensburg Lecture, perhaps it can now be agreed that Pope Benedict, in cooperation with men like Marcello Pera, has been trying to give the world a precious gift: a vocabulary through which a serious, global discussion of both the crisis of technological civilization in the West and the crisis posed by jihadist ideology and its lethal expressions around the world can be engaged by believers and nonbelievers alike — the vocabulary of "rationality" and "irrationality." If Europe began to recover its faith in reason, then at least some in Europe might, in time, rediscover the reasonableness of faith. And in any event, a renewed faith in reason would provide an antidote to the spiritual boredom from which Europe is dying, and thus open the prospect of a new birth of freedom in Europe and throughout the West.

Benedict XVI has been trying to remind the world that societies and cultures are only as great as the nobility of their spiritual aspirations. It is not an act of ingratitude toward the achievements of the Enlightenment to suggest that the soul-withering secularism — the exclusivist humanism — that has grown out of one stream of Enlightenment thought threatens the future of the West, precisely because it prevents us from giving an account, to ourselves and our children and grandchildren, of the noble political ends embodied in the Western democratic tradition. As Marcello Pera put it in *Without Roots*, "Absolute [worldliness], supposing there is such a thing, is an absolute vacuum in which neither the happy majority nor the creative minorities can exist."[24]

No Faith, No Future

It remains to be seen where the conversation initiated by Joseph Ratzinger and Marcello Pera leads, or whether Pera's political-cultural initiative begins to get a purchase on the cultural high ground in Europe. Some would argue that it is already too late, that the demographic tipping point has been reached and that, as Mark Steyn puts it, with "the successor population...already in place — Islam — ...the only question is how bloody the transfer of real estate will be."[25] But if Europe's two culture wars are not to result in the accelerated emergence of Eurabia, surely something like the Ratzinger/Pera conversation must be expanded, and soon.

The alternative construction of Europe's future reality was graphically displayed in August 2005 when former British Foreign Secretary (and Iraq War critic) Robin Cook died. The funeral service was held in the historic "High Kirk" of Edinburgh, St. Giles, and led by the former Anglican primate of Scotland, Bishop Richard Holloway, who some years ago wrote a book attempting to reconcile his readers to what he termed the "massive indifference of the universe." Holloway later described Robin Cook's funeral in these terms: "Here was I, an agnostic Anglican, taking the service in a Presbyterian church, for a dead atheist politician. And I thought that was just marvelous."[26]

What, however, is so marvelous about such a blithe indifference to first things? Nihilism rooted in skepticism, issuing in moral relativism and comforting itself with a vacuous humanitarianism: not only is that not "marvelous," that is what has been killing Europe, demographically, and that is what is paralyzing Europe in the face of an aggressive anti-humanism fueled by a distorted theism. Those who love Europe, and what it has meant and still could mean for the world, had better hope that it's Joseph Ratzinger, Marcello Pera, and their allies, not Richard Holloway and his fellow debonair nihilists, who prevail in the contest to resolve Europe's two culture wars.

Acknowledgments

While I am, of course, solely responsible for the arguments, claims, and animadversions in this book, I am grateful to many friends and colleagues for helping shape these explorations in political theology through their advice, criticism, suggestions, and support:

Elliott Abrams; the Adorers of the Sacred Heart of Jesus of Montmartre at Tyburn Convent, London; Robert Andrews; Paul Belien; James H. Billington; Joseph Bottum; Carl Braaten; Rémi Brague; Jacek Buda, O.P.; Don J. Briel; Rocco Buttiglione; Romanus Cessario, O.P.; Joseph Augustine DiNoia, O.P.; Jean Duchesne; Avery Cardinal Dulles, S.J.; João Carlos Espada; Kevin Flannery, S.J.; John Lewis Gaddis; Hillel Fradkin; Mary Ann Glendon; James M. Harvey; Mark Henrie; Russell Hittinger; Robert Jenson; James Turner Johnson; Leon Kass; the late Penn Kemble; Douglas Kmiec; Neal Kozodoy; Charles Krauthammer; the late Jean-Marie Cardinal Lustiger; the late Elizabeth Maguire; Eugene McCarthy and the board of the McCarthy Family Foundation; Gilbert Meilaender; Celestino Migliore; Richard John Neuhaus; David Novak; Michael Novak; Edward T. Oakes, S.J.; Oliver O'Donovan; Charles Paternina; Marcello Pera; Robert Pickus; Norman Podhoretz; Charles Reed; Robert Royal; David Ryall; Christoph Cardinal Schönborn, O.P.; Michael Sherwin, O.P.; William E. Simon Jr., J. Peter Simon, James Piereson, Sheila Mulcahy, and the board and staff of the William E. Simon Foundation; Nathan Tarcoff; J. H. H. Weiler; M. Edward Whelan III; Thomas D. Williams, L.C.; Robert

Louis Wilken; Rowan Williams; R. James Woolsey; and Maciej Zięba, O.P.

By extending me the courtesy of lecture invitations, the following institutions helped make these essays possible: the Archdiocese of Vienna; the Columbus School of Law at the Catholic University of America; the Center for Catholic and Evangelical Theology; the John M. Olin Center for Inquiry into the Theory and Practice of Democracy, and the Committee on Social Thought, both of the University of Chicago; the Catholic campus ministry of Columbia University, New York; the Ethics and Public Policy Center, Washington; the Pontifical Gregorian University, Rome; the Institute for Political Studies of the Catholic University of Portugal, Lisbon; Princeton University; the Pontifical Atheneum Regina Apostolorum, Rome; the Institute on Religion and Public Life, New York; Tyburn Convent, London; and the International Security Studies Program of Yale University.

The deep influence on my thinking of the late Pope John Paul II, with whom I had the privilege of being in extensive conversation for almost fifteen years, should be obvious. Our discussions, which touched on many of the subjects explored here, were not without occasional disagreements, but those disagreements were marked by the mutual understanding and respect that ought to characterize all serious intellectual encounters. As Joseph Cardinal Ratzinger, Pope John Paul's successor, Pope Benedict XVI, suggested that I think of this sort of writing as a distinctive form of apologetics; I am grateful to him for his encouragement.

Thanks, too, to John Jones and Gwendolin Herder of the Crossroad Publishing Company for thinking that there was a "there" there in essays older and newer, and for their patient work in bringing this volume to press. My agent, Loretta Barrett, took care of the temporalities, as an older generation of Catholic theologians would have described them, and I remain in her debt. Stephen White, my assistant, did yeoman service in preparing the manuscript. Over the decade and a half in which these essays were gestated, the priests and people of St. Jane Frances de Chantal Parish in Bethesda, Maryland, were a steady and welcome source of support and challenge.

During the years in which these essays were prepared, I was immeasurably blessed by the assistance and friendship of a remarkable group of assistants. It is a pleasure and a privilege to dedicate this book to them.

Finally, in sequence but not in affection, my abiding thanks to my wife, Joan, and to my children — Gwyneth Susil, with her husband, Robert, and son, William; Monica; and Stephen.

George Weigel

Washington, D.C., June 27, 2007
Commemoration of the
Ukrainian Martyrs of World War II

About the Author

Crossroad is honored to welcome George Weigel to our list.

Mr. Weigel, Distinguished Senior Fellow of the Ethics and Public Policy Center, is a Catholic theologian, the premier biographer of Pope John Paul II, and one of America's leading public intellectuals.

A native of Baltimore, Mr. Weigel was educated at St. Mary's Seminary College in his native city and at the University of St. Michael's College in Toronto. In 1975, Weigel moved to Seattle, where he was Assistant Professor of Theology and Assistant (later Acting) Dean of Studies at the St. Thomas Seminary School of Theology in Kenmore. In 1977, Weigel became Scholar-in-Residence at the World Without War Council of Greater Seattle, a position he held until 1984. In 1984–85 Weigel was a fellow of the Woodrow Wilson International Center for Scholars in Washington, D.C. There he wrote *Tranquillitas Ordinis: The Present Failure and Future Promise of American Catholic Thought on War and Peace* (Oxford University Press, 1987). Weigel is the author or editor of nineteen other books, including *The Final Revolution: The Resistance Church and the Collapse of Communism* (Oxford, 1992); *The Truth of Catholicism: Ten Controversies Explored* (HarperCollins, 2001); *The Courage To Be Catholic: Crisis, Reform, and the Future of the Church* (Basic Books, 2002); *Letters to a Young Catholic* (Basic, 2004); *The Cube and the Cathedral: Europe, America, and Politics without God* (Basic, 2005); *God's Choice: Pope Benedict XVI and the Future of the Catholic Church* (HarperCollins, 2005); and *Faith, Reason, and the*

War Against Jihadism (Doubleday, 2007). Weigel has written essays, op-ed columns, and reviews for the major opinion journals and newspapers in the United States and is a contributor to *Newsweek*. A frequent guest on television and radio, he is also Vatican analyst for NBC News. His weekly column, "The Catholic Difference," is syndicated to sixty newspapers around the United States. His scholarly work and his journalism are regularly translated into the major European languages.

From 1989 through June 1996, Weigel was president of the Ethics and Public Policy Center, where he led a wide-ranging, ecumenical, and inter-religious program of research and publication on foreign and domestic policy issues. From June 1996, as a Senior Fellow of the Center, Weigel prepared a major study of the life, thought, and action of Pope John Paul II. *Witness to Hope: The Biography of Pope John Paul II* was published to international acclaim in the fall of 1999, in English, French, Italian, and Spanish editions. Polish, Portuguese, Slovak, Czech, and Slovenian editions were published in 2000. A Russian edition was published in 2001, a German edition in 2002, and a Romanian edition in 2007; a Chinese edition is in preparation. A documentary film based on the book was released in the fall of 2001 and has won numerous prizes. Weigel has been awarded ten honorary doctorates, the papal cross *Pro Ecclesia et Pontifice*, and the *Gloria Artis* Gold Medal by the Republic of Poland. He serves on the boards of directors of several organizations dedicated to human rights and the cause of religious freedom and is a member of the editorial board of *First Things*. George Weigel and his wife, Joan, have three children and one grandchild, and live in North Bethesda, Maryland.

Notes

Introduction: Against Several Grains

1. *Being Right: Conservative Catholics in America,* ed. Mary Jo Weaver and R. Scott Appleby (Bloomington: Indiana University Press, 1995), pp. 138–62.

2. John Courtney Murray, S.J., *We Hold These Truths: Catholic Reflections on the American Proposition* (Garden City, N.Y.: Doubleday Image Books, 1964), p. 50.

3. Ibid., p. 51.

Chapter One: The Free and Virtuous Society

1. The text of the *Letter to Diognetus* may be found in *The Apostolic Fathers,* 2nd ed., trans. J. B. Lightfoot and J. R. Hammer, ed. and rev. by Michael W. Holmes (Grand Rapids: Baker, 1989), pp. 296–306. *Lumen Gentium* cited *Diognetus* in describing the Christian's place in "the world" (cf. *Lumen Gentium,* 38), while the *Catechism of the Catholic Church* (at 2240) cites *Diognetus* on the duties of Christian citizens.

2. Hans Urs von Balthasar, *Truth Is Symphonic: Aspects of Christian Pluralism* (San Francisco: Ignatius Press, 1987), p. 87.

3. H. Richard Niebuhr, *Christ and Culture* (New York: Harper & Row, 1956).

4. For a fuller analysis of the principle of subsidiarity, see my essay "Catholicism and Democracy: The Other Twentieth-Century Revolution," in *Soul of the World: Notes on the Future of Public Catholicism* (Grand Rapids: Eerdmans, 1996), pp. 107–10.

5. This experience of a nascent civil society was critically important in the collapse of European communism; the emergence of a resistance community as an alternative form of civil society to communist fakery was brilliantly analyzed by several key figures in the resistance. See, for example, Václav Havel, "The Power of the Powerless," and Václav Benda, "Catholicism and Politics," in Havel et al., *The Power of the Powerless* (Armonk, N.Y.: M. E. Sharpe, 1990), and Józef Tischner, *The Spirit of Solidarity* (San Francisco: Harper & Row, 1982). See also Jacques Maritain, *Christianity and Democracy* (San Francisco: Ignatius Press, 1986).

6. Readers interested in a summary of each of these texts may consult my *Witness to Hope: The Biography of Pope John Paul II* (New York: HarperCollins, 1999 and 2005).

7. John Paul II, *Laborem Exercens,* 4, 25.

8. Ibid., 6.

9. Ibid., 25–27.

10. John Paul II, *Sollicitudo Rei Socialis,* 15.

11. Ibid., 15–16, 45.

12. Ibid., 28.

13. Ibid., 16–17.

14. John Paul II, *Centesimus Annus,* 42, 51.

15. Ibid., 46.

16. Ibid., 44–52.

17. Ibid., 42.

18. Ibid., 13, 46, 49.

19. Ibid., 32.

20. Ibid., 58, 52. For further discussion, see Richard John Neuhaus, *Doing Well and Doing Good: The Challenge to the Christian Capitalist* (New York: Doubleday, 1992), especially chapter 8, "The Potential of the Poor."

21. John Paul II, *Veritatis Splendor,* 96.

22. John Paul II, *Evangelium Vitae,* 20, 18, 56.

23. For a fuller account of this evolution, see my essay "Catholicism and Democracy: Parsing the Other Twentieth-Century Revolution," in *Soul of the World: Notes on the Future of Public Catholicism* (Grand Rapids: Eerdmans, 1996), pp. 99–124.

24. For a concise survey of the European intellectual foundations of Catholic social doctrine, see Franz H. Mueller, *The Church and the Social Question* (Washington: American Enterprise Institute, 1984).

25. For one example of this process at work, see Mary Ann Glendon, *Rights Talk* (New York: Free Press, 1993).

26. St. Augustine provides this definition of "peace" in *The City of God,* xix, 13. For discussion of the evolution of this idea, its abandonment in recent years, and intellectual steps toward its resuscitation, see my *Tranquillitas Ordinis: The Present Failure and Future Promise of American Catholic Thought on War and Peace* (New York: Oxford University Press, 1987).

27. These questions are discussed at greater length in chapter 7 below.

28. On these points, see William McGurn, "Pulpit Economics," *First Things* 122 (April 2002), pp. 21–25.

29. A remarkable book by a Danish statistician, Bjørn Lomborg, should be required reading for all those interested in developing Catholic social thought in the

decades ahead. Not only does Lomborg (a lifelong Green and man of the Left) provide an ocean of data refuting the environmental and economic prophets of gloom; he does so in a way that does not ignore, but rather engages with great moral earnestness, the genuine questions of choice that have to be made in concretizing our commitments to empowering the poor and preserving and enhancing the environment. See Lomborg, *The Skeptical Environmentalist: Measuring the Real State of the World* (Cambridge: Cambridge University Press, 2001).

30. Francis Fukuyama, *Trust: The Social Virtues and the Creation of Prosperity* (New York: Free Press, 1995), p. 11. See also my essay, "Capitalism for Humans," *Commentary,* October 1995, pp. 34–38.

Chapter Two: The Sovereignty of Christ and the Public Church

1. *Redemptor Hominis,* 21, 2.

2. On "deification," see two volumes by Jaroslav Pelikan: *The Emergence of the Catholic Tradition, 100–600* (Chicago: University of Chicago Press, 1971), pp. 155, 233–34, and *The Spirit of Eastern Christendom, 600–1700* (Chicago: University of Chicago Press, 1974), pp. 10–12, 14, 34–35, 46, 227, 247, 259–60, 267–68, 290.

3. Dorothy L. Sayers, Introduction to *Dante: The Divine Comedy, Purgatory* (London: Penguin Books, 1955), p. 37.

4. Office of Readings, December 30; from the treatise "On the Refutation of All Heresies," by Hippolytus.

5. See Luke 9:28–36 and parallels.

6. Hans Urs von Balthasar, *The Glory of the Lord,* vol. 3: *Studies in Theological Styles — Lay Styles* (San Francisco: Ignatius Press, 1986), p. 100.

7. See Robin Lane Fox, *Pagans and Christians* (New York: Knopf, 1986).

8. See my study *The Final Revolution: The Resistance Church and the Collapse of Communism* (New York: Oxford University Press, 1992). For an anecdotal ecumenical review of the phenomenon, see Barbara von der Heydt, *Candles behind the Wall* (Grand Rapids: Eerdmans, 1993).

9. For a journalistic account of this moral revolution, see Timothy Garton Ash, *The Uses of Adversity* (New York: Vintage Books, 1990).

10. See Acts 2.

11. The *Catechism of the Catholic Church* discusses this aspect of the basic Christian confession of faith in paragraphs 784–975. The Nicene-Constantinopolitan Creed, which is widely used in the liturgy, includes unity and apostolicity among the distinguishing "marks" of the Church ("... *unam, sanctam, catholicam, et apostolicam Ecclesiam*").

12. See Ephesians 4:4–6

13. Charles W. Colson, *The Body* (Dallas: Word, 1992), p. 68. Questions of ecclesiology are among the most urgent in the new evangelical-Catholic dialogue in America. See, for example, Richard John Neuhaus, "The Catholic Difference," in Neuhaus and Charles Colson, eds. *Evangelicals and Catholics Together: Towards a Common Mission* (Dallas: Word, 1995), pp. 175–227. See also "The Communion of Saints: A State of Evangelicals and Catholics Together," *First Things,* March 2003.

14. *Gaudium et Spes,* 40:

> Proceeding from the love of the eternal Father, the Church was founded by Christ in time and gathered into one by the Holy Spirit. It has a saving and eschatological purpose which can only be fully attained in the next life. But it is now present here on earth and is composed of men; they, the members of the earthly city, are called to form the family of the children of God even in this present history of mankind and to increase it continually until the Lord comes. Made one in view of heavenly benefits and enriched by them, this family has been "constituted and organized as a society in the present world" by Christ, and "provided with means adapted to its visible and social union." Thus the Church, at once, "a visible organization and a spiritual community," travels the same journey as all mankind and shares the same earthly lot with the world: it is to be leaven and, as it were, the soul of human society in its renewal by Christ and transformation into the family of God.
>
> That the earthly city and the heavenly city penetrate one another is a fact open only to the eyes of faith; moreover, it will remain the mystery of human history, which will be harassed by sin until the perfect revelation of the splendor of the sons of God. In pursuing its own salvific purposes not only does the Church communicate divine life to men but in a certain sense it casts the reflected light of that divine light over all the earth, notably in the way it heals and elevates the dignity of the human person, in the way it consoles society, and endows the daily activity of men with a deeper sense and meaning.

15. On this, see Pope John Paul II, homily at Camden Yards, Baltimore, October 8, 1995.

16. Richard John Neuhaus, Foreword to George Weigel and Robert Royal, eds., *Building the Free Society* (Grand Rapids: Eerdmans, 1993), p. xvi.

17. See Acts 2:13–41.

18. See *Gaudium et Spes,* 16, and the discussion of this point in chapter 6 below.

19. See William Lee Miller, *The First Liberty: Religion and the American Republic* (New York: Knopf, 1986).

20. Fyodor Dostoevsky, *The Brothers Karamazov,* trans. Richard Pevear and Larissa Volokhonsky (New York: Vintage Books, 1991), pp. 254–55, 256–57.

21. See Dumas Malone, *Jefferson the Virginian* (Boston: Little, Brown, 1948), p. 188.

22. Instruction on Christian Liberation and Freedom, 44.

23. Richard John Neuhaus, *The Naked Public Square: Religion and Democracy in America* (Grand Rapids: Eerdmans, 1984).

24. Robert Bellah, "Civil Religion in America," in *Beyond Belief: Religion in a Post-Traditional World* (New York: Harper and Row, 1970), pp. 168–89.

25. *Redemptoris Missio,* 39.

26. On Nietzsche's analysis of the spiritual crisis of European civilization, see Frederick Copleston, S.J., *A History of Philosophy,* vol. 7 (Westminster, Md: Newman Press, 1963), pp. 390–420.

27. *Gaudium et Spes,* 76.

28. Ibid., 1.

Chapter Three: Diognetus Revisited

1. The phrase, though not the time-frame, is from Raymond E. Brown, S.S., *The Churches the Apostles Left Behind* (New York: Paulist Press, 1984).

2. For the text of the letter see *The Apostolic Fathers,* 2nd ed., trans. J. B. Lightfoot and J. R. Hammer, ed. and rev. by Michael W. Holmes (Grand Rapids: Baker, 1989), pp. 296–306. To provide patristic warrant for their teaching that "each individual layman must witness before the world to the resurrection and life of the Lord Jesus, and a sign of the living God" (*Lumen Gentium,* 38), the Fathers of the Second Vatican Council cited *Diognetus* 6.1. The *Letter to Diognetus* is also referenced three times in the *Catechism of the Catholic Church:* on the duties of Christian citizens (2240); on the right to life of the unborn (2271); and on the "public" meaning of the Lord's Prayer as directed to the One who is "in heaven" (2796).

3. *Letter to Diognetus,* 6.

4. Ibid., 5.1–10. The author of *Diognetus* goes on to make clear that the "unusual character" of their citizenship had some unusual consequences for Christians:

They love everyone and by everyone they are persecuted. They are unknown, yet they are condemned; they are put to death, yet they are brought to life. They are poor, yet they make many rich; they are in need of everything, yet they abound in everything. They are dishonored, yet they are glorified in their dishonor; they are slandered, yet they are vindicated. They are cursed, yet they bless; they are insulted, yet they offer respect. When they do good, they are punished as evildoers; when they are punished, they rejoice as though brought to life. . . . Those who hate them are unable to give a reason for their hostility. (Ibid.)

5. *Catechism of the Catholic Church,* 1818, 1817.

6. Hans Urs von Balthasar, "Church and World," in *Truth Is Symphonic: Aspects of Christian Pluralism* (San Francisco: Ignatius Press, 1987), p. 98.

7. *Letter to Diognetus*, 6.7.

8. See Francis Fukuyama, "The End of History?" *The National Interest* (Summer 1989), pp. 1–18.

9. A temptation that goes back, on some readings of the New Testament, to the original apostolic band. See, for example, Dorothy L. Sayers's portrait of Judas in *The Man Born to Be King* (San Francisco: Ignatius Press, 1990).

10. See Balthasar, "Church and World," p. 98.

11. Hans Urs von Balthasar, "The Three Forms of Hope," in *Truth Is Symphonic*, pp. 190–92.

12. Hans Urs von Balthasar, *The Glory of the Lord*, vol. 1: *Seeing the Form* (San Francisco: Ignatius Press, 1982), p. 36.

13. Contemplation and action are thus not antinomies. "Contemplation melds into action, or it is not contemplation," according to Balthasar. Cited in Edward T. Oakes, S.J., *Pattern of Redemption: The Theology of Hans Urs von Balthasar* (New York: Crossroad, 1994), 147.

14. Thus John Paul II, in the 1991 social encyclical *Centesimus Annus*, asserts that the social doctrine of the Church "is not an ideology" (46) and has been developed "not in order to recover former privileges or to impose [the Church's] own vision" of the right ordering of politics (53), but as an "indispensable and ideal orientation" (43), a horizon of reflection radiating from the "care and responsibility for man" entrusted to the Church by Christ (53), and thus constituting a "valid instrument for evangelization" (54).

15. Balthasar, "Church and World," p. 96.

16. *Lumen Gentium*, 1.

17. Cited in Christoph Schönborn, O.P., "The Hope of Heaven, the Hope of Earth," *First Things* 52 (April 1995), pp. 32–38.

18. See Murray, *We Hold These Truths*, p. 43.

19. John Paul II, *Tertio Millennio Adveniente*, 37; on the 21st century as a "springtime of the Gospel," see *Redemptoris Missio*, 86.

20. John Paul II developed this point further in his 1995 encyclical on ecumenism, *Ut Unum Sint:*

> In a theocentric vision, we Christians already have a common martyrology. This also indicates the martyrs of our own century, more numerous than one might think, and it shows how, at a profound level, God preserves communion among the baptized in the supreme demand of faith, manifested in the sacrifice of life itself. The fact that one can die for the faith shows that the other demands of the faith can also be met. I have already remarked, and with

deep joy, how an imperfect but real communion is preserved and is growing at many levels of ecclesial life. I now add that this communion is *already* perfect in what we all consider the highest point of the life of grace, *martyria* unto death, the truest communion possible with Christ who shed his blood, and by that sacrifice brings near those who once were far off (cf. Eph. 2:13). [*Ut Unum Sint,* 84, emphasis added]

21. On martyrdom as the "form" of discipleship, see John Paul II, *Veritatis Splendor,* 90–94.

22. *Gaudium et Spes,* 22.

23. John Paul II, Homily at Camden Yards, Baltimore, October 8, 1995.

24. See Richard John Neuhaus, "Joshing Richard Rorty," *First Things* 8 (December 1990), pp. 14–24.

25. The Deists among the Founding Fathers were not, for example, overly concerned about the world's redemption. But as the bishops of the United States argued at the Third Plenary Council of Baltimore in 1884, the American Founders built better than they knew. Or, as John Courtney Murray put it three-quarters of a century later, the success of the American democratic experiment rested, not on the thin epistemological and anthropological foundations of "eighteenth- century individualistic rationalism," but on the moral culture of a people who had "learned [their] own personal dignity in the school of Christian faith," whether they recognized that patrimony or not. (See Murray, *We Hold These Truths,* pp. 45, 50.)

The American democratic experiment, like every other one, depends for its legitimation on warrants it cannot produce in and of itself. For all the inadequacies of their philosophical position, the Founders still knew that they had to give an account of their actions, before "nature's God" and in honor of "a decent respect to the opinions of mankind" (as they put it in the Declaration of Independence). The peculiar danger of our present circumstances is the denial, by philosophers and political theorists, of the very possibility of such warrants and such an account.

26. On this point, see Richard John Neuhaus, "Can Atheists Be Good Citizens?" *First Things* 15 (August/September 1991), pp. 17–21.

27. See Balthasar, "Church and World," p. 96.

28. Ibid.

29. See ibid.

30. See John Paul II, *Address to the Fiftieth General Assembly of the United Nations Organization,* October 5, 1995. See also my essay "Are Human Rights Still Universal?" *Commentary,* February 1995, 41–45. For a reflection on how this problem asserts itself in U.N. forums today, see Mary Ann Glendon, "What Happened at Beijing," *First Things* 59 (January 1996), pp. 30–36.

31. *Letter to Diognetus,* 7.4.

32. The defense of religious freedom, viewed from this angle, is thus an expression of the Church's commitment to the core Catholic social-ethical principle of subsidiarity.

33. In his homily at Camden Yards, Baltimore, on October 8, 1995, Pope John Paul II cited this as "the basic question before a democratic society."

34. Thus the Church's contesting for genuine pluralism becomes another expression of the Church's commitment to subsidiarity.

35. *Catechism of the Catholic Church,* 1913.

36. This was empirically demonstrated at the 1994 Cairo World Conference on Population and the 1995 Beijing World Conference on Women, where a populist Church challenged the plans of an international cultural-bureaucratic elite to impose a certain construal of human sexuality on the entire world in the name of feminist ideologies that have little or nothing to do with how 95 percent of the world's women actually live.

37. See, for example, section 5 of *Centesimus Annus,* "State and Culture."

Chapter Four: The Paradoxes of Disentanglement

1. Robert Louis Wilken, *The Christians as the Romans Saw Them* (New Haven: Yale University Press, 1984).

2. Cited in Christoph Schönborn, O.P., "The Hope of Heaven, the Hope of Earth," *First Things* 52 (April 1995), pp. 32–38.

3. See Russell Hittinger, "The Supreme Court v. Religion," *Crisis,* May 1993, pp. 22–30, and Nathan Lewin, "The Church-State Game: A Symposium on *Kiryas Joel,*" *First Things* 47 (November 1994), pp. 39–40.

4. For an extended discussion of these problems, see my book, *The Cube and the Cathedral: Europe, America, and Politics without God* (New York: Basic Books, 2005).

5. It is interesting to recall that H. L. Mencken, a lifelong agnostic, assayed a withering critique of liberal theology in his obituary column in praise of the intellectual consistency of the Presbyterian fundamentalist J. Gresham Machen:

> [Machen] fell out with the reformers who, in late years, have been trying to convert the Presbyterian Church into a kind of literary and social club, devoted vaguely to good works. . . .
>
> It is my belief, as a friendly neutral in all such high and ghostly matters, that the body of doctrine known as Modernism is completely incompatible, not only with anything rationally describable as Christianity, but also with anything deserving to pass as religion in general. Religion, if it is to retain any genuine significance, can never be reduced to a series of sweet attitudes, possible to anyone not actually in jail for felony. It is, on the contrary, a corpus

of powerful and profound convictions, many of them not open to logical analysis....

What the Modernists have done... [is] to get rid of all the logical difficulties of religion, and yet preserve a generally pious cast of mind. It is a vain enterprise. What they have left, once they have achieved their imprudent scavenging, is hardly more than a row of hollow platitudes, as empty [of] psychological force and effect as so many nursery rhymes" [H. L. Mencken, "Doctor Fundamentalis," *Baltimore Evening Sun,* January 18, 1937].

6. See Jacques Maritain, *Christianity and Democracy* (San Francisco: Ignatius Press, 1986).

7. See Richard Wightman Fox, *Reinhold Niebuhr: A Biography* (New York: Pantheon Books, 1985).

8. See my essay "John Courtney Murray and the Catholic Human Rights Revolution," in *Catholicism and the Renewal of American Democracy* (New York: Paulist Press, 1989).

9. *Centesimus Annus* is discussed at length in my *Witness to Hope* (New York: HarperCollins, 1999).

10. See my study *The Final Revolution: The Resistance Church and the Collapse of Communism* (New York: Oxford University Press, 1992).

11. See Schönborn, "The Hope of Heaven, the Hope of Earth," p. 34.

12. C. S. Lewis, "The Weight of Glory," in *The Weight of Glory and Other Addresses* (New York: Macmillan, 1990), p. 19.

13. The formulation is adopted from Richard John Neuhaus, "What the Fundamentalists Want," *Commentary,* May 1985.

14. Weiler's analysis is discussed at length in my book *The Cube and the Cathedral.*

15. See Neuhaus, "What the Fundamentalists Want," p. 43.

16. See Murray, *We Hold These Truths,* p. 34.

17. Richard John Neuhaus, "Can Atheists Be Good Citizens?" *First Things* 15 (August/September 1991), p. 21.

18. Ibid., p. 20.

19. Richard John Neuhaus, "The Public Square," *First Things* 42 (April 1994), p. 67.

20. See Alasdair MacIntyre, *After Virtue* (Notre Dame: University of Notre Dame Press, 1981), and Richard John Neuhaus, "The Truth about Freedom," *Wall Street Journal,* October 8, 1993.

21. See Neuhaus, "The Truth about Freedom." I explore the relationship of "giving an account" to the current crisis of civilizational morale in Europe in *The Cube and the Cathedral,* and to the post-9/11 international environment in *Faith, Reason, and the War Against Jihadism: A Call to Action* (New York: Doubleday, 2007).

22. James Madison, "To the Honorable the General Assembly of the Common-wealth of Virginia: A Memorial and Remonstrance," in William Lee Miller, *The First Liberty: Religion and the American Republic* (New York: Knopf, 1986), pp. 359–64.

23. Here is John Paul II in his apostolic letter announcing the Great Jubilee of 2000, *Tertio Millennio Adveniente:*

> Another painful chapter of history to which the sons and daughters of the Church must return with a spirit of repentance is that of the acquiescence given, especially in certain centuries, to intolerance and even the use of violence in the service of truth.
>
> It is true that an accurate historical judgment cannot prescind from care-ful study of the cultural conditioning of the times, as a result of which many people may have held in good faith that an authentic witness to truth could include suppressing the opinions of others or at least paying no attention to them. Many factors frequently converged to create assumptions which jus-tified intolerance and fostered an emotional climate from which only great spirits, truly free and filled with God, were in some way able to break free. Yet the consideration of mitigating circumstances does not exonerate the Church from the obligation to express profound regret for the weaknesses of so many of her sons and daughters who sullied her face, preventing her from fully mir-roring the image of her crucified Lord, the supreme witness of patient love and humble meekness. From all these painful moments of the past a lesson can be drawn for the future, leading all Christians to adhere fully to the sublime principle stated by the [Second Vatican] Council [in the Declaration on Re-ligious Freedom, 1]: "The truth cannot impose itself except by virtue of its own truth, as it wins over the mind with both gentleness and power" [*Tertio Millennio Adveniente*, 35].

24. Justices Anthony Kennedy, Sandra Day O'Connor, and David Souter, in *Casey v. Planned Parenthood of Southeastern Pennsylvania*, 112 Sup. Ct. 2791 (1992), at 2807.

Chapter 5: Is Political Theology Safe for Democracy?

1. Richard John Neuhaus, "What the Fundamentalists Want," *Commentary* (May 1985).

2. Mark Lilla, *The Stillborn God: Religion, Politics, and the Modern West* (New York: Alfred A. Knopf, 2007).

3. Rémi Brague, *The Law of God: The Philosophical History of an Idea*, trans. Lydia G. Cochrane (Chicago: University of Chicago Press, 2007).

4. Lilla, *The Stillborn God*, 58.

5. Ibid., 23.

6. Lilla's construal of "political theology" is also called into question by his suggestion that Iranian president Mahmoud Ahmadinejad was engaging in "the language of political theology" when he ranted on about "the sounds of the shattering and falling of the ideology and thoughts of the liberal democratic systems." If theology, as Anselm of Canterbury suggested a millennium ago, is "faith seeking understanding," whatever else President Ahmadinejad was engaging in, it wasn't theology.

7. Mark Lilla, "The Politics of God," *New York Times Magazine,* August 19, 2007.

8. Ibid.

9. Lilla, *The Stillborn God,* 77.

10. Winston S. Churchill, *The Gathering Storm* (London: Cassell & Co., 1948), 10.

11. Lilla, "The Politics of God."

12. Ibid.

13. Ibid.

14. Ibid.

15. Brague, *The Law of God,* 4

16. Ibid., 4–5.

17. Ibid., 6.

18. Ibid.

19. Ibid., 223.

20. Ibid., 227.

21. Ibid., 237.

22. Ibid., 231–35.

23. Ibid., 257.

24. Ibid., 257–58.

25. Ibid., 262.

26. Lilla, *The Stillborn God,* 304.

27. Ibid., 302.

28. Lilla, "The Politics of God."

29. See chapter 12 below.

30. At the beginning of *The Stillborn God,* Mark Lilla notes that "readers will notice the absence of modern Catholic thinkers from this study. . . . Telling the Catholic story would require another book." If the analogy be permitted, writing any part of the history of the Western debate over religion-and-politics without a serious wrestling with Catholic sources, especially modern and contemporary Catholic sources, is a bit like writing the history of baseball without mentioning the National League. This lacuna creates all sorts of problems for Lilla's analysis. Perhaps

the greatest — which provides another sharp challenge to Lilla's Hobbes-centered thesis — is that modern Catholic social doctrine, from the late 19th century to the present, but especially in the years since Vatican II and through the teaching of John Paul II, provides a powerful argument on behalf of pluralism, religious freedom, civility, tolerance, the rule of law, and is marked by a notable modesty in applying divine warrants to prudential judgments. By using the natural law tradition creatively, modern Catholic social doctrine gets its adherents to a thick defense of the democratic project without a Great Separation that, ultimately, sunders human life and consciousness in an unsustainable way.

Chapter Six: Popes, Power, and Politics

1. See Rocco Buttiglione, *Karol Wojtyła: The Thought of the Man Who Became Pope John Paul II* (Grand Rapids: Eerdmans, 1997), pp. 1–20.

2. The latter form of interference continued even after the popes lost their temporal power. Emperor Franz Joseph vetoed Cardinal Mariano Rampolla's candidacy in the papal conclave of 1903 — a veto pronounced, ironically, by Karol Wojtyła's predecessor as archbishop of Kraków, Cardinal Jan Puzyna.

3. Robert A. Graham, S.J., *Papal Diplomacy: A Study of Church and State on the International Plane* (Princeton: Princeton University Press, 1959), p. 157.

4. Owen Chadwick, *A History of the Popes, 1830–1914* (Oxford: Clarendon Press, 1998), p. 39.

5. For this and several other points above I am indebted to Professor Russell Hittinger.

6. Chadwick, *A History of the Popes,* p. 330.

7. See, for example, *The Pius War: Responses to the Critics of Pius XII,* ed. Joseph Bottum and David Dalin (Lanham, Md.: Lexington Books, 2004).

8. See Owen Chadwick, *Britain and the Vatican during the Second World War* (Cambridge: Cambridge University Press, 1986), pp. 86–100.

9. See Pierre Blet, S.J., *Pius XII and the Second World War: According to the Archives of the Vatican* (New York: Paulist Press, 1999), pp. 48–49, 55, 58, 60.

10. See *Christus Dominus,* 20. This concrete "separation" of Church and state was made legally binding within Latin-rite Catholicism by the 1983 Code of Canon Law, which confirmed that "No rights and privileges of election, appointment or designation of bishops are hereafter granted to civil authorities" [Canon 377.5].

11. Montini and Casaroli were also concerned about what might happen in underground local churches cut off from the supervision of Rome, a concern which, in some instances, proved warranted.

12. See George Weigel, *Witness to Hope: The Biography of Pope John Paul II* (New York: HarperCollins, 1999), pp. 327–28.

13. Author's interview with Cardinal Jean-Marie Lustiger, October 24, 1996.

14. John Paul combined a robust faith in the power of religious and moral truth with a commitment to the independence of the resistance movements he inspired. Thus in 1983 the Pope refused to cut a deal with the Polish government behind Solidarity's back, when some suggested making the Polish Church the state's formal interlocutor and letting Solidarity wither and die. For John Paul, this was a matter of principle, not simply of prudent tactics. The Church did not demand control of the political forces its teaching had helped create; that was not the Church's role, according to the evangelical vision of Vatican II.

15. It was not an accident that this text was the psalm antiphon at the great Mass in St. Peter's Basilica marking Karol Wojtyła's fiftieth anniversary of priestly ordination.

16. *Lumen Gentium*, 25.

17. In addition to its Permanent Observer status at the U.N., the Holy See is represented diplomatically at the European Union, the Organization for Security and Cooperation in Europe, and the Organization of American States.

Chapter Seven: Two Ideas of Freedom

1. Michael Ignatieff, *Isaiah Berlin* (New York: Henry Holt, 1999), p. 225.

2. Although Berlin notes that negative liberty is "not, at any rate logically, connected with democracy or self-government. Self-government may, on the whole, provide a better guarantee of the preservation of civil liberties than other regimes. ... But there is no necessary connection between individual liberty and democratic rule." [Isaiah Berlin, "Two Concepts of Liberty," in Berlin, *The Proper Study of Mankind* (New York: Farrar, Straus and Giroux, 2000), p. 202.]

3. Ignatieff, *Isaiah Berlin*, p. 226.

4. Ibid., p. 228.

5. Norman Podhoretz, "A Dissent on Isaiah Berlin," *Commentary*, February 1999, p. 34.

6. Berlin, "Two Concepts of Liberty," p. 206.

7. This summary is adapted from Servais Pinckaers, O.P., *Morality: The Catholic View* (South Bend, Ind.: St. Augustine's Press, 2001), p. 74.

8. Ibid., p. 71.

9. Murray, *We Hold These Truths*, p. 43.

10. Josef Pieper, *Scholasticism: Personalities and Problems in Medieval Philosophy* (South Bend, Ind.: St. Augustine's Press, 2001), p. 150.

11. Servais Pinckaers, O.P., *The Sources of Christian Ethics* (Washington: Catholic University of America Press, 1995), p. 242.

12. Ibid., p. 339.

13. On this point cf. ibid. pp. 348–49, and Pinckaers, *Morality,* p. 66.

14. For a lengthy discussion of freedom of indifference, see Pinckaers, *The Sources of Christian Ethics,* pp. 327–53; a summary chart contrasting freedom for excellence and freedom of indifference may be found in Pinckaers, *Morality,* p. 74.

15. Berlin, "Two Concepts of Liberty," p. 193.

16. Ibid., p. 194.

17. Ibid., p. 203.

18. Ibid., p. 216.

19. Ibid., p. 219.

20. Aldous Huxley, *Brave New World* (New York: Bantam Modern Classics, 1968), pp. 119–20.

21. Murray, *We Hold These Truths,* p. 9.

Chapter Eight: Thinking World Politics

1. See, for example, John Eppstein, *The Catholic Tradition of the Law of Nations* (Washington: Catholic Association for International Peace, 1935).

2. See Joseph S. Nye, *Soft Power: The Means to Success in World Politics* (New York: Public Affairs, 2004).

3. See, for example, John Lewis Gaddis, *The Cold War: A New History* (New York: Penguin Press, 2005), for an analysis that does justice to the role of both hard power and soft power in bringing the Cold War to a successful resolution in favor of the forces of freedom.

4. On this point, see Gregory M. Reichberg, "Is There a 'Presumption Against War' in Aquinas's Ethics?" *The Thomist* 66 (2002), pp. 337–67.

5. See Anne-Marie Slaughter, "A Chance to Reshape the U.N.," *Washington Post,* April 13, 2003.

6. Cited in David Rivkin and Lee Casey, "Leashing the Dogs of War," *The National Interest* 73 (Fall 2003), p. 59.

7. John Courtney Murray, S.J., "Things Old and New in *Pacem in Terris,*" *America,* April 27, 1963, p. 612.

Chapter Nine: Moral Clarity in a Time of War

1. Leo Tolstoy, *War and Peace,* trans. Louise and Aylmer Maude, III.2.21 (New York: Knopf, 1992), p. 460.

2. Robert D. Kaplan, *Warrior Politics: Why Leadership Demands a Pagan Ethos* (New York: Random House, 2002).

3. See Brian C. Anderson, "Men o' War," *National Review,* February 25, 2002, p. 46.

4. This story is recounted in a slightly more generic form in Murray, *We Hold These Truths,* p. 262.

5. One publicly prominent exponent of this view was Pope John Paul II. Prior to his pontificate, he analyzed the capacity for moral action as the distinguishing characteristic of the human being in *Osoba y czyn, oraz inne studia antropolog- iczne,* Tadeusz Styczeń, Jerzy W. Gałkowski, Adam Rodziński, and Andrzej Szostek (Lublin: KUL Press, 1994). This is the revised Polish edition of Karol Wojtyła's prin- cipal philosophical work; the presently available English translation is inadequate. *Osoba y czyn* is intelligently discussed in Kenneth L. Schmitz, *At the Center of the Human Drama: The Philosophical Anthropology of Karol Wojtyła/Pope John Paul II* (Washington: CUA Press, 1993), and Jarosław Kupczak, O.P., *Destined for Liberty: The Human Person in the Philosophy of Karol Wojtyła/John Paul II* (Washington: CUA Press, 2000).

6. Anderson, "Men o' War," p. 48.

7. Johnson's major works include *Can Modern War Be Just?* (New Haven: Yale University Press, 1984); *The Quest for Peace: Three Moral Traditions in Western Cultural History* (Princeton: Princeton University Press, 1987); and *Morality and Contemporary Warfare* (New Haven: Yale University Press, 1999).

8. See Johnson, *Morality and Contemporary Warfare,* pp. 35–36.

9. *Summa Theologiae* II-II, 40.1.

10. Ramsey's principal works in this field were *War and the Christian Conscience* (1961) and *The Just War* (1968). James Turner Johnson describes Ramsey's specif- ically Christian understanding of the just war tradition in these terms: "Ramsey argued that Christian just war theory is based on the moral duty of love of neighbor. The obligation to protect the neighbor who is being unjustly attacked provided jus- tification for Christians to resort to force; at the same time, love also imposes limits on such force, requiring that no more be done to the unjust assailant than is necessary to prevent the evil he would do, and that no justified use of force can ever itself directly and intentionally target the innocent" [James Turner Johnson, "The Just War Tradition and the American Military," in Johnson and George Weigel, *Just War and the Gulf War* (Washington: Ethics and Public Policy Center, 1991), pp. 8–9].

11. On this point, see James Turner Johnson, "Just Cause Revisited," in *Close Calls: Intervention, Terrorism, Missile Defense, and "Just War" Today,* ed. Elliott Abrams (Washington: Ethics and Public Policy Center, 1998), p. 27.

12. New York: Oxford University Press, 1987.

13. Augustine, *De Civitate Dei,* XIX, 13.

14. Pope John Paul II made important contributions to this idea, especially in his World Day of Peace message in 1981 [see *Ways of Peace: Papal Messages for the World Day of Peace 1968–1986* (Vatican City: Pontifical Commission "Iustitia et Pax," 1987), pp. 147–61]. The Pope's 2002 World Day of Peace statement refines the discussion of the components of *tranquillitas ordinis* further by teaching that there is no peace without justice and no justice without forgiveness. Forgiveness helps create the conditions of civil society in which the peace of order, composed of justice and freedom, can flourish. In a comment on the message, Richard John Neuhaus notes, "The title of the message has it right: there is no peace without justice, and temporal justice is secured by the acknowledgment of a transcendent judgment that reveals our need to be forgiven and to forgive. This is said [by the Pope] without any blurring of the line between good and evil, or any obscuring of the duty to defend the innocent. Rather, it anticipates the day when, beyond the present battles, there may be a new order based on a shared recognition of God's justice and mercy. Some call that idealistic. The right word is prophetic" [See John Paul II, "No Peace without Justice, No Justice without Forgiveness," in *Origins* 31:28 (December 20, 2001), pp. 461–66; Richard John Neuhaus, "The Public Square," *First Things* 120 (February 2002), p. 88].

15. See Johnson, "Just Cause Revisited," for a historical survey and contemporary arguments.

16. The debate over "humanitarian intervention" launched in the 1990s by the Somali famine and the genocidal violence of an imploding Yugoslavia also remains to be completed, and bears on the development of the just cause criterion. Addressing the U.N. Food and Agricultural Organization on December 5, 1992, Pope John Paul II spoke of humanitarian intervention as a "duty of justice" in cases of impending or actual genocide, or mass starvation caused by political upheaval or ethnic conflict. But the Pope did not specify precisely why this is a moral duty, on whom that duty falls, or how it is to be fulfilled. Development is, again, required.

Can we argue that the mass murder of innocents (or the starvation of entire peoples) constitutes an unacceptable affront to world order and a challenge to international security that must be met? That might have arguably been true in Yugoslavia, but it seems a stretch in regions more marginal to mainstream world politics — no matter how much we deplore (as we should) situations like the Somali famine or the genocide in Rwanda. If, as the Pope proposed, there is a "duty" of humanitarian intervention in these cases, then perhaps it is time to revisit the old notion of "punishment for evil" as satisfying the criterion of "just cause" for the resort to armed force in the vindication of justice and the peace of order. That would not resolve other questions posed by the assertion of a "duty" of humanitarian intervention, but it would get the just cause debate tethered to what are likely to be an increasing number of "real-world" situations in the 21st century.

17. On this point see the editorial "In a Time of War," *First Things* 118 (December 2001), pp. 11–17.

18. On the intellectual origins and class "location" of modern terrorism, see Walter Laqueur, *Terrorism* (Boston: Little, Brown, 1977).

19. David S. Yeago, "Just War: Reflections from the Lutheran Tradition in a Time of Crisis," *Pro Ecclesia* 10, no. 4 (2001), pp. 414–15 (emphases in original).

20. *Catechism of the Catholic Church*, 2309.

Chapter Ten: Just War and the Iraq Wars – I

1. On Saddam's depredations, see Kanan Makiya, *Republic of Fear: The Politics of Modern Iraq*, updated edition (Berkeley: University of California Press, 1998).

2. The chief exception among established just war scholars was James Turner Johnson, who made his dissent from (and disdain for) the prevailing consensus clear in *The War to Oust Saddam Hussein: Just War and the New Face of Conflict* (Lanham, Md.: Rowman & Littlefield, 2005).

3. I have been making this case for some twenty years, beginning with *Tranquillitas Ordinis: The Present Failure and Future Promise of American Catholic Thought on War and Peace* (New York: Oxford University Press, 1987).

4. Professor William T. Cavanaugh offered a perfect example of this forgetting when he wrote, in an essay critical of my understanding of the just war tradition, "Weigel and others regard the just war theory as a tool of statecraft. The Catholic tradition, in contrast, has understood the just war theory as an aid to moral judgment in the most serious of moral matters: the taking of human life" [William T. Cavanaugh, "At Odds with the Pope: Legitimate Authority and Just Wars," *Commonweal*, May 23, 2003]. Why, one wonders, this sharp juxtaposition between "statecraft" and "moral judgment?" In classic Catholic political theory, as distinct from various "realist" theories, statecraft is precisely about the exercise of moral judgment in the public realm.

5. "Countering Terrorism: Power, Violence and Democracy Post 9/11: A Report by a Working Group of England's House of Bishops," September 2005, pp. 40–46.

6. Kaukab Jhumra Smith, FoxNews.com, November 10, 2005.

7. *www.wcc-coe.org/wcc/what/international/iraqstatements.html.*

8. See Drew Christiansen, S.J., "Of Many Things," *America*, November 15, 2004.

9. Johnson, *The War to Oust Saddam Hussein*, p. 32.

10. Mark J. Allman, "Postwar Justice," *America*, October 17, 2005.

11. See, among many other examples, the pre-invasion manifesto, "Disarm Iraq without War: A Statement from Religious Leaders in the U.S. and the U.K." [*www.unitedforpeace.org/article.php?id=2837&printsafe=1*].

12. Michael Walzer, "So Is This a Just War?" in Walzer, *Arguing about War* (New Haven: Yale University Press, 2005), pp. 160–61.

Walzer's position after the invasion echoed the position of the Administrative Committee of the U.S. Conference of Catholic Bishops, which, in its September 2002 letter to President Bush, urged "continued diplomatic efforts aimed, in part, at resuming rigorous, meaningful [weapons] inspections; effective enforcement of the military embargo; maintenance of political sanctions and much more carefully focused economic sanctions which do not threaten the lives of innocent Iraqi civilians, non-military support for those in Iraq who offer genuine democratic alternatives; and other legitimate ways to contain and deter aggressive Iraqi actions" [*www.usccb.org/sdwp/international/bush902.htm*]. Kenneth Pollack made an extended argument against the feasibility of "sanctions plus" or "little war" in *The Threatening Storm: The Case for Invading Iraq* (New York: Random House, 2002); the USCCB letter failed to wrestle with Pollack's arguments in any serious way, suggesting, yet again, that the U.S. bishops' pronouncements on issues of war and peace reflect a narrow range of inputs.

13. Cited in Drew Christiansen, S.J., "Of Many Things," *America,* September 13, 2004.

14. Mere weeks before the war began, for example, Prime Minister Blair and his attorney general, Lord Goldsmith, were still wrangling over whether yet another Security Council resolution was legally required to take military action against Saddam Hussein, or whether Security Council Resolution 1441 (the last in the series of Iraq disarmament resolutions) authorized the use of force in the face of Iraqi defiance. Lord Goldsmith's secret memorandum to Blair, which was subsequently leaked to the press, also noted the unsettled nature of the debate over whether the 1991 ceasefire resolution (Resolution 687) terminated or merely suspended the Security Council's 1990 authorization of the use of force in Resolution 678 — and further noted that the resolution of that question had at least something to do with the question of what Resolution 1441 did or did not mean (which the attorney general admitted was unclear both from the text and from the statements made by those voting for 1441 at the time).

15. As James Turner Johnson has put it, "Where authority to resort to force is concerned, the continental European view emphasizes the role of the United Nations as a kind of supersovereign entity, privileges the strong prohibition against the resort to force by states in Article 2 and the conditional character of the statement of the right of self-defense in Article 51, and reserves to the collective action of

the Security Council any decision to use force to respond to threats to international peace and order, as provided in Articles 39 and 42. In this view, states have ceded the right to determine for themselves when they may employ force, and the black-letter law of the Charter now imposes this as a duty. In the United States and Britain, by contrast, the common-law tradition influences the interpretation of what actually is the content of international law, including the status of the United Nations as an organization and the black-letter provisions of the Charter. From this perspective, things often look different" (Johnson, *The War to Oust Saddam Hussein*, p. 127).

16. See Jim Hoagland, "2006: A Pivot for History?" *Washington Post*, January 1, 2006.

17. Executive Summary, *Comprehensive Report of the Special Advisor to the DCI on Iraq's WMD*, p. 1.

18. "Saddam's U.N. Payroll," *Wall Street Journal*, October 28, 2004, p. A14.

19. See *Iraq's Legacy of Terror: Mass Graves*, U.S. Agency for International Development, January 2004, and *Humanitarian Arguments for War in Iraq*, ed. Thomas Cushman (Berkeley: University of California Press, 2005). For a counterargument, see Ken Roth, "War in Iraq: Not a Humanitarian Intervention" [*http://hrw.org/wr2k4/3.htm*].

20. See Pollack, *The Threatening Storm*, pp. 18–25, for the unhappy tale of U.S. policy toward Iraq in the 1980s.

21. See Bob Woodward, *Plan of Attack* (New York: Simon and Schuster, 2004), with particular reference to the activities of Prince Bandar bin Sultan, the longtime Saudi ambassador in Washington.

22. See Stephen F. Hayes, "Saddam's Terror Training Camps," *The Weekly Standard*, January 16, 2006, pp. 22–25.

In the aftermath of the war, al-Qaeda saw new opportunities in a post-Saddam Iraq, as was illustrated by a letter from al-Qaeda's second-ranking figure, Ayman al-Zawahiri, to the al-Qaeda leader in Iraq, Abu Musab al-Zarqawi, which was intercepted by U.S. intelligence and released in October 2005. The letter indicated that al-Qaeda's strategic purpose in Iraq is to seize control of the country as the new base from which to create the revived Islamic caliphate that is al-Qaeda's ultimate goal.

23. See, among many other analyses of this failure, Richard Kerr, Thomas Wolfe, Rebecca Donegan, and Aris Pappas, "Issues for the U.S. Intelligence Community," *Studies in Intelligence* 49:3 (2005), pp. 47–54.

24. See James Q. Wilson, "Defending and Advancing Freedom: A Symposium," in *Commentary* 120:4 (November 2005), pp. 66–67.

25. For Walzer's pre-war arguments for steps-short-of-invasion, see Walzer, *Arguing about War*, pp. 153–59. Walzer's proposals for an intensified "little war" seem perilously close, in real-world effect if not in his intention, to a siege, which he

rightly condemns as "the most massively destructive form of warfare"; see "Justice and Injustice in the Gulf War," in *Arguing About War,* p. 85.

26. NSS-2002, p. 1.

27. Ibid., p. 15.

28. Ibid., pp. 4, 6, 25–28.

29. Ibid., p. 6.

30. Ibid., p. 15.

31. Ibid., p. 16.

32. Johnson, *The War to Oust Saddam Hussein,* p. 116.

33. For numerous examples of this dynamic at work, see John Keegan, *The Iraq War* (New York: Alfred A. Knopf, 2004); Karl Zinsmeister, *Boots on the Ground: A Month with the 82nd Airborne in the Battle for Iraq* (New York: St. Martin's Press, 2003); and Karl Zinsmeister, *Dawn over Baghdad: How the U.S. Military Is Using Bullets and Ballots to Remake Iraq* (San Francisco: Encounter Books, 2004).

34. Walzer, *Arguing about War,* p. 163.

35. Johnson, *The War to Oust Saddam Hussein,* pp. 17, 141–43.

36. See Niall Ferguson, *Colossus: The Price of America's Empire* (New York: Penguin Press, 2004), especially pp. 290–95.

37. Pope Benedict XVI, "Address to the Vatican Diplomatic Corps," *L'Osservatore Romano* [English Weekly Edition], January 11, 2006, pp. 4–5.

Chapter Eleven: Just War and the Iraq Wars – II

1. Johnson, *The War to Oust Saddam Hussein,,* p. 22.

2. William V. O'Brien, *The Conduct of Just and Limited War* (New York: Praeger, 1981).

3. Walzer, *Arguing about War,* p. 163.

4. Ibid.

5. Michael R. Gordon and General Bernard E. Traynor, *Cobra II: The Inside Story of the Invasion and Occupation of Iraq* (New York: Pantheon, 2006), p. 138.

6. Fouad Ajami, *The Foreigner's Gift: The Americans, the Arabs, and the Iraqis in Iraq* (New York: Free Press, 2006), pp. 165, 155.

7. Although General Tommy Franks, the commander of Operation Iraqi Freedom, wanted to try, in one instance. Tired of Syrian interference, Franks memorably said to a colleague, General David McKiernan, "Find out where the knobs are to shut off the oil to Syria — they've been [expletive deleted], they're going to continue to be [expletive deleted], so I want to turn off their oil" (cited in *Cobra II,* p. 436).

8. Robert Kaplan, *Imperial Grunts: On the Ground with the American Military, from Mongolia to the Philippines to Iraq and Beyond* (New York: Vintage Books, 2006), p. 332.

9. Ajami, *The Foreigner's Gift*, p. 79.

10. Max Boot, *War Made New: Technology, Warfare, and the Course of History, 1500 to Today* (New York: Gotham Press, 2006), p. 403.

11. David H. Petraeus, "Learning Counterinsurgency: Observations from Soldiering in Iraq," *Military Review* (January–February 2006).

12. Boot, *War Made New*, p. 414.

13. Dean Acheson, *Present at the Creation: My Years in the State Department* (New York: W. W. Norton, 1987), p. xvii.

14. Charles Frankel, *Morality and U.S. Foreign Policy* (New York: Foreign Policy Association, 1975), p. 52.

15. Ajami, *The Foreigner's Gift*, p. xix.

16. Bernard Lewis, "Freedom and Justice in Islam," *Imprimis* (Hillsdale College), September 2006.

Chapter Twelve: Is Europe Dying?

1. See J. H. H. Weiler, *Un'Europa Cristiana: un saggio esplorativo* (Milan: Biblioteca Universale Rizzoli, 2003).

2. For Manent on "depoliticization," see "Current Problems of European Democracy," *Modern Age* (Winter 2003), p. 15.

3. Chris Brook, "£1,300 Just to Change a Few Church Light Bulbs," *Daily Mail,* October 19, 2005.

4. "No More 'Christ' with a Capital C in the Netherlands," Catholic News Agency, October 19, 2005.

5. "Atheist Teacher Wins Catholic School Discrimination Case," *Scotland Today,* March 9, 2006.

6. On Flemish euthanasia: Chris Gacek, "Half of Infant Deaths in Flanders Were Euthanasia," *Daily Telegraph,* April 9, 2005; on Belgian legal battle, see *www.brusselsjournal.com/node/31.*

7. See *www.brusselsjournal.com/node/794.*

8. See *www.brusselsjournal.com/node/676*; *www.brusselsjournal.com/node/696.*

9. See *www.brusselsjournal.com/node/676.*

10. Charlemagne, "The Fertility Bust," *The Economist,* February 9, 2006.

11. Bruce Bawer, *While Europe Slept: How Radical Islam Is Destroying the West from Within* (New York: Doubleday, 2006).

12. Mark Steyn, "Needing to Wake Up, West Just Closes Its Eyes," *Chicago Sun-Times,* February 26, 2006.

13. Henrik Bering, "CBS Does Denmark," *Weekly Standard,* March 6/March 13, 2006.

14. Joseph Ratzinger and Marcello Pera, *Without Roots: The West, Relativism, Christianity, Islam* (New York: Basic Books, 2005). All subsequent quotes from Ratzinger and Pera are from this slim but very suggestive volume.

15. Chantal Delsol, *Icarus Fallen* (Wilmington, Del.: ISI Books, 2003), p. 3.

16. The manifesto may be found at *www.perloccidente.it/doc_english.php.*

17. Joseph Ratzinger, *Christianity and the Crisis of Cultures* (San Francisco: Ignatius Press, 2006).

18. Ibid., p. 27.

19. Ibid., pp. 30–31.

20. Ibid., p. 43.

21. Ibid., pp. 47, 49.

22. Ibid., pp. 50, 51–52.

23. Ibid., pp. 18–19.

24. *Without Roots,* p. 106.

25. Mark Steyn, "Hello, Dolly; Sayonara, Japan," *National Review,* February 27, 2006.

26. John Lloyd, "Last of the True Believers," *FT Magazine,* December 17–18, 2005.

Index

Of Related Interest

George William Rutler
COINCIDENTALLY

From the Da Vinci Code and Roswell to E Pluribus Unum and the pyramid on the back of every dollar bill, we all are fascinated by secrets, codes, and coincidences. George Rutler — EWTN speaker, *Crisis* magazine columnist, and reigning Catholic wit — offers his reflections on the coincidental links that connect the most far-flung parts of our worlds. Topics cover the gamut of human life, from Louis Farrakhan and Edgar Allan Poe to Benjamin Franklin and the propensity of Scottish physicians to dominate the Nobel Prizes for Medicine.

Fr. George Rutler is best known as the host of a weekly program on EWTN and the pastor of Our Saviour in midtown New York City, where he lives.

0-8245-2440-3, hardcover

crossroad

Of Related Interest

Lorenzo Albacete
GOD AT THE RITZ
Attraction to Infinity

"Lorenzo Albacete is one of a kind, and so is *God at the Ritz*. The book, like the monsignor, crackles with humor, warmth, and intellectual excitement. Reading it is like having a stay-up-all-night, jump-out-of-your-chair, have-another-double-espresso marathon conversation with one of the world's most swashbuckling talkers. Conversation, heck — this is a papal bull session!"
— Hendrik Hertzberg, *The New Yorker Magazine*

"Monsignor Albacete has a keen insight into the mystery of God and a wonderful sense of humor even when he is speaking about very heady subjects. Perhaps it is precisely this sense of humor — and wonder — that bring people of all faiths to Msgr. Albacete's writings to find there a source of goodness and strength."
— Theodore Cardinal McCarrick
of Washington, D.C.

0-8245-1951-5, hardcover

crossroad

Of Related Interest

Christopher Ruddy
TESTED IN EVERY WAY
The Catholic Priesthood in Today's Church

"*Tested in Every Way* brings together a wide variety of voices on the state of the contemporary priesthood. Christopher Ruddy works a small miracle in gathering disparate viewpoints, weighing the hard facts, and connecting it all with Scripture and church tradition to provide a remarkably engaging study of the Catholic priest today. This new study is essential reading."
— James Martin, S.J., author of
My Life with the Saints

0-8245-2427-6, paperback

Check your local bookstore for availability.
To order directly from the publisher,
please call 1-800-707-0670 for Customer Service
or visit our Web site at *www.cpcbooks.com*.
For catalog orders, please send your request to the address below.

THE CROSSROAD PUBLISHING COMPANY
16 Penn Plaza, Suite 1550
New York, NY 10001

crossroad